Survivors of Addiction

Addiction is something that affects many different people from all walks of life and can be difficult for a therapist to treat, and the client to conquer. In this book fifteen people who have formerly had serious addictions speak about their experiences.

Survivors of Addiction draws on first-hand narratives to provide an overview of how and why people become addicted, and explores what happens after the addiction is left behind. Divided into four parts it covers:

- being caught up in addiction
- how and why users stop being addicted
- the early days after surviving addiction
- long-term outcomes.

By considering psychodynamic and Jungian perspectives as well as the clinical vignettes, this book examines the process of recovery from addiction. It will be key reading for therapists, clinicians and healthcare workers who encounter addictions in their day-to-day professions and will also be of great interest to those who are or have been addicted, and their families.

Mary Addenbrooke, Ph.D. is a Jungian analyst who has worked in the field of substance misuse and a professional member of the Society of Analytical Psychology.

Survivors of Addiction

Narratives of Recovery

Mary Addenbrooke

Routledge
Taylor & Francis Group

LONDON AND NEW YORK

First published 2011 by Routledge
27 Church Road, Hove, East Sussex BN3 2FA

Simultaneously published in the USA and Canada
by Routledge
711 Third Avenue, New York NY 10017

Routledge is an imprint of the Taylor & Francis Group, an Informa business

Copyright © 2011 Mary Addenbrooke

Typeset in Times by Garfield Morgan, Swansea, West Glamorgan
Printed and bound in Great Britain by TJ International Ltd, Padstow,
Cornwall
Paperback cover design by Andrew Ward

British Library Cataloguing in Publication Data
A catalogue record for this book is available from the British Library

Library of Congress Cataloging-in-Publication Data
Addenbrooke, Mary, 1938-
   Survivors of addiction : post-Jungian narratives of recovery / Mary
Addenbrooke.
       p. cm.
   Includes bibliographical references and index.
   ISBN 978-1-58391-724-4 (hardback : alk. paper) –
ISBN 978-1-58391-725-1 (pbk. : alk. paper) 1. Addicts–Rehabilitation–Case
studies. 2. Substance abuse–Treatment–Case studies. 3. Alcoholics–
Rehabilitation–Case studies. 4. Drug addicts–Rehabilitation–Case studies.
I. Title.
   HV4998.A317 2011
   616.86'03–dc22
                                                                2010042155

ISBN: 978-1-58391-724-4 (hbk)
ISBN: 978-1-58391-725-1 (pbk)

Dedicated to the memory of Dr. Raj Rathod, in appreciation of his insight and dedication to his patients and his friendship to his colleagues.

Contents

Preface

This book is a tribute to the work of an eminent consultant psychiatrist, Dr. Raj Rathod, who died in 2007. The book started as a joint project with him and would not exist without him. I shall forever be grateful to him as an esteemed colleague and friend. His contribution as a psychiatrist was immense. He also initiated the gathering of the case studies upon which the book is based. Raj spent his professional life treating addicted people and conducting research in many aspects of the subject. He grew up in India and recalls his mother giving him and his brother and sisters opium pills to keep them quiet. He was also exposed to celebratory LC-bhang drinks in his late teens and he had been addicted to tobacco. As a young medical student, he was saddened by the death of his first landlord from alcohol-related problems. After coming to the UK, he had a Freudian analysis. Not only was he an inspirational teacher for the World Health Organization, but he also challenged his own staff to go the extra mile in terms of learning about addiction and gaining an understanding of the people who fall under its sway. His approach was to wait to get in touch with the emotional experiences of his patients; he was genuinely interested in what these experiences meant for the patient. He was not caught up in the everyday experiences they had, but could look beyond that. He had the analytic attitude of not responding in kind, yet he was present for the person he was with.

I am a Jungian analyst, coming from a Scottish family in which one set of grandparents signed the Temperance Pledge, having observed at first hand the havoc caused by alcohol binge drinking among sailors on shore leave. My father was a lifelong heavy smoker who died of lung cancer. In my teens, I was introduced to alcohol rather in the French fashion, as a part of family dinners on a Saturday evening, learning to appreciate how well-chosen wines enhanced the enjoyment of the various stages of the meal. Since then I have always enjoyed alcohol.

I worked as part of a team of therapists in the Substance Misuse Project at Crawley Hospital. We were all trainees at the hands of our patients, as well as therapists to them. Over the years they have taught us much about ourselves. Just as addictions generally develop over a considerable space of time, so also recovering is a process of reorientation in life. An advantage of continuing to work in a specific location over a number of years is that one can observe people's evolving development. We were impressed by the richness of their experiences and we believe that professionals have much to learn from their views. We have been privileged to be entrusted with their confidences during our interviews with them.

Acknowledgements

Thanks are due to all those who helped in the production of this book. Professor Andrew Samuels at the Centre for Psychoanalytic Studies at the University of Essex supervised the PhD thesis which formed a starting point for this book. Ms. Juliet Addenbrooke, Dr. Peter Bermingham, Mr. George Bright, Dr. Michael George, Ms. Alex Goodwin, Ms. Lilly Harrington, Mr. Steve Holbrook, Mr. Francis Hope, Dr. Jean Knox, Ms. Alison Masters, Dr. Anthony Parker, Ms. Fiona Ross, Mr. Sam Rustom and Dr. Norah Smith all gave generously of their time and expertise in reading the text and commenting on it. Mr. Alan Rosenbach and Dr. Michael George were co-leaders of the Relapse Prevention Group. Professor Renos Papadopoulos advised on methodology. Miss Joan Slater, Librarian at the Society of Analytical Psychology, assisted in conducting a literature search. Many of my colleagues at the SAP have spurred me on with their enthusiasm for research and writing.

Especial thanks are due to John Simopoulos, Alan Rosenbach and Peter Addenbrooke for their encouragement.

Appendices 1 and 2 were written by Dr. Rathod. Figures 1 and 2 originally appeared in a handbook produced by members of the Substance Misuse team for educational purposes with the support of the League of Friends of Crawley hospital.

Introduction

This book has been written to give voice to people who have experienced severe, chronic addiction but have left it behind. Fifteen people, formerly addicted to either alcohol or injectable heroin, speak about their experiences. The hope is to dispel the overwhelming pessimism that often greets the topic of addiction and to explore the processes of recovery. The fifteen narrators have all had contact with a local NHS treatment facility in the UK. Thirteen of them left their addictions behind them years ago, whereas two were still addicted, having had periods when they were drug-free for a considerable number of years.

The concept of recovery from the aftermath of any serious long-term condition raises questions as to what extent recovery is possible; whether the individual can expect to return to the life they had before disaster struck; and, if lasting damage has been caused to others or to themselves in the course of the experience, whether they can discover ways of facing and living with this. There is a further question which is sometimes overlooked: can they expect to have gained anything in the course of experiencing and surviving the disaster?

This book is written especially for people who are or who have been addicted, as well as for people in their families (parents, partners, children, other relatives) and for those who care about their well-being. Among the latter, I hope the book may be of use to anyone who works with addicted individuals or their relatives. I have come across many therapists who appreciate taking a closer look at addiction and recovery. Interested professionals may find the book useful in enabling them to understand addiction from the client's point of view. Health workers may be interested, because a significant proportion of people admitted to hospital or attending accident and emergency departments are there directly or indirectly because of alcohol or drug problems. Last but not least, readers who drink alcohol for pleasure without causing harm to themselves or anyone else, or who experiment with other drugs from time to time, may be intrigued by what happens to those who fall into the trap of being addicted. Addictions cast a long shadow, over both the person who has been addicted and those close to them.

Chapter 1 sets the scene, focusing on the context, the drugs in question and the former patients whose narratives are presented, including a brief description of the treatment offered and the research which took place within the service. Three members of staff, all involved in both offering day-to-day treatment and in research, were keen to discover more about what recovery really entails from the patient's point of view. The psychodynamic principles which most aptly apply to addiction are outlined. While much psychological treatment focuses, rightly, on cognitive approaches, unconscious forces play a key role both in addiction and in treatment. The narratives illustrate the psychodynamics at work as the narrators describe what they believe promoted their recovery as well as what hindered it. The ideas of C. G. Jung are given particular prominence because of his indirect but powerful influence on the beginnings of Alcoholics Anonymous. Although the chapters from this point on follow a chronological sequence from addiction towards recovery, I hope the reader will not feel too constrained by this, opting, if they wish, to read the narratives in any order.

The four parts of the book deal with different stages of the process of moving out of addiction. To consider recovery in a vacuum would be meaningless, so Part 1 presents three narratives which illustrate what it is like to be enmeshed in the throes of addiction, with the final chapter in this part focusing on the nature of addiction itself. Four narrators in Part 2 describe why and how they stopped drinking or using drugs after many years of being addicted. They speak about how they came to a turning point, what it was like, and its significance afterwards. The question as to the usefulness of the concept of *rock bottom* is discussed in the final chapter in this part. The challenging early days after stopping are illustrated by four narratives in Part 3. People who have been chronically addicted face a formidable task at this stage, to rebuild shattered lives and forge relationships in a different style from those in the days of their addictions. A final chapter explores the significance of this crucial stage. The narrators in Part 4 illustrate what has happened to them in the long term. The first is still addicted, and his story is told by presenting an interview with his former psychiatrist, who had not seen him for many years. Three others, by contrast, have built on the experiences of their early recovery. They tell how they view their former addictions and how they have each forged a new path. A final chapter draws together the psychological processes involved.

Appendices containing information for the reader are added. Appendix 1 delineates the consequences of addiction to alcohol, Appendix 2 those of addiction to heroin. Appendix 3 points readers in the direction of further reading and sources of information, while Appendix 4 lists the Twelve

Steps of Alcoholics Anonymous, which are quoted to at several points in the book.

A note on terminology

While specific terms relating to addiction will be explained briefly as they occur in the text, here are some general guidelines. Throughout the book the term *drug* is used in preference to the more precise but cumbersome expression 'chemical substance', and it should always be understood to include alcohol. Alcohol can be used in the way that 'drugs' are, that is, to produce a desired psychological effect. For someone addicted to alcohol, the whole point of drinking is the effect that it will have on the body and the brain. In general terms, *using* a drug implies taking it to achieve an effect on one's mood, but the term also has a specific meaning: people who inject any drug refer to their injecting as 'using', as opposed to smoking, swallowing or snorting it. The term *addict* is avoided, because the word has judgmental overtones and tends to suggest that this is all that is worth saying about that person. The words *stop* and *stopping* are used in some places in a technical sense as shorthand for stopping or quitting drinking or drug injecting. A further question was how to designate those who offer treatment. The team at the hospital was multidisciplinary and it included volunteer counsellors, some of whom were professionally trained, while others were not strictly speaking professionals. Therefore the term chosen is *therapists*.

Chapter 1

Setting the scene

In Western society, availability and use of alcohol and drugs is widespread and increasing, as are the problems associated with misuse. Much has been written about the multiplicity of causes of addiction but in this book the focus is on what happens to the individual at and after the end of addiction. How is it that some people who appear to be inextricably trapped in long-term addiction actually come to a point of stopping? What happens then? What challenges face them, and how do they succeed in facing them? Where do they go from there? Is life forever marred by their past addiction?

While many people experiment with chemical substances and do not become addicted, for a variety of reasons others do. They may or may not seek help, but they commonly feel ashamed of what has happened to them. Is it all self-inflicted? While people love to enjoy the euphoric results of being drunk, high or spaced out, they tend to frown on those who fall into the trap of addiction. This is partly because it is not easy to know how to deal with someone who is intoxicated. It is frightening. How do you respond when someone is out of his or her mind? So people with drug addictions tend to be feared and scapegoated. Sometimes they do indeed live up to their worst reputations, but when someone who has been chronically addicted comes to the end of the line with their drinking or drug using, it is fascinating to discover what actually happens. All the narrators here said that one of the reasons they did not mind what they had said being made more generally public was that it might help somebody else. Looking back, they were appalled at the way they behaved when they were in the worst throes of their addictions.

The attitudes and expectations of family, friends and society at large have a powerful influence on the outcome for the individual, as with many other psychological problems. In the case of addiction the problem has been brought about to some degree by the person's own choices so it may not be easy for those affected or for bystanders to get away from a punitive, intolerant attitude. Extremely negative expectations tend to predominate. In the narratives that follow, the reader will have the chance to consider how much personal choice and responsibility is involved in addictions and in overcoming them. This is of profound importance in finding one's own way of relating to people who are addicted. Some professionals, for example, have misgivings about engaging with people who are or have been addicted, either because they are rightly wary of people who are liable to turn up in intoxicated states, or because addiction can recur even after a long period. The intention is that by presenting the experiences and views of people who are now successfully rebuilding their lives free from former addictions we can see that those who have been addicted can not only recover, but thrive and develop. An important question is why this should be so and how it comes about. It goes against the common assumption that the outcome for addicted people is inevitably hopeless.

The narrators

In the course of work in a National Health Service Drug and Alcohol Treatment Service over a period of years, a group of us, all interested in discovering more about the long-term outcome of treatment, had the opportunity to trace the progress of former patients, in many cases long after they had finished treatment. They each have their own ideas about the challenges that faced them and about what helped them. The narrators are not people who have merely dabbled in drugs or been binge drinkers. They were all chronically addicted to either alcohol or heroin, in addition to other psychotropic drugs which can be taken orally or injected, or to all of these. They speak from their own particular perspectives, formed by time, geography, their childhood backgrounds and their social setting, as well as by their personalities. It is inspiring to talk to people who have overcome great hardship and suffering. In the course of recognising their own vulnerability and finding ways to deal with it, many of them have re-evaluated their lives. If you look at a section in a library about addiction, the vast majority of books will be written by theoreticians or those who offer treatment. At the hospital we wanted to restore the balance and let the words of patients and former patients be heard.

The narrators have all been addicted to either alcohol or heroin, or to both. In addition, they nearly all smoked tobacco, and the heroin injectors would use cocktails of drugs according to what was readily available and affordable. They sometimes injected other drugs, such as Ritalin or cocaine, instead of or in addition to heroin, as well as taking other drugs orally, particularly benzodiazepines, such as Valium, to give them an added hit. If at certain times they couldn't get drugs, they drank more.

Alcohol and heroin share certain unique characteristics. Both, if taken in sufficient quantity over a period of time, will induce a need that is both mental and physical. In cases of chronic use, they produce physical withdrawal symptoms which can be so severe that they require medical intervention or special care in the first days after stopping. These drugs share the characteristic of producing *physical tolerance*. This means that you need to keep increasing the amount you use or drink to produce the effects you experienced when you started experimenting. This tends to lead to physical, mental and social problems. Both drugs, when used without due caution, cause harm which can be life threatening, as can withdrawal from alcohol (see Appendices 1 and 2). Other drugs that are commonly misused, such as cocaine, ecstasy and amphetamines, produce psychological withdrawal symptoms, but because alcohol and heroin both produce physical as well as psychological withdrawal symptoms, there are added complications in stopping using them. If an individual comes under the thrall of any of these drugs, his or her lifestyle is likely to be radically affected, which means that they will need to make a radical readjustment when they stop. Many people, but not all, need help to stop. When people stop without formal treatment, this is called *spontaneous remission* or *self-initiated recovery*. Some of the narrators talk about their experiences of this.

Treatment perspectives

The treatment of patients consisted of outpatient or day-patient care to offer a forum in which to consider the need for change and help in reducing risks. Inpatient care was offered, either in cases of overdose or treatment of serious health problems arising from the addiction, or for detoxification. After patients had completed this initial stage of their treatment, there was a long-running weekly group, mainly for people who were intent upon achieving and maintaining abstinence from either drugs or alcohol. This was not a time-limited group, for once a person had been accepted into the group, they could attend again without a formal assessment. We intended this to create a sense that there was somewhere they could come when they felt desperate, either because they had had a lapse or a relapse, or because they were afraid they were about to have one, or because of a new crisis in their lives. The group set its own rules, one of which was that if someone who came had a positive breathalyser reading for alcohol, they spent time with one of the group leaders individually. They were then either encouraged to come to the next meeting without having taken any drugs or alcohol, or were offered an individual outpatient appointment at another time. At that time there was no available test for drugs other than alcohol which would give an immediate result, but members of the group were pretty astute at spotting signs of drug use. Their suspicions were voiced and became part of the proceedings of the group. We learned an enormous amount from being facilitators of this group, and over a period of ten years there were only five main facilitators – another factor which helped build a sense of trust all round. Quite a few of the members of the hospital group were members of the Alcoholics Anonymous (AA) Fellowship, which could at times arouse bitter arguments in meetings. The positive aspect, however, was that these members could help to introduce others who wished to try AA or, later, when it was established locally, Narcotics Anonymous (NA). The significance of the influence of AA is an important part of the story and some relevant features of its work and ethos are described below.

One aspect of the service was unusual: there was no prescribing of methadone or any other opiate substitute. The psychiatrist in charge of treatment did not believe in its efficacy. Therapy and one-to-one support were the means of treatment, before and after inpatient or outpatient detoxification under medical supervision. In thinking about how best to help someone who came for treatment, we kept away from dogma by keeping one very clear idea in mind, which was the parity of importance between the person and the problem. The relationship between therapist and patient is ever changing and is, in our view, the key to treatment. When treatment of people who are addicted becomes rigid and stereotyped, there tends to be poor attendance at clinics. Patients want to be regarded as individuals, and they need to feel valued by their therapists. It is unlikely that the narrators would have been so generous in giving interviews had they not felt that their views were taken seriously and were regarded as useful in adding to an understanding of addiction.

Addiction has physical, psychological and social effects because people not only become addicted to the drug itself but also become entirely enmeshed in the addicted lifestyle. Cognitive therapy, in its aim of requiring the individual to think about what they are doing, plays a vital role at many stages of treatment. The specific cognitive approaches of motivational interviewing (Miller and Rollnick 2002) and of relapse prevention (Marlatt and Gordon 1985) were employed at different stages, but it became apparent, when talking to colleagues, that behind the cognitive approach there often lies an enduring curiosity. This relates to the paradoxical picture presented by someone who seems unwilling or unable to escape from a path of enslavement to favoured drugs, while doing him or herself considerable overt harm. Unconscious motivation speaks loud and clear in people's actions, and therefore it is hoped that the psychodynamic perspective will also be of interest to those who work primarily in other ways because it enriches an understanding of what is going on throughout any treatment process. Of the three principal therapists at the time when these narrators received treatment, the lead psychiatrist had had a Freudian analysis, one facilitator of the relapse prevention group had group analytic as well as nursing training, and the other facilitator, the author, is an analytical psychologist. Coming from different analytic schools and different professional disciplines, we each brought our own perspective as therapist and as research writer.

Psychological principles

It may be helpful to outline here the most relevant psychological concepts which informed our understanding of these patients, especially for those readers who are less familiar with this field. Although cognitive approaches were part of our repertoire, especially in motivating patients to think about the need to change and in aiming to prevent relapses, behind this lay a constant awareness of the power of unconscious factors to undermine rational thinking and 'catch us out' in our well-laid treatment plans. On the other hand, unconscious factors of a different colour were clearly of great benefit in our interactions with the patients. What follows is a personal choice of concepts which are particularly relevant in considering the process of addiction, treatment intervention and recovering. I have chosen to use everyday terms wherever possible because some psychodynamic terms seem to me to be mystifying to all but specialists in that field. For readers who wish to pursue the ideas further I have added a few key references in Appendix 3.

The field of psychodynamics is basically concerned with elucidating the positive and negative psychological influences on the human developmental process in terms of psychological growth. Intrinsic in this picture is the varied character of our relatedness to others. On the positive side, it is recognised that *good enough* care and nurture from the beginning of life to its very end provides a *containing* or stabilising function. From this springboard can arise not only development of human potential, but also resilience in situations of difficulty and particularly the capacity for looking after oneself, i.e. *self-care*. Deficits or disruptions in nurture, on the other hand, produce a need to protect oneself from unbearable anxiety or distress, and then *defence mechanisms* spring up. These play a part in the development of an addiction – people want to compensate for and blot out their woes, as will be apparent in many of the narratives. Of course we all need psychological defences to survive in life, but sometimes these defences can come to rule our lives.

If all goes well enough in an individual's development, he or she can develop a sense of *self-agency* and purposefulness in life. We can have long-term, rather than immediate goals. If things go well, we become able to tolerate frustration, to accept the reality of imperfections in others and to take account of our own weaknesses. Such capacities enable us to relate to others and to be confident that we have a continuing place in the minds of others.

Relationship with others, including a need to be intimate with them at certain times and to distance oneself at other times, goes alongside relationship with oneself and a capacity to be self-aware, a capacity diminished during addiction, as many of the narrators describe. This includes tolerating the fact that we all have many facets to our personalities, a sort of network of varied facets which sometimes feel cohesive, sometimes divisive, which can make us feel torn or conflicted. In addiction there is a curtailment of this variety, as only the addicted part of the personality thrives at the expense of other aspects of the individual.

In relation to others, we may at times need to *identify* strongly with someone else, to take something we need from them, just as we did in our infancy. There are times, too, when we find ourselves re-enacting elements of an earlier relationship with someone in the present. In a treatment setting, this is called *transference* (on the part of the patient), or *counter-transference* (on the part of the therapist). This implies something very different from a rational response to the other person. We may find ourselves unwittingly reacting to them according to what we once felt towards someone significant in our early lives. The reaction can be of a fluctuating and infinitely varied complexion. According to how aware of this factor therapists can allow themselves to become, this phenomenon can be of great benefit in the treatment; but if, as therapists, we remain in its grip without due awareness, it causes unforeseen trouble. Unacknowledged transference or countertransference often lies at the heart of the reason patients fail to turn up for appointments.

If development proceeds sufficiently well in an individual's childhood, adolescence and adulthood, two further benefits accrue, the first being the growth of the *capacity to imagine*. 'Things' don't need to be concrete – we can picture them as images, hold them in mind, and, as it were, play with them. Further to this is the capacity for *symbolic thinking*, where we can appreciate the interplay of the real with the imaginary in the arts or indeed in everyday life. In addiction, these capacities either fail to develop or they are suppressed, so that life loses its sparkle and the need to take more of the drug grows stronger in compensation.

Other relevant concepts are *fixations* (attachment to certain objects or rigid patterns) or *repetition compulsions* (seemingly becoming unable to escape from re-enacting former patterns of emotion and behaviour). These can make us lose heart and feel blocked in life, overwhelmed by our problems. Time and time again, in spite of our best intentions, we find ourselves trapped in situations which replicate unhappy times from our earlier days. We can become stuck in these rigid attitudes or in repetition of former patterns, against our better judgment. This could be said of many people who are addicted.

Finally, throughout the narratives, there appear certain patterns which are *archetypal* in human life. Three that recur are the archetype of the lost child, embodied in those who have been abandoned and deeply traumatised in childhood; the archetype of the negative hero, embodied in those who followed an exciting but reckless path during their adolescence; and the archetype of the wounded healer, embodied in those who are no longer addicted and who, though damaged by their previous addiction, work tirelessly to help others. Archetypal patterns hold a special power to affect us, whether we observe them in the lives of others or realise that we are held in their sway ourselves. They are powerful unconscious motivating factors for good or ill in life.

The contribution of C. G. Jung

Jung had a particular interest in development in adult life. To describe this, it is necessary to say something about his view of the psyche. He observed that many people are restricted by their need to meet the demands or supposed demands of the outside world by presenting a fine *persona* to the world. He also saw that there are parts of ourselves, not necessarily 'bad', of which we are largely oblivious. These he called the personal *shadow*. Some of the narrators in this book were initially plagued by the need to present a fine persona, and so drank or used drugs to assuage their disappointment in themselves – so making matters worse. Others fought against any awareness of their shadow side, so in fact ended up omnipotently fighting the world. They were terrified of their own vulnerability. These are somewhat simplified examples of what promoted their addictions, but give some idea of what they had to face when they left their addictions behind. Accepting shadow aspects of the psyche, hitherto only glimpsed, is part of what Jung had in mind when he wrote about *individuation*. Those narrators who left their addictions behind many years ago illustrate the effects of individuation in practice. They not only allowed themselves to know and accept their weaknesses, but also put them to good use. They have discovered how they really want to lead their lives, using their true strengths, which for many years had become obscured or had never developed.

Jung treated many patients who were addicted to alcohol in the course of his working life. However, as he wrote in a letter only a few months before his death in 1961 to one of the founding members of AA who had contacted him, he had not committed his ideas in writing earlier for fear of being generally misunderstood. He intuitively sensed that as well as being a defence against anxiety, addiction to alcohol represented a 'spiritual thirst' which had gone awry (Jung 1976: 623). The reader is invited to consider to what degree this applies to the narrators here. A further idea of Jung's was that the isolation in which an addicted individual exists puts him or her 'outside the protective wall of human community' (Jung 1976: 624). This is a vital but little-mentioned aspect of addiction, which also has repercussions at the stage of leaving the addiction behind. In practical terms, Jung saw no point in offering formal analysis to a person in the grip of an addiction, and in one case he made the suggestion to a former patient who had relapsed that he should put himself in a position to experience a conversion, though offering no guarantee that this would help him to stop drinking. In fact Roland Hazard, the ex-patient, did contact an evangelical Christian group, the Oxford Group, back in his native USA, and did experience a 'conversion'. He was later influential in the beginnings of AA. An intriguing question is whether leaving an addiction behind leads on to a total reorientation in life, similar to that ensuing after a religious conversion, or whether the changes are limited to patterns of behaviour. Jung believed that the yearning for a life over and above the mundane is what makes us human. This is highly relevant to the question of the deficits in life which might increase an individual's vulnerability to becoming addicted, to the restriction of experience in addiction where life revolves around a chemical, and, above all, to what promotes recovery.

Alcoholics Anonymous

As many of the narrators became members of AA, I shall say a few words about the 'Fellowship', as it and its fellow groups are known. The idea is a simple one, but it has been effective in helping millions of people worldwide. There are three premises on which it is based: first, it has only one aim – to help those in trouble with alcohol; second, it carries no funds and has no affiliation to any other group or organisation; and finally, its starting point is that the individual needs to abandon his or her omnipotence and acknowledge powerlessness over alcohol. Four basic principles underlie the spiritual programme of AA, called the Twelve Step Programme (See Appendix 4). These involve first acknowledging that you don't always know best (which may or may not involve acknowledging a Higher Power, however one envisages God); that you make up as best you can for the harm you caused when you were addicted; that you go on thinking about what your are doing, rather than regarding the change after stopping as being the end of the story; and finally, that you help others, in reciprocity for the help you yourself have received. AA is regularly attacked in the press on the grounds that its members replace one addiction with another, by becoming dependent on AA. In response to this, it is worth remembering that being dependent on people is generally less toxic than being dependent on a drug. There is an important distinction between dependence and attachment, too. In the case of the narrators here, it is interesting to observe whether those who have no involvement with AA or NA tread a different or a similar path in the process of recovering.

Research into the long-term outcome of addiction

There were two practical reasons why people who had been treated by the service were invited to give interviews. The most compelling was that the team at the hospital wanted to find out what happened to them following their treatment. What was the use of putting enormous effort into our work if it all turned out to be for nothing? We wanted to learn. We had studied the theories and knew what others had written about the various modes of treatment, but we wanted to test those theories, particularly our own pet theories, to see what the patients themselves thought at the time, and how they fared afterwards. Long term is often taken to mean a year or two. Yet addiction is claimed to be notoriously difficult to escape, and recidivism in the form of *relapse* is known to be common. Many of our former patients continued to have lapses or relapses far beyond two years, so we were keen to look at a longer time span.

The lead psychiatrist first applied this idea in the early 1970s to eighty-six heroin injectors who formed a cohort of people to be followed (Rathod 1972, 1977). They were not selected at random, but were the eighty-six consecutive referrals to the service over a period of months who were confirmed by clinical tests to be injecting heroin and other drugs. These people were followed up until 2005, and the study includes the causes of death of the nineteen known to have died. Interestingly, the majority of those died of the direct consequences of either alcohol or methadone use, though of course their immune systems would have been compromised by their former or continuing heroin use. We could get no information whatever on three people, and two had emigrated. However, of the others who are still alive, most were discovered to have been abstinent for many years, and were living settled lives. The follow-up period was thirty-three years (Rathod *et al.* 2005).

The second reason for asking people to give interviews was that in the 1980s our service obtained a government grant for three years to undertake educational activities locally. The final session of each of the study days and weekend workshops for members of the public and groups of statutory workers comprised interviews of former patients by their therapists, followed by questions from the audience. These interviews were video recorded and if the interviewee later agreed to the recording being kept for educational purposes, having viewed it, then it was retained. Otherwise, it became their personal property. We found these video recordings invaluable for training volunteer counsellors and for our own learning process. Further interviews were audio-recorded for a separate outcome study when we wished to look at how people who had been treated for drink problems viewed their treatment in retrospect and how they had fared since. This study identified themes discernible in the various stages of addiction and recovery (Addenbrooke 2004). Sometimes people were interviewed soon after they had completed their treatment and then long afterwards. This was particularly illuminating for us. While we recognise the hazards of generalising from a small number of cases, the fifteen people quoted in this book are part of a larger number in our collection. Rather than reporting on measurable markers of change, the aim is to let the narrators express their own thoughts.

We had a rare opportunity to tap a rich seam. The former patients who gave interviews had nothing to gain in monetary terms. They had all had the experience of knowing people, particularly in some cases those close to them, who had a poor understanding of addiction. They wanted to help correct some of the misunderstandings. The impression we got was that they could look back on the times when they had been firmly challenged or had had a tough time facing their difficulties with the staff without too much rancour. They all wanted to give something back, which is in itself a gain.

The presentation of the narratives

The words of the narrators are quoted verbatim, apart from the removal of excessive repetition, some 'ums' and 'ers', and any discourse which wanders far from the theme in question. The interviewers invited the narrators to tell their stories as they wished. Each narrative is followed by some background information and comments are offered as a starting point for thinking about psychological aspects of the case.

Specific narratives have been chosen to illustrate various stages because they are particularly illuminating, but these are not taken out of context – the narrators tell their stories as they wish. Becoming addicted, being addicted, coming to the point of stopping, and going on from there form a continuum, and different people simply say more about one stage than another, according to what is most vivid for them. I believe that it is easier for a reader to become involved imaginatively with one person at a time, so the reader is invited to observe what life was like after addiction from the very start of the book when three people speak about their experience of being addicted. Conversely, three of the narrators in the final section on the long-term outcome depict very clearly what life was like for them while they were addicted, and one narrator was still addicted when he came to talk to us. I hope that this will provide a patchwork, creating a picture of how change evolved in each individual's life.

It could be argued that these people had a vested interest in painting a dramatic picture with themselves as the heroes at the centre of the narratives. If this is so, one reason is that telling their stories with this slant may help them to retain their belief in themselves and their sobriety. A professor of psychology who spent a long period in a hospital ward following a stroke observed how being able to talk to one another about their experiences transformed the morale of the patients, including himself (Richman 2000). There is, however, another way of looking at it. Many of the narrators explicitly said to us that they wanted their words to be of help to other people in the same situation and therefore wanted to give as honest a picture as possible.

Chronic addiction is far more than a behavioural or secondary problem. Rather than being a constant state, it is a process, ever developing in one direction or another. Because addiction tends to push people to the margins of what Jung termed 'the protective wall of human community' (Jung 1976: 624) it is not only the drug use that has to change if people are to succeed in leaving their addictions behind. Jung's idea that alcoholism was a 'spiritual thirst' rather than being merely a defence has specific implications for what happens in the period of rebuilding after addiction is left behind.

Part 1

Lost in the labyrinth of addiction

The following pages present three people all of whom describe how they fell under the influence of their favourite drug, and how they fell further and further into a lifestyle dominated by that drug. You will see how effective the addicted lifestyle is in trapping people. In each case you can observe how the original motivation for using the drug gets lost and changes into something quite different. The narratives show what addicted people feel about themselves as well as what happens to their relationships, and to what extent their preoccupation with the drug comes to obscure any concern they have for others. What appears in technicolour is the destructive influence of the addiction over most aspects of their lives.

Chapter 2

A shameful secret

Anna was sent to the hospital by her GP because she felt desperate about her drinking and the troubles it was causing her, although she had continued to present a respectable face to the world. She was admitted for detoxification and here she is speaking to her former psychiatrist fifteen months later. She shows how life can be for someone who has been drinking increasingly over the years with serious effects. Although she felt that things in her life were going very wrong, she didn't realise until she was far down the line that she could do anything about her drinking.

Alcohol was the problem that brought me to the hospital. I went to the doctor thinking that I was drinking too much and that I had a problem. I didn't know about alcoholism. I didn't know about alcoholics. I went to see my own GP and the very next day he asked me to come and see you. You asked me what I was drinking, how much, how frequently and you asked me if I'd like to come into the hospital to dry out. With that, I came in the next day. You wanted me to come that day, but I had to get another drink. So – that night I had a last drink.

The thing that took me to my GP was that I just couldn't cope any longer, really could not cope with my life. Every morning when I got up, I never had a hangover, for the twenty years that I was drinking, but I had blackouts. I never ever remember any one of the five days going to work, how I got there, how I left home. I never felt drunk and I carried on a very responsible job.

Nobody spotted anything. My boss was absolutely shocked when I told him, because I functioned very, very well. You know, I think, being as I am, maybe I was a good actress. That's why I went to the GP – I couldn't keep this act up any longer. I needed help. I was desperate for it. What I really could no longer cope with was myself, with the lie I was leading. I got fed up with my own lies. I felt very, very guilty.

I became conscious of the fact that drink was affecting my life. The last six months of my drinking I was doing horrendous things. In one instance I attacked, sexually tried to attack, my friend's husband. At the time I did it I didn't know anything about it. These were the blackouts. Whatever other people were doing in drink, coming home from various places, I would join them. Really disgusting things, you know.

And the next day when my husband would tell me about these things, I couldn't believe it. And I went to these places and checked up, and I just got fed up with going around apologising. I became disgusted with myself. Oh, very much so.

At that time I was drinking a litre bottle of Liebfraumilch, to start with, and then the bottle of whisky, a fully bottle of whisky, straight after, every day. Five thirty in the evening was my first drink. I never drank by day, only Saturdays and Sundays. I don't know how long I'd been drinking alcoholically. I would think maybe ten years out of the twenty. Alcoholically – I would say it's when you've *got* to have it. I would say that's probably when it must have become a problem, but I didn't know, of course, I thought it was normal. I was drinking just to get me out of my misery, so I could get a good night's sleep. The pressures became so horrendous. I just couldn't cope. So I thought, 'Well if I have my two bottles, I shall sleep tonight.'

I just thought my problems might go away, you know – I had a son born with Hirschman's disease, and he was in Great Ormond Street Hospital for two years and I stayed with him. I left my elder son with my mother in Wales where I was born and brought up. I didn't think Dan was going to live, and I just couldn't cope with this problem. I'm a farmer's daughter and I was very, very shy – London was a big, wicked city to me. Living down there in the sticks, you know, you thought if you went to Cardiff for the day, you were emigrating! You know, coming to London, and I just drank and drank and drank, but in saying that you see, Dan is twenty-one now – so that's going back a while.

My first husband left me as soon as Dan was born – twenty-one years ago. I was married to him for about four years before he left me. He just found someone else. I didn't have a drink problem then. I coped with it and with the children. I wasn't taking any drugs at that time. I've had a nervous condition right through my life, really, and my doctor prescribed Valium and various things for my nerves for as long as I can remember. Valium, Librium – that type of thing. The largest dose of Valium or tranquillisers, 50mg a day, I was taking for many, many years.

I was born in Wales. I never knew my father. What happened was that my mother already had one illegitimate child, my brother, and my grandmother was a very staunch Wesleyan. She asked my mother if she was pregnant, and she said *no*. There's this Home, and as soon as my grandmother realised that she was pregnant, which was several months on, because my mother was lying – she put her in the Home, and there I was for adoption. I was born in 1943 and the Italians were over here because the war was on, and I do believe my father was an Italian prisoner of war, but this is only what I've heard from my grandparents. I have no definite facts. I was in the Home until I was two – so I understand. Then my mother met this farmer. She was going to work on his land, and after they got together he came to the Home and adopted me and brought me up as his own child. I had a wonderful, wonderful childhood. He always said to me that I was very lucky because he chose me, you know? I idolised him; absolutely idolised him. I have never felt bitter or stigmatised because of the way I was born and adopted, because up to the age of two I wasn't really that aware of it, and at school there were a lot of children born in 1943 who didn't have fathers. I loved the farm life, so in some ways I was very fortunate.

It's very hard to put a time to it, now, but I would say I'd been drinking alcoholically for something like ten years. I tried many times to cut down or say, 'I won't drink today,' and I failed. I tried to drink just the wine, which I didn't like too much anyway. I tried to drink later in the evening, instead of coming straight in from the office and running to the cupboard and getting my first drink. I'd go shopping, but I couldn't even cope with that. I got such terrible shakes. I tried just going on the Liebfraumilch, but the Liebfraumilch did nothing for me. I couldn't afford to pay for two bottles, my salary was taken up with one bottle, so I'd get something cheaper to subsidise it.

After my detox in the hospital I went to Portugal to convalesce the day after. I threw myself into wet places, to try and conquer the battle as soon as possible, and I succeeded, fortunately. I didn't find it too hard the first couple of weeks. The first couple of weeks were fine for me. There was no problem in Portugal. It was about three months after. Well, for one thing, your memory gets very short. You know, the honeymoon period was over, and being a good girl – 'See how clever I am! I'm not drinking now.' And then your memory gets short of the time on the ward. You forget the sweating, the horrors, the hallucinations, the nightmares of the drinking. And then you think – perhaps it wasn't so bad. But you do remember the last drink and it *was* so bad. I coped by going to AA meetings. And I also came to the hospital group for quite a while. I felt very threatened because in the group some people were bragging about controlling their drink. That upset me very, very much. You know, I really wanted to join them, to see if I could control mine. But you taught me that in my case it wasn't on. It's either everything or nothing. Absolutely. No. One drink to me would be one bottle again immediately. And I realised that.

Since I stopped being anaesthetised I am more aware. I have many problems. My husband has been back in intensive care. He had a heart attack, another heart attack, about twelve months ago. He's got over that, fortunately. But two of my children have serious problems. I am still battling with all these problems. Oh yes. I definitely have not got another drink in me. I drank for enough years *with* these problems and they did not go away. No.

I do think part of the reason I drank was that I have felt very guilty about the children. That it was my drinking that caused their problems. Although they came into a reasonably clean, tidy house, and the meal was there, I mean, I just kept to my chair at night. I wouldn't talk to anyone. As long as I had my two bottles, you know, and when they asked, 'Mummy, can I have a tenner?' I couldn't get it out of my purse quick enough. My conscience. So I was paying them off all the time.

Now, today, they don't get any money. But I haven't won my children back yet. My eldest son has got an awful lot of respect for me. I've *almost* got him back, you know? Almost. But the other two – no. It's going to take quite a bit of time and working. At least I feel more respect for myself, now, I can lift my head now and walk anywhere, you know, I don't care. I'm pleased that I'm a sober alcoholic.

Anna started drinking when her baby's life hung in the balance and he was in the care of the medical and nursing staff. She was far from home and far from anyone who could look after her. This situation echoed all too clearly the start of her life when she was left in the children's home. The *lost child* archetype was being re-enacted. Far from home, seeking treatment for her ill child, Anna again felt abandoned. Although the hospital allowed her access to her baby and provided care for him for two years, it seems there was no support for her. At this point she discovered a substitute mother, alcohol, which soothed her and helped her to obliterate her anxiety over her baby in hospital and the older child she had left at home with her mother. She drank to blot out the unbearable feelings of loneliness and abandonment, stranded far from her home with a child she believed to be dying.

This narrative centres on different aspects of mothering. Going back two generations, her strict grandmother refused to accept a grandchild born out of wedlock, and so forced her daughter to abandon her own little daughter. However, Anna's mother was able to rescue her from the orphanage by choosing a husband who gave Anna a home and affection. Anna herself was not so fortunate in her choice of husband, for he left her when she herself was a young mother.

It is the nature of alcohol to exert a continuing attraction, and what started out as a temporary prop became an increasingly demanding element in her life. Without fully realising what was happening, by the time she was again married, with teenage children and a full-time career, she had become addicted. When her children were growing up, she was filled with shame because she knew that she was failing them as a mother. Being trapped in this pattern compounded the problem. Later she drank to blot out the realisation of what her drinking had done to her and specifically to her relationship with her children. Her guilt towards her children was heavy and painful, and the more ashamed she felt at not being able to reduce her drinking when she tried to do so, the more secretive and remote she had to become. She bought her children off so that she could drink in peace. Alcohol in truth separated her from her family. She loathed herself. She felt helpless. She didn't think there was anything she could do about her drinking.

It is amazing how successful she was at fooling people who she worked closely with in an office about the extent of her drinking. They had absolutely no idea that she was having blackouts and was arriving at work in the mornings with not a clue as to how she got there. This is an example of how much someone may be drinking without this being obvious even to close colleagues. She never felt drunk because she kept herself well topped up, and she was able to carry out a responsible job, valued and respected by her boss.

All through her drinking days, she lived in a vicious circle of guilt and disgust at herself. She says that she tried many times to stop or cut down, but her attempts all failed, a further source of shame. The vicious circle is like this: drinkers often know how much harm their drinking is doing to others and consequently feel disgusted at themselves. Then they drink to hide away from their guilt. Anna was trapped. She felt ashamed, so she had to try to conceal the effects of her drinking. She loathed herself. She felt helpless. She didn't think there was anything she could do about her drinking.

It is also surprising that she seems so naive about her reliance on prescription drugs over the years. She actually says that she wasn't taking any drugs at the time, as if prescribed drugs didn't come into the picture. She says nothing about stopping that drug use, but somehow she did manage it, as she was not being prescribed any drugs at the time of her interview, just smoking tobacco very heavily. It remains unclear whether this was denial on her part or whether she never discussed the impact or these drugs in conjunction with her drinking with her doctor or her therapist. The joint impact of tranquillisers and heavy drinking would have been considerable, as the drugs and alcohol potentiate the effects of one another.

Her take on addiction is very clear. She says that you are addicted 'when you've got to have it'. As to her thinking about the reasons for her drinking, again she is clear: 'I was drinking just to get out of my misery.' This fits exactly with the views of Edward Khantzian, who has worked with many addicts, that addiction is a defence against mental pain or anguish in those who have not been able to develop a sufficiently strong capacity for caring for themselves in difficult situations (Khantzian 2003). Maybe she has always been more committed to caring for others than for herself.

She is not the only person to mention having felt absolutely impelled to have 'one last drink' or 'one last fix' before stopping. More unusual, however, is her attitude to drinking environments immediately after stopping, when she says, 'I threw myself into wet places.' This is something definitely not recommended for those who have just stopped and want to 'stay stopped'. She seems to have known what she could cope with. It was as if she wanted to immerse herself in the atmosphere of bars and clubs ('wet places') to show herself that she could remain unaffected. When she says that she hasn't got another drink in her, she implies that with one drink she would be plummeted back into her addiction.

Although at the time of this interview Anna had only been abstinent for fourteen months, this represents an achievement which runs counter to the depressing expectation that drinkers inevitably revert to drinking. She readily faced up to her difficulties once she had sought help. In fact, to the present day, she has not returned to drinking and she has persevered in finding ways to support her family through their problems.

It was the desire to atone for what she perceived as her inadequate mothering that eventually motivated her strongly to leave her addiction behind. To speculate on what has helped Anna in leaving her addiction behind, one factor is definitely her strong transference feelings, both positive and negative, on to the staff at the hospital. Just as she was rescued by a loving mother and stepfather in difficult circumstances, so she has allowed herself to be rescued by the hospital staff. In the course of her treatment, sometimes she expressed fury at the staff, but she was able to work through this and begin to understand herself and her anger. She is also a committed member of AA. She has continued to maintain contact with both sources of help. It is perhaps also partly her intrinsic resilience which has enabled her to become strong in the face of difficulties.

In conclusion

Knowing and not knowing

It is often said that addicted people deliberately deny the severity of their addictions, but something more subtle may be at work, for addiction itself blinds the individual to the reality of their situation. It can take time and patience for the person themselves and for their therapist to see the true picture.

Most people who leave their addictions behind have to live in the same environment in which they led their addicted lives – the pressures are still there. Unpleasant memories of detoxifying tend to fade over time and act less as a deterrent to lapses. Knowing and understanding the characteristics of addiction and the risk of relapsing are a vital part of recovery.

Shame

It is regrettable that Anna did not admit the extent of her drinking to the doctors who prescribed tranquillisers to her over the years, but it is equally regrettable that doctors failed to probe this sufficiently. She might have had help with her drinking habits at a far earlier stage. Those who are addicted are often successful at hiding their habits for a long time. This is dangerous, because the need for secrecy and the sense of shame play into and exacerbate one another. This can stop people from looking at their situation head on and from seeking a solution to their problems.

Early traumas and their aftermath

Trauma early in life is often echoed later, although the individual is not willingly re-enacting the role of victim. The trouble is that the emotions evoked are doubly painful because they resound, just as echoes do. Anna's case demonstrates how a person can start to face up to her past rather than continuing to hide from it in addiction. Early traumatic experiences need not prevent successful recovery, which involves continuing to face and find a resolution to personal problems.

The Lost Child *searching for rescue by the* Good Mother

Anna's life story is rich in examples of this archetypal theme: her mother and stepfather rescued her; her son was rescued by the children's hospital; she sought rescue from feeling abandoned in alcohol; our hospital rescued her alcoholic self, and she could then start to rescue her own children once she stopped drinking. At yet another level, in her inner life, Anna can be said to have been searching for the Good Mother within herself, so that she could not only be a mother to her own children, but also to the vulnerable part of herself.

Chapter 3

Down and out

Gerald had been in and out of alcohol treatment units and psychiatric hospitals for years before he came to our hospital on the recommendation of the local AA. Here, in his forties, he is talking to one of the facilitators of the relapse prevention group which he had attended since the time of his referral, as well as having individual appointments. In this narrative, as with others in this book, events are not recounted in the order in which they occurred; rather, Gerald chose his own way to tell his story. As he says, he was addicted not only to alcohol, but also to drugs such as codeine which he could buy 'over the counter' without a prescription.

My wife asked me to come back here from Northern Ireland, which is where I originally hail from. I'd been doing well in Northern Ireland. I wasn't drinking or taking tablets. Nothing. I didn't want to come really, but, ah, when there's a chance to get your children back and your wife. . . And for a couple of months I was doing all right, and then she said, 'Leave!' You see, I got married in a church years ago, but I have found out in AA that a practising alcoholic, or anybody that thinks that way, *they don't get married – they take hostages.* So when she finally wised up – not that I liked it at the time, I took it hard – she did me the service of my life by getting divorced from me, because it made me sit down and think. But it was not enough at that time to actually stop me drinking.

Back in Ireland I was again in a mental hospital, under Section[1]. When I found out that I couldn't leave the hospital I went crazy. The doctor there told me, 'You're in here for the remainder of your life. Your parents are dead, and now your wife's gone. You're a danger to yourself. So we'll keep you for the remainder of your life. Just knock about here.' I said, 'Good, good,' but I was scheming straight away – how I was going to deal with this guy and get out. I got out! Four hours later I was out on the main road. I hailed a bus, and got off down the road to Southern Ireland, so the British authorities couldn't touch me. See? And when the forty days were up, I came back to Northern Ireland and by that time the Police couldn't touch me. Having schemed my way out of hospital, I started drinking more or less straight away. I'm cross-addicted. It's mostly cough mixtures and tablets, but all sorts of drugs too. Yeah, I went back on everything straight away.

When I was six I had asthma. Doctors put me on ephedrine[2]. And up till I was about nine, I was taking this and I found I got better results from it if I took it liquid. I didn't know why I couldn't sleep and why I was seeing things when I got into the drinking. I was first drinking when I was five, then by the time I was nine, once a month – though there was no drink allowed in our house – I would drink approximately once a month. I was taking the bottles to bed with me, two bottles of wine. I would drink in bed, you see? At about fourteen I schemed my way out of school. Left home in Northern Ireland and came to this country, see, and really started drinking heavily – all the time. When I couldn't get drink and I had no money, I would shoot off to the doctor and be lying, and would get tablets and medicine – and I would buy stuff. I would take it – if it moved, I took it; if it didn't move, I took it – as long as it changed my mood. You see? *Anything*, no matter what it was. I couldn't stick the pain of not drinking. I took an easier, softer method. I would use anything at all.

After I returned to Northern Ireland, I slept out for a little while, and then I went back on tablets and cough mixtures and stomach mixtures and drink. And it all just led on from there. Eventually I went back to an organisation called AA and they started to tell me things. For the first time in my life, I started really listening. See, all my life, I thought I knew everything. I knew it all. AA told me something – I knew they were telling the truth, but I would argue. I'd do it *my* way. It was the wrong way! I used to go to these AA meetings and say, 'Well, I'm not drinking. I'm all right.' I'd have loads of tablets down me. I didn't know I was eating the booze. I was drinking it in cough mixtures and all kinds of medicine. But when I returned here from Ireland again, AA arranged for some AA people to meet me when I got off the plane, and they told me I also had to go to certain meetings and find out about my drinking at the hospital.

Over the years that I've been involved with this hospital, it's been difficult on both sides, at times. I started going each week to the Relapse Prevention meeting doped up on tablets and all sorts of other things I could get me hands on. I was sitting there, even though I'd passed the Breathalyser, being shaken awake. I was falling asleep with Heminevrin[3], and all those things I was taking. I was always taking something. You see? I was lying to myself. I found that out, at the end of the day. I was going to one of the meetings one day, sitting at the table – I was always fighting and talking – I could tell everybody else how to stop drinking by staying away from it, and you said to me, 'And what about you?' And I went home and started thinking of it. Physical things had started happening to me. You see? I was getting a lot of pain and bleeding and stuff. I said to myself, 'I'd better do something.'

So I came back into this AA and joined up and said, 'Now I'll start listening.' They taught me, 'Take the cotton wool out of your ears and put it in your mouth!' They taught me how to count to one. I was forty-four years of age before I learned how to count to one. You see, the curious thing in my life is that I could never face the truth. If you threw a question at me fast, I'd instinctively or impulsively lie to you. I could choose to spend my life lying. I did what I wanted, always scheming. And even today, if my daughter asks me something, I'll lie. And I'll have to say, 'Look, I'm sorry, that was a lie.' I find it hard to get out of. But if I want to stay clean, I have to learn the truth myself, and eventually the truth'll come out to other people. So I find this quite hard at present, although all I have to do is a day at a time. So that's it.

Over the years the pattern of my drinking and staying dry in between has changed, since I've been at the hospital. Sometimes it's quite difficult. I used to think I was wicked, I was weak. I'd have a craving for a drink, for the tablets, or whatever. I'd be bolshie, I'd say, 'All right, I'll have it.' The thing is, I'd suit myself at these times. Nowadays I think, 'I'll drink tomorrow. I'll take this stuff tomorrow. Not today. I'll not touch it today.' Stay away from one drink, from one tablet, no matter what it is, for one day at a time. If I can't do it for one day, I'll do it for half a day. One hour. Ten minutes. *Don't touch nothing today!* And that's how I have to work – on a daily basis, a daily reprieve. So I found this strategy with my self-help group.

I come to the clinic, and it is helping me. I kept going to this meeting here at the hospital for five years, you know, and I found out – I was watching people there five, six years of it, and I found that the people that went there consistently and persistently, they stayed off it. There was a turning point. It's something that I gave a lot of thought to, acknowledging that alcohol and the other drugs were causing my problems. I always thought all my life that the most important thing in my life was that I had to get some money, I had to get a job, had to see about getting the wife back, see my children, but the doctor here said, 'Look, that's not your problem. Your problem is drink and the other things you take. Work on this.' And I am an 'instant' person. I want everything yesterday. So nothing changed suddenly. I just got sick of being sick. And the physical stuff started taking over. I said to myself, 'You'll kill yourself here.' As I said, I started listening. At last. And then I came to realise that if you don't know everything and stop being God. . . You see? I said, 'I don't know everything.' I found out – I used to say, 'I'll do it by self-will, willpower.' I found out, I know today, that if I try to do it by willpower alone, then willpower's a total liability. I need help. I have to ask for help and to listen to the people that are trying to help me, and do what they suggest. I couldn't do it on my own.

It's only two and a half years since I acknowledged that I had a problem. I thought everybody in life drank, took stuff, but especially drink – the way I did. It was the most natural thing in the world to have hangovers, to have blackouts, to get locked up – in prison and stuff. It was just par for the course with the people I was mixing with.

When I was in Ireland previously, I'd been in some kind of treatment for my drink problems. I'll tell you what made me acknowledge it. I was in a bed in the hospital one night. It was on a Sunday. I was having convulsions. The doctors came and they said, 'We'd better send for a sky pilot.' And I said, 'Why, what's wrong now?' And they said, 'We can do nothing for you. You'd better see a clergyman.' So I said, 'Send me a clergyman quick.' And a clergyman came to hear my last confession. And I said, 'I don't want to hurt your feelings, but get me somebody else, like.' And he sent for his mate and he came and heard my last confession. And I said, 'Get me somebody else.' He got another priest then to hear my confession, but this priest knew me. He was a young chap, I'd known him for about four years, and as he was going out the door, he said, 'You'll be all right, you know.' And I said, 'Yeah,' and then he said, 'Would you like me to get the bishop?' And I was thinking, 'That's an idea,' you see! Scheming, and all. And, ah, then he said, 'You'll be all right. Just lie there.' And these convulsions kept coming. They frightened me, really frightened me. So I'd better do something. And that's the first time really, because I was always frightened at the end of the day that I'd have to get my wife back and get me children. I was lying there. There was no way out of this now. It really does matter if I die this way. And that's really when it struck home to me.

Well, I lived in a group home for five years, and now I have a little flat, and my daughter, she's living there too. The others are with their mother, after the court took its time to give me access to see them. You see? It takes patience just to think of it. But I had to get on top of my problem, drinking and other things first, before the other things could start to happen. And it's all happening, see.

My daughter had a problem with glue sniffing, or Tippex sniffing and stuff, and tablets, you see. The doctor's tablets. I don't question. I found out, you see. When I did speak to her, she said, 'Well you can't talk about these things.' And that's quite right. But I know today, you see, if I act the heavy father, and put my foot down and all, it'll only drive her away, so, I just have to – I told her, I told her once, I told her twice, and if she wants to do it, it's her choice. She does it. See? And who am I? – I can't say too much. And that's it.

I feel that gradually since I stopped drinking and since I stopped taking tablets, which I was very good at getting, things are improving for me. It's terrific. You see, today I can shave myself, have a bath today, have a shower, dress myself. I shaved this morning, and I had an egg for breakfast, you know, and I can remember the time when I couldn't do that. I couldn't walk right. Couldn't stand up. Not just with the physical sickness after the drink, and stuff – I couldn't get my mind together. I didn't know what was going on. I was drinking in this town one time for five weeks, and I went in to the doctor and he said, 'What happened?' And I said, 'Well, I don't know, but I started drinking yesterday.' He said, 'Do you not know you were in the hospital overnight? You've been drinking for five weeks.' And I thought I was only drinking for one day. Because of blackouts. Once I left Victoria to go back to Belfast and it took me nine weeks going from Victoria to Belfast! And when I ended up in Cheshire in hospital, drinking, I met this big fellow – I kept dribbling, see, and he said, 'You're coming to have a wet brain[4], did you not know?' I said, 'No.' And still I went back to it. It stopped me for a little while – the fear. But I still went back to the drink.

I found out, you see, all my life I was angry. I hated people. Anger is a luxury no way I can afford today. Since then they had to teach me. I have to love everybody. I don't have to like everybody, but I have to love them. So it's self-survival. Anger is a luxury I can't afford. Get rid of it. Just leave it there. And, that's it. I'm very wealthy today. I've no money, but I've found peace. If I've got no peace, I grieve people round me. I don't know what happened, this feeling of anger and hatred's just gone. See, I'm getting off all these things. I was an alcoholic before I ever took a drink, I know today. It's not just a matter of putting down the drink. It's a matter of walking on anger, hatred, fear, resentment – all these other things.

You see, it's AA − A for '*accept*'. It's also A for '*action*'. I accepted that I had a problem with drink; I accepted that I was an alcoholic very early on in life, years ago. But I sat round meetings and sat round hospitals, and sat round different places, waiting for somebody to wave a magic wand and do something about it, to stop it, and cure me. I found out − going to this AA, it told me − if you sit around and do nothing, something rubs off; something sets in − rigor mortis! It's only when I'm doing the action, trying to look after myself, that it started coming, doing things. That was it.

Even when Gerald is silent, there is a sense of energy bursting out of this man. His gaze and expression are compelling. He likes to hold forth and to be the centre of attention. He has never lain down under troubles, but has fought back from the days of his early childhood onwards. At the chronic stage of his drinking, Gerald embodied the stereotype of a person who has lost all sense of themselves, who is right down in the gutter. At many points in his adult life, anyone catching sight of him would simply have written him off as a hopeless drunk, with destitution and Korsakoff's syndrome, colloquially known as 'wet brain', just around the corner. It is amazing that Gerald has survived at all, because this is against the odds in view of his prolonged serious alcohol and drug abuse.

Gerald has a definite view of his alcoholism: 'I was an alcoholic before I ever took a drink,' because 'I couldn't stick the pain of not drinking.' Like Anna, Gerald drank to alleviate his mental distress. He discovered he could soothe himself with alcohol as well as with the drugs he was prescribed for his asthma. This became a way of coping which also laid down the pattern of being secretive and lying. He says that drink was not tolerated in the family when he was a child. Was this through financial constraints only? Perhaps there was some other very good reason for there being no alcohol at home. He doesn't say. Extreme attitudes for or against drinking give a child little chance to develop a sensible attitude towards alcohol. It is not uncommon to find that these children are at risk of falling prey to problems with alcohol. They miss out on seeing people enjoying alcohol as part of a balanced lifestyle. It may be that someone in the household has had troubling experiences with alcohol, either in themselves or in someone close to them. The reasons are usually complicated, but Gerald is not the only narrator whose parents would not tolerate alcohol in the home. Another point he mentions is the way he dealt with his medication as a child, which suggests very inadequate parental supervision amounting to neglect.

Later in his life the use of alcohol and other drugs which are available either over the counter or on prescription from more gullible doctors became intertwined. When Gerald couldn't get the one, he'd get the other. Although he gives no details, it seems clear that as a child love and attention were in short supply. He left home at the age of fourteen, and from then on he lived in an environment where 'everybody drank', and drank heavily, a situation which no doubt reinforced his idea that this was quite normal. He sees his alcoholism as primarily part of his personality, particularly in terms of dealing with his anger and fear, and his admitted tendency to 'want everything yesterday', but the circumstances of his life and his social environment cannot be overlooked in forming a view of his reasons for drinking as he did.

Gerald's experiences raise some interesting questions for therapists. Anyone who has had to develop such an independent streak in order to survive needs to be very firmly challenged. He recounts the tale of how the third clergyman at last stood up to him on what he believed to be his deathbed. He was clearly able to lead hospital staff a merry dance, and this priest not only challenged his wheedling ways, but saw beneath them to Gerald's terror that he was actually going to die. He *was* wheedling, but he was also flailing around in real panic and desperately needed someone to say *stop* and to say that if he would just lie there, he could get through the convulsions and come out the other side. As it turned out, this episode was an important marker in Gerald's waking up to the possibility of taking what was happening to him seriously in ways other than simply being a victim.

More recently Gerald was faced by his therapist with the idea that it was important to sort his drink problem out first, before tackling other areas of his life. In the group he also learned that he had a duty to sort himself out before he could help to sort out anyone else's problems. He noticed for himself that people who continued to attend the group were able to stay away from drinking.

It is in lives like Gerald's that AA is often the first port of call in a crisis. Members of AA are used to those who have reached the point of having memory blanks and have seen them recover. The meetings provide a context within which an individual can start thinking. The value of the mutual trust and respect between the hospital staff and AA was never clearer than in Gerald's case. What spoke most clearly from AA to Gerald? He himself loves words. He is a great raconteur. Clearly he relishes the sound and the personal resonance of AA slogans such as, '*Take the cotton wool out of you ears and put it in your mouth.*' He gives us a glimpse of the techniques, embodied in slogans, which AA offers to those who want to steer clear of relapsing into alcoholism – such as '*Willpower is a total liability*'; taking tablets is '*Eating the booze*'; '*A is for accept and A is for action*', that is, it's no good simply paying lip service or having good intentions. He embraced the injunctions of AA like those of a firm but benevolent parent. AA and the hospital group provided an ongoing container for him. Short-term treatment on its own would have been pointless. He needed to develop trust in a reliable 'family', and trust takes time to grow. In the early part of his life, thinking came into the picture very little. One might speculate that Gerald had not been brought up in such a way as to be reflective. Perhaps his parents had not helped him to *name* his feelings – maybe they had not even understood them. As a child he was unwell with asthma. He doesn't say anything about either of his parents or about his siblings. He may have used alcohol to give himself bodily sensations in place of emotional feelings. Something was lacking, but he didn't know what. Drink and drugs gave him a buzz.

Anyone whose life has been as full of drama as Gerald's is likely to thrive in an environment like AA meetings where drama is the substance of the chair's utterances. At every meeting what happens is that one member takes the chair, recounting his or her personal story, and by the very nature of addiction that story is likely to be dramatic. Gerald can relish this atmosphere, and he can feel at home in it – no longer the despised, embattled outsider. At AA he can meet plenty of other people who have been similarly disadvantaged, as well as those who have started life with the proverbial silver spoons in their mouths, but have thrown it all away in their alcoholism and landed up with nothing at all but a bitter aftertaste. The slogans he heard were spoken by people who know the score. In the hospital group, he often used to get himself in trouble by banging the AA drum too stridently. Other members of the group were intimidated by this ardour, but for him, it was a lifeline at a time when he was drowning. It was up to us, as facilitators, to stay calm and absorb some of the fiery feelings churning around so that people could feel safe enough in the group.

His achievements Gerald measures in simple terms – he can look after himself and he can keep his life on the rails now. He highlights a crucial element in recovering from addiction when he says, 'It's not just a matter of putting down the drink. It's a matter of "walking on" anger, hatred, fear, resentment.'

In conclusion

Belief in the possibility of recovering from addiction

Even people whose childhoods are blighted by trials such as ill health or neglect, who start misusing drugs at a very early age and proceed to full-blown addiction, may leave it behind. The turning point may take a long time coming and the route may be circuitous, but it can come about. Gerald's survival and recovery follow an archetypal pattern found in literature all over the world – the resilience of a valiant individual who starts out with few advantages but succeeds in surmounting difficulties against the odds.

Therapeutic challenges

The therapist of such a patient needs a belief in the possibility of recovery, and should challenge the patient's lonely conviction that he or she knows best. Empathic listening alone is merely the start with some patients. Among these are people who have had to develop thickets of defences simply to survive, and have become alienated from what Jung calls 'the protective wall of human community' (Jung 1976: 624). In Gerald's case, his therapist won by convincing him to deal with his alcohol and drug addiction first, before trying to set in order other chaotic aspects of his life. At the relapse prevention group, we made it clear to him how much we valued him, just as much as we valued more compliant members, but he did not have things all his own way. In fact he had to be ejected from the group twice under threat of police intervention, but this firm boundary was an aspect of the safe family he found there.

Cognitive awareness in recovery

The need for someone who has stopped drinking or drug using to develop awareness and vigilance is a theme which recurs in many of the narratives. This is where a group can be particularly potent, by its emphasis on getting to know about addiction and what triggers relapse. Members of a group will bring their individual perspectives on what tempts them to lapse and what they do about this. Some will say they are blown away by emotion, some by drinking or drug-using environments, some for no reason whatsoever that they can discern. The seemingly simple slogans of AA are a useful buffer when temptation looms.

Loneliness

It is a moving experience to observe someone thaw out from being a lonely outsider. When Gerald speaks about how he lived as a young man, his choice of the word *scheming* gives the feel of how he had to exist in a world which he felt could never understand him and would certainly never give him what he wanted. Certain factors made a difference: first, being reined in from his wild ideas by the young priest who was not taken in by him and later by the therapist who saw through his embattled persona, and second, the acceptance he met in AA and at the hospital here.

Notes

1 Certain 'sections' of the Mental Health Act in the UK necessitate individuals to be compulsorily detained in psychiatric hospitals for various specific periods of time.
2 Ephedrine is medication for asthma prescribed as a bronchodilator.
3 Heminevrin is the trade name for Clomethiazole, a hypnotic drug prescribed for short-term use to attenuate alcohol withdrawal symptoms.
4 See Appendix 1: Alcohol.

Chapter 4

Ambivalence second time round

Bernadette first received treatment at the hospital for her drug injecting habit in her teens and early twenties when she lived nearby. She was one of the ex-patients who took part in the most recent longitudinal study (Rathod *et al*. 2005). She agreed to be interviewed and to bring us up to date on her progress. She is now in her forties and lives some distance away in a smaller town in a more rural setting where she has developed an addiction to a different substance.

I don't drink every day. It's just that when I pick up that drink, I can't stop. It's binge drinking. When I was back in my home town for a fortnight a while back, apart from about three days, I was pissed every day. But here, I never drink every day. In the last twelve months I've had sleeping pills to take the edge off the 'come down'. And I've smoked cannabis and I've had a bit of speed, but only occasionally, not as much as once a week.

As for the drug situation I more or less stopped when I was living in my home town, because – it sounds stupid, but it's true – I got bored with it. I got bored with the people that were coming round, the same old people, the same old thing, and I got frightened. I mean, the fear was just as big on drugs as it is on alcohol now, really. I wasn't frightened of the trouble I'd get into – it wasn't that. It's more that you feel like your life's out of hand completely – you've got no control over what you're doing. And when you do wake up, you realise what the place looks like. There are bodies all over the place. The place looks like a bomb's hit it. It's filthy dirty and you've wasted your money. You've got no money left. It's complete fear of not living in any sort of order – I think that's the only way I can describe it.

There was one stage when I was taking an awful lot of speed[1]. I was picking it up on prescription. I used[2], but I mainly used speed. I've tried morphine, but I didn't like it. It made me so sick, whereas other people that I spoke to said it was total euphoria, for me it was total sickness. But I was injecting speed quite dreadfully. I used to like the rush[3]. I got terrible come downs[4] from anything that I was taking. We used to, I mean, people that I know used to raid chemists' and there was loads of Valium all over the place, so when I wasn't speeding I was Valiumed up anyway, because I've a fear of come downs.

I remember one stage I'd had so much of it, and you've got to remember now that I had little children in the middle of all this. I was living up the road from the Lamb and Flag – everybody from there was on something, you know? My house was just full of people. I never had a minute to myself. The kids *were* a factor, because at the end of it all, some logic starts coming through, and I remember I said, 'If somebody comes round here for drugs, tell everybody down that bloody pub, "The next person that comes round here, with drugs, for drugs or anything to do with drugs, they'll get this bucket of water over their head."' It happened to be Terry Blackwell and I tipped this bucket over him. It had come to such a stage in my head – I was frightened, terrified. The kids weren't getting enough attention. It was just a horrifying state of affairs.

There wasn't any particular person that was relevant to my stopping that made me open my eyes to it. No. But the one thing, if anything comes through, it's your upbringing, so, if anything, it's your father – do you understand what I'm saying? It's that little voice in your head that says, 'What you're doing is wrong.' When I came to, at the end of the day, the loathing with myself became more than the enjoyment of the drug, I think. That's what it boils down to. At the end of the day I didn't want to keep loathing myself. I loathed what I was doing to the children and I could see I wasn't going to get anywhere in life at all because of the people that I was with. You get people speeding[5] a lot and they talk about the same thing over and over again. So there's nothing new coming out of it. There's nothing exciting about it in the end – it's just boring.

When I gave up speed and injecting, I still dabbled here and there in the beginning. And I've taken methadone linctus. So it was a gradual coming off. What I'd like to say about it is, I mixed with these people, and that was my scene. Right? And when you've got no other friends in life, that's your scene – how do you walk away from it? You don't walk away from it and be on your own, do you? You have a turning point, but you can't, you don't leave the whole lot behind in one go. No. You'd have to go and lock yourself in the – somewhere – for a long, long time to do that.

I sometimes still feel like using. I actually go through the movements of injecting. That might sound daft to you, but actually, I do it even now. Occasionally, I'll get that feeling. It's not strong enough to make me go out and look for it. I have a drink instead. It's easier to get hold of. If you want the honest to God's truth, I think drink is easier to come by. If I wanted to go and find gear[6] now, I've been off the scene for so long, I don't know where I'd go. I'd probably get it if I wanted to desperately enough, but, I mean, by that time I could have gone down the pub half a dozen times, couldn't I? I don't know anybody round here that uses.

Nowadays I've got something that's legal, it's the drink. It's easily obtainable; you don't have to have a load of bloody junkies round your place. The company I keep seems a bit more respectable with alcohol. You can put on a modicum of respect-ability – do you understand what I'm saying to you? But you can't really, because in the end you're going to show yourself up anyway. I mean, I'm barred from every pub round here. Now I'm even partly barred from The King's Head. They don't like me there. They tolerate me. One little step out of line and I'd be out of there like a shot. I've really barred myself in the end. If I drink nowadays, I drink away from this area or I drink indoors.

The very first time I had any treatment was in this hospital. I'd have been sixteen or seventeen. You could get hold of drugs and stuff there though you weren't supposed to. I really don't know what we did there. They introduced me to AA, but I didn't understand anything that was going on. There were bits I remember. There was this woman called Maggie, who made an awful lot of sense to me, but I didn't take it in, really. There was a load of people talking about their experience of drink, but none of it sunk in, to be honest with you, except maybe for Maggie. I just sat there and I was, like, 'Who are all these people and what are they doing here? And what am I doing here?' I giggled a bit because I felt stupid. That was about it, really. The funny thing was, I knew there was something wrong with me that was making me drink and use too much. It was some personal problem. Later, when the kids were taken into care, I didn't think it was a long-term problem. It could be quite easily put right by ten days in detox, and then I'd come out and never drink again. That was my thinking on it, which was just a load of shit. But at that time, that's what I thought was going to happen. All I had to do to get cured was have ten days off the drink and that's it. I'm cured!

Nowadays I'd get away with murder in my home town. Everybody knows me. I can go in any bar. 'Oh, it's Bernadette!' Nobody takes a blind bit of bloody notice. And everybody I know drinks there. Everybody drinks – or takes drugs. So I'm no different from them. But when I moved down here it was completely different. The people I met didn't drink like I drank. I started to realise there was something wrong, with me. Then I started doing dim flips[7]. So it was becoming really clear to me that I wasn't right. I'd think, 'Oh well, I've had a good night on the piss. Oh sod it, I don't care.' But then I'd start abusing people. I've got an awful bloody tongue on me. I'd start verbally abusing people. I'd wake up the next morning, remembering that I'd met a couple of friends, and I'd abused them verbally. In the end I didn't have any friends any more, did I? 'What am I doing?' I thought, 'There is a helpline.' So I phoned up AA. I'd done that a few times really. They said, 'Well, get to a meeting.' 'Yeah,' I said, 'But I'm off the booze now. So I won't bother.' And then gradually, bit by bit, it started to sink in, 'I want to stop, but I can't stop it. I can stop it for days, then I'm back on it.'

Some little light started to come through and I started to realise I wasn't like other people. It didn't matter whether it was binge drinking or not. Once I'd had that first drink, I wasn't happy until I was completely sozzled and didn't know what I was doing, until I'd insulted and upset and demanded and phoned up people and told them what they were – in other words, been a right so and so. I started to realise that there was something wrong with me.

It took me a little while after that, then I started going to meetings. I started to listen to what they were saying, and I began to realise I wasn't the only one in the world who had done this. There were lots of people out there that had done it. Lots and lots of people and they weren't mad, they were very nice people. None of them were scruff bags. There were all sorts of people there that were doing the same things as me. There were lots of binge drinkers there. All the same. They'd caused riots all over the place. Their families were not speaking to them for life because of what they'd done. I got something out of the meetings. It dawned on me that I'm an alcoholic. So then I thought, 'If I know what I am, maybe I can do something about it.' Up to then, I think I'd been in a complete state of denial about who I was. It's so deceptive that you don't know what you're doing to yourself. And it's the same with the drugs. I had just swapped it. I'd swapped it for something that seemed a bit more respectable.

My thought was, 'Ah good, at least I know what I am. I'm an alcoholic. There is help there. And people have stopped drinking.' So, in a way, I got a bit of hope from that. But then I stopped going and when I started drinking again I was referred to a residential centre. They took me in there. Their treatment is based on the Minnesota method[8]. It's the most intense thing I've ever been through. But I bullshitted my way through that – I've got to admit it now. I was very clever, because I didn't open up. I knew exactly what they wanted out of me, and I gave it to them. I did dry out, and I stayed dry for another three months, till I went to my home town, then I picked up a drink.

This was two Christmases ago. I know in myself, I can stop drinking if I go back to AA, but. . . It's like AA says, you have to come to your rock bottom. Now luckily, so far I've stayed off rock bottom. I haven't got the wolves at the door. I haven't had my face messed up. As yet, I've not done any of that. I've not got run over in a drunken stupor and woken up with broken legs. None of these things have happened to me – yet. But I have caused riots with people, and I'm a nasty piece of bloody work when I've been drinking. I don't like that side of me, but as yet I haven't hit my rock bottom. It's bound to come. I know it is.

I went to a meeting last Wednesday. I was pissed when I walked in there. I stopped the meeting actually, because one of them got up and said, 'Oh, we're so glad to see you.' And I said, 'Well, I'm pissed.' 'It doesn't matter Bernadette, you're here.'

It's emotions that set it off. I'm a very emotional person. I cope partly by having a drink and I do have other ways of coping temporarily. I do believe in a Higher Power. I've always believed in God to a certain extent, anyway. And to a certain extent I rationalise the situation and I know what I should do in it. But in the end the emotions get the better of me.

Yeah – it's reasonable, my home, it's comfortable. I've had to struggle quite a bit to get it that way, I've deprived myself a lot to get it that way. But at the end of the day, I sometimes wonder if it's the surroundings that are really important, and I don't think they are – it's your own state of mind. I look around sometimes and I'm terribly lonely, terribly frightened. I'd rather have a feeling inside me that was much more contented. If this all disappeared tomorrow, I'd be extremely insecure, because it has given me some sort of security. It has given me that, but, all this inside is still going on, and I can still sometimes look at it and think, 'I'm not happy.'

And peace. I don't think I'm going to get it all the time. No, I have a feeling of insecurity. You lose your spiritual self. You can say things and do things that you regret doing. I mean all these sort of things. They tell you in AA that when you're drinking you're spiritually, mentally, physically sick. And you are.

It's like being two people really, being an addict, isn't it? One side of you wants the addict side, and the other side wants the side that isn't. It is like split. Yeah, it's very schizophrenic. You've got the side of you that knows what's right and what's wrong, and you do know, everybody knows, underneath it all, and yet you've got the side of you that behaves so badly.

Bernadette's childhood was marred by tragedy, a trauma which set off a downward spiral, for her mother died when she was eight years old. She identifies now with her mother in being house-proud, and although she remembers rather little about her, she says she 'screamed' at her death. After this she and her two younger siblings were under the care of her strict grandmother, and it was the view of the psychiatrist who treated her as a teenager that she was given far too much responsibility at too early an age. She feels very protective of her father, who was always warm towards the children, but he was perhaps too permissive. She wished that he had taken a firmer line over their truanting and shoplifting. Both she and her brother were sent to approved schools because they truanted from school and ran away from home. Too early in life she had to step into a parental role. She felt she had to shoulder responsibility for all her family, at the same time as suffering the misery of unresolved grief. Her entry to further education foundered because just as she was about to enter college, her brother got into trouble with the law and consequently her father was 'in pieces'. She never held any job for more than a few weeks. It seems that her bereavement caused her pain which nothing and no one could assuage.

At the age of sixteen, one evening she was drunk, and wrote a poem:

> Why does anybody have to lose themselves, because there is no escape?
> Why do I place myself on some forbidden shelf?
> Why can't I be like everybody else?
> When somebody cares I don't want to know, and when somebody hurts me, it's because they don't understand.
> Why do I hate myself above all things and why does this sorrowful bell have to ring for me? Why can't I be free?
> Why does everybody hate me, or at least, why do I think they do?
> When I cry, it's never teardrops of pity.
> They are teardrops of helplessness and pain.

Her grief for her mother's death was never really understood or taken into account by those around her, as is far from uncommon when children lose a parent. People find it hard to empathise, because children often show their grief in ways very different from adult mourning. They may act out feelings of outrage, loss, confusion, and pain in dangerous ways, including drug use, without any concern for the consequences. Bernadette was a child who needed help far earlier on.

At the age of fourteen she started experimenting with stimulants, cannabis and LSD, in a search for thrills to compensate for her lack of stability. She had a desperate need to be part of the 'in crowd'. It was a search for excitement as a way out, as well as a defence against unhappiness; it is easy to see how she became part of a set of drug users in a culture where drugs were easy to come by. She started to experiment, as adolescents do, and found that the effect shielded her from the impact of her pain. So the drug using is a protection against the suffering. It could equally be understood as a misguided attempt to find a way out of her unsatisfying situation, an attempt to find a better answer.

Bernadette is still a bewildered child. She doesn't know what she wants: she wakes up thinking she wants to stop drinking, but as the day goes on, she's not so sure. She thinks she wants to stop, but *just not yet*. The trouble is, as she says, that her emotions get the better of her. She knows a great deal about addiction, but some of this knowledge she has used in deceiving therapists at the residential centre, her desire to please stopping her from being open. People are often unable to make use of the treatment they are offered.

She presents a picture of someone in the grip of ambivalence, blaming her addiction to alcohol: 'It's so deceptive that you don't know what you're doing to yourself.' Although one part of her wants to stop, another part doesn't, so she has no peace of mind, but feels lonely and frightened. Living with an enthusiastic drinker doesn't help. Nor do her lovely surroundings, the home she has created, which simply helps to distract her from making any radical change. There are some hopeful signs for the future. She was impressed that members at the AA group were pleased that she came along again, even though she was drunk. She is full of shame, which may push her to make changes in the future. She may again pay attention to echoes of her father's voice, as she did when she left her previous addiction behind. But at present her drinking is a way of continuing to be a child, a lost child.

Her own children were taken into care because her house was used by a crowd of drug users at one stage. What had started as a desire to be popular and a key figure in a peer group ended for her in a completely chaotic life. Underneath the boredom, which she says was the trigger to her giving up, lay fear – fear of having no control over what she was doing and of not living in any sort of order. She knew it was a dead end, but it is very hard to give up a lifestyle when all your friends are involved in it. When people talk about giving up drugs, it is not just the drugs you have to give up. Another problem early on was that she had a misguided idea that if she undertook a detox programme for ten days, that would be that.

AA came into her life at a point when, as a teenager, she couldn't make any sense of it, but she has returned to make use of it more recently. This is often the way. Someone will attend a meeting or two and strongly resist what they see and hear; yet later, maybe years later, they will respond in a different way. At her first contact she hadn't a clue what it was all about. She felt embarrassed and giggled a lot. Now she knows a great deal about AA. It's there for her. She dips in and out. From what she says, I gather it's not AA she's critical of, but more her own ability to benefit from what it offers.

It is not uncommon to find that someone who has been addicted to one drug later becomes addicted to another. She is well aware that her addiction is of equal severity to her former amphetamine injecting. She has changed to a substance she sees as more 'respectable', even though she is far from respectable once she gets drunk. There is a geographical aspect to this, for it is easier for her to drink than go searching for drugs in her new environment. She assuages her cravings to use drugs with alcohol. In a long-term study in the USA, half of a cohort of 298 heroin users substituted alcohol after they stopped using heroin on a daily basis (Lehman et al. 1990).

It is embarrassing to contemplate how it must feel to be publicly banned from one pub, let alone several. How does that impact on your feelings as you go shopping in the town, only to meet regulars who know all too well what has gone on? The difficulty when you reach the very margins of what is socially acceptable in such an exposed, public way is how on earth to draw back. Self-esteem plummets. One understandable response is bravado, a determination not to care, not to feel, to plunge on headlong. People talk about addicts lying, but often shame may be at the root of it, as it was with Anna. As therapists we need to develop the sensitivity to sense shame and encourage patients to give it expression.

I suspect that at present, apart from drinking, Bernadette has little idea of how to care for herself. Perhaps the hollow facade now is a replica of the one she had to adopt after her mother's death. Maybe her spiritual thirst was for a time before her mother died. She feels dissatisfaction with how things are, but feels trapped. Many people who are addicted express the hope of changing how much they use or drink, rather than making other sorts of life changes. This reflects a preoccupation with the drug, which is described in great detail compared with the way they speak about other aspects of their lives. Bernadette feels ashamed of being on the outside, socially, because of her drunken behaviour. She can't conform, but would like to. At present she can keep up appearances a lot of the time, but underneath all that she is lonely and frightened. She is just about holding on to her present modus vivendi, but she is massively ambivalent – it could go either way.

Feeling ashamed may be a good sign. When she was approaching the lowest point in her addiction to injectable drugs, she recalled her father's words. In crises the remembered words of an inner figure may speak influentially. Feelings aroused by the memories of the love and concern of her parents were reawakened. This represents a veering away from relating in an addicted way to a drug in favour of relating to people. Perhaps as well as responding to a superego demand, a demand of conscience, it is also because the concept of a world peopled by loving figures, including herself, is still alive within her.

In conclusion

The purpose of 'using' drugs

Bernadette makes a basic statement about why people use any drug: it changes the way you feel. This change has a dual nature. You can damp down painful emotions in such a way as to defend against them, and/or you can make yourself feel good, thus finding some temporary satisfaction.

The effect of the context in which drugs are used

The social environment plays an important role in which particular drug is chosen. While at various stages of their lives people may wish to identify with or to keep within the norms of their environment, others will choose to rebel against these norms to exert their desire for independence or simply for an added thrill.

Low sense of self-worth

Many addicted people hate themselves and what they are doing. They work hard at hiding the fact and at presenting a fine persona to the world. A sense of low self-worth can precede an addiction, but addiction itself can cause or enhance it. It may be hard for people who have never been addicted to empathise with those whom they perceive to be perversely bringing about their own downfall and it can be extremely helpful for those in this situation to meet others in a similar position. This can be at groups for friends and relations of addicted people, where they can hear about practical strategies for dealing with the inevitable problems, as well as gaining a greater understanding of addiction in order to feel less isolated. Groups for friends and families of addicted people such as Al-Anon can have great influence on the outcome for the addicted person as well as for the person who attends the group (See Appendix 3).

Initial rejection of AA

It is not uncommon for people who attend AA or NA to feel at first that it is not for them. Yet it may be that although they reject it, something or somebody makes an impact which is remembered later. Bernadette, having lost her own mother, came across an inspiring maternal figure there. Years later she returned.

Ambivalence

The final part of this narrative gives a picture of the ambivalence of those who know they could make changes, but can't quite make a move – yet. Therapists are often presented with this dilemma.

Notes

1 The stimulant amphetamine sulphate is most commonly taken orally, but it can also be injected.
2 *Used* is slang for 'injected a drug'. This terminology can be confusing because of the more inclusive term *drug using*, which does not imply taking drugs by injection.
3 The *rush* is a term for the sudden intense experience resulting from injecting a drug.
4 *Come downs* are withdrawal symptoms.
5 *Speeding* implies taking stimulant drugs.
6 *Gear* is slang for any injectable drug, most commonly heroin.
7 *Dim flips* are the temporary blackouts which are a common feature of habitual heavy drinking. The drinker has no recollection of what was taking place or what they were doing.
8 The Minnesota Method is based on the notion of treating the whole person – body, mind and spirit – and on the idea that addicted individuals can help one another. It originated in 1949 with a guest house named Hazelden for alcoholic men in Center City, Minnesota, where the founders insisted that residents should attend to the details of daily life, tell their stories and listen to each other, in order to help them to shift from a life of isolation to a life of dialogue. From this seemingly simple beginning, the model has had a profound influence on the treatment of addiction worldwide. The Twelve Steps of AA are intrinsic to the model.

Chapter 5

Lost in the labyrinth of addiction

Range of drug use and addiction

Becoming addicted is like being lured into a dark, encompassing labyrinth, as many were drawn into the Cretan labyrinth of the Minotaur. The term 'addiction' refers both to a *state* and the *process* of arriving at that state. When we give careful thought to the different stages of the process of becoming addicted, whether we are considering our own or someone else's addiction, we come to realise how vast is the change that occurs between the early and later stages of using drugs or drinking. People often use the term *addiction* very loosely, for example, when they are referring to heavy

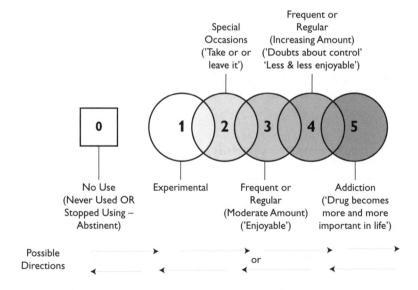

Figure 5.1 Range of drug use

Source: Reprinted by permission from Rathod, 1992 (ed.), *Substance Abuse – A Layman's Guide*, p. 24

but irregular drug use such as binge drinking. Though the edges are blurred, it is helpful to look at the stages on the way to addiction.

The range of drug use can best be compared to a bus journey with many stages between the two termini. The starting point may be called a 'No Use' terminal. This can mean either 'never having used' or 'not currently using'. Few of us can claim never to have used, as inadvertently most of us have been exposed to passive smoking, and many of us have been exposed to drugs as foetuses if our mothers used drugs when they were pregnant, because drugs such as alcohol, heroin or tobacco cross the placenta. Addicts who have given up use and are abstaining totally also belong to the 'No Use' category. The first stage along the route is where the use is 'one off' or experimental. The second stage is where the use is occasional and the person can take it or leave it. The third stage is where the use is regular but moderate while entailing little risk of harm. The user can still take it or leave it. The fourth stage is where there is regular or frequent *excessive* use, with the possibility of potential harm, and the user finds it impossible to curtail their use for any appreciable time. The ability to control their intake is strained and the drug fails to produce the desired effects in small doses. This is because tolerance of the drug has increased and enjoyment is on the decline so that larger doses are required to achieve the desired effects. The fifth stage is the last stage: the person is addicted and cannot function normally without the drug and experiences withdrawal symptoms if deprived of the drug for any length of time. The drug has become necessary simply for the user to feel 'normal'. It is important to bear in mind that these various stages, that is, levels of use, overlap. The journey is flexible, in that one can get off at any stop and either stay there or make the return journey, but the problem is that the ability to control drug use declines as the journey progresses. A further, controversial, question is whether, having reached the final stage, it is possible to retrace one's steps partially or whether a return to 'No Use' is the only viable alternative.

The triangular model of addiction

After Bernadette moved to a different area, her addiction switched to alcohol, an easier drug to come by in her new social setting. This pattern supports a triangular theory that society, the drug and the characteristics of the individual all play a vital part in shaping an addiction. In order to understand how an addiction has developed, it is important to keep in mind the relevance of seeing the personality of the addicted individual not only in a familial but also in a *social* context, both past and present. These factors are interactive and exercise both promotional as well as controlling influences on each other. A crucial point is that without all three facets of the triangle, drug misuse cannot occur.

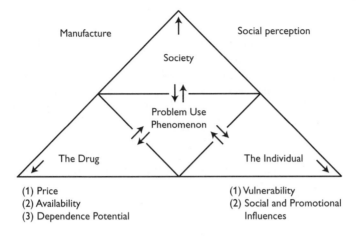

Figure 5.2 Promotion and control of drug use

Source: Reprinted by permission from Rathod, 1992 (ed.), *Substance Abuse – A Layman's Guide*, p. 22

Society

While in the UK society prohibits the use of certain drugs regarded as highly dangerous and regulates the use of others through controls such as price and the restriction of prescription, the manufacture of potentially harmful drugs such as alcohol, tobacco and tranquillisers yields high financial benefits, through both taxation and employment. Legal restrictions have a high cost to society in terms of the criminal justice system and of fostering a clandestine economy. On the other hand, enjoyment of drinking alcoholic drinks, for example, is a traditionally accepted enhancement of social life accompanied by intricate and varying rituals according to the setting. Part of becoming adult involves learning how to fit into this picture and advertising plays a part in moulding attitudes. At the same time, attempts are made to minimise harm through societal measures by education against the abuse of drugs, legal measures and the provision of treatment services. Whenever there is state regulation of the manufacture, import, sale or prescription of any substance, a clandestine economy with all its attendant problems springs up in response.

Society overtly scapegoats addicted people. Sylvia Brinton Perera has written about the nature and origins of scapegoating, describing it as a form of denying shadow aspects of oneself by projecting these into others. She shows how individuals can come to identify with the scapegoat by taking on personal responsibility for the rejected qualities of others and play out their identification in self-rejection, motivated by a deep sense of guilt and shame (Perera 1986: 31).

The Drug

Whether a particular chemical with mood-altering potential is regarded as a medicine or as a poison depends upon the setting, the intention of the user and the manner of use, and this determines the legal status of the substance. Perceptions affect definitions of drugs and these are never static. If introduced as a new drug, for example, coffee would probably be a restricted substance and social attitudes towards the smoking of tobacco have changed vastly over the past thirty years. Other factors which govern consumption are availability and price. Supply reduction strategies take various forms, principally interception at the point of entry into the country and legal sanctions against possession and supply in the case of 'illegal' drugs, as well as control of prescription. As far as harm caused by abuse is concerned, as opposed to adverse drug reactions, the dependence potential of each drug has implications in relation to addiction. Heroin, cocaine and tobacco are highly potent in terms of immediacy of producing the desired effect and are of comparatively short duration of action, leading to frequency of use. All dependence-producing drugs are excreted or metabolised fairly quickly and almost all psychoactive drugs that are abused and lead to dependence produce their effects within minutes rather than hours and have a short 'half-life', that is, the time during which the drug would have lost half of its potency.

The individual

Each individual has greater or lesser vulnerability to land in trouble through misuse of drugs. Family background and personal psychological and physical make up can each play a part. Fashion exerts powerful incentives for adolescents in particular because of the desire to be accepted by peers, and exploration is part of growing up. This holds good in relation to drug use as in everything else. However, when assessing the causative potential of these factors, the problem is that addiction is accompanied by a variety of changes in lifestyle and behaviour patterns so that it is difficult to be sure whether these pre-dated the abuse of a certain drug or are the consequences of the addiction. In the USA one study found that about 78 per cent of adolescents with conduct disorders who were being treated for drug problems had had their first conduct disorder symptom prior to their initiation to drug use (Hser et al. 2003). Similarly, in this locality, Mott and Rathod (1976) showed that many adolescents who became drug dependent had been in trouble with the law or had attended child guidance clinics prior to their experimentation with drugs. It may be said that in these cases their vulnerability is increased by their previous history and lifestyle.

Vulnerability to addiction

All three narrators in this part of the book experienced significant disturb-
ances or losses in childhood. As they grew up, Gerald and Bernadette found
common currency in adolescent groups of peers, Gerald in a crowd of
heavy drinkers, Bernadette in a group experimenting with illegally obtained
drugs. Belonging to a group gave each of them a sense of stepping away
from a home they were keen to leave behind. The cohesive element in each
of these groups was the drinking or drug experimentation, a risky element
for anyone who had a weight of unhappy emotions to blot out. Some
people in these groups no doubt grew out of the need for drugs, and
eventually settled into a less drug-fuelled way of life as adults, but Gerald
and Bernadette were more vulnerable to becoming addicted, not only
because of their unhappiness, but also because their upbringing had left
severe deficits in their capacity to look after themselves. It seems that as a
child Gerald had been left to get on with life pretty much on his own, while
Bernadette had been expected to care for her younger siblings. The pattern
was different for Anna, for she had had a childhood where she was well
cared for once she had been rescued from the orphanage. In addition to
this, she started drinking at a different stage in her life from the other two.
Her need to defend against painful feelings came at a point when she had
already started to build her own family group, and although this was
disrupted by the desertion of her husband and the illness of her baby, she
never lost it completely.

Secrecy and isolation during addiction

The labyrinth of the addicted lifestyle is easy to get lost in. Simply maintaining an adequate level of supplies of the drug takes more and more time
and attention, so other vital features of life begin to fade into insignificance
by comparison. The problem is that by that stage few addicted individuals
want the world to see how little control they now have over their need for
the drug, whether the drug is legally acceptable or not – a thoroughly
humiliating state of affairs. It generates a crippling sense of shame and one
way of dealing with shame is bravado. Therapists would do well to be wary
of being fooled by this. It often demands patience and a very canny attitude
to unravel the layers of concealment of the true state of affairs.

As an addicted person becomes more and more reliant on a substance, so
other considerations go by the board, including relationships, jobs, health,
and finances. The balance is overturned. There is little sense of belonging or
of mutuality in intimate relationships. If offers of help fail, a downward
spiral ensues. It is both the sense of shame and rigorous denial which drive
someone who has developed an addiction further into isolation. Most
people who have been addicted will tell you that they did not have real

friends while they were addicted – instead they may have had people around them who, consciously or unconsciously, supported their addiction in one way or another, people, in other words, who did not increase their sense of shame. So although an alcoholic may be always keen to go off to the pub, this is because it is the place where he or she will feel in company with people who are drinking. Anyone who tries to restrain or dissuade the drinker is regarded as a spoilsport.

After a time, the drug-using no longer brings a sense of belonging to and identifying with a chosen group of friends and acquaintances in the way it did at the start. Current relationships with partners, parents or children tend to be poorly maintained or unsatisfying. This also operates not only at a social but also at a personal level, because having to hide one's habits is isolating. Some people hide their drug use at home, while others hide in a crowd of people who are also using, or who sympathise. In addition to this, the drug may be illegal. All this pushes the person into greater and greater isolation from relationships and friendships. Jung understood how part of the destructive power of addiction was that the person ended up being outside the protectiveness of being part of a family or a group of any sort (Jung 1976: 624).

In love with the drug

A group of Freudian analysts who were leaders of substance misuse services in New York produced a book edited by Angelo Smaldino called *Psychoanalytic Approaches to Addiction* (Smaldino 1991). It highlights an element in addiction the implications of which no one had emphasised so clearly up to that time. In general, patients in treatment, whether analytic or not (and whether this is consciously acknowledged or not), experience a transference of feelings onto their therapist. That is to say, they tend to experience their therapist in a way they have experienced a former important caregiver or authority figure, usually a parent. In psychoanalytic therapies this transference, along with its counterpart, the countertransference of the therapist, form the basis for exploring the problems presented. With people who are addicted, however, something different happens. Because their predominant feelings are felt towards the object of their addiction, they are apt to discount their therapist to a large degree at the start of the treatment (May 1991: 2). They are primarily having an intense love/hate affair with their drug or with their gambling or whatever it is they are addicted to, so their need for intimacy with people, in the meantime, becomes severely curtailed (Liebeskind 1991: 65). In a similar way, it is not uncommon for people involved in violent relationships to refuse to leave their partners behind, even if they are at risk of serious injury. It is the same with addiction. However much harm the addiction is causing, its fascination ensnares.

Difficulties in treatment

This goes some way towards explaining why some therapists may tend to feel that people who are addicted are unsatisfactory patients who are difficult to help – prone to sudden disappearances, denying the obvious, giving contradictory messages, etc. It can be hard for therapists to tolerate what appears to be a lack of success. They may then tend to blame their patients if things go wrong. Once they understand their patients' transference to the object of addiction, the therapist can become prepared to wait for that individual's readiness to return to acknowledging the value of relationship with people. What Smaldino and his colleagues noticed was that this did happen over time if the therapist was patient and stood firm.

The initial motivation for using drugs alters partly because of the build-up of tolerance. People need to have more and more of the drug in their search to obtain the same effect as they did in the beginning, but that has its price, in more than purely monetary terms, because at the same time there is a build-up of adverse effects, both physical and mental. And there is the fear of withdrawal symptoms if you stop.

Defensiveness and defences

Edward Khantzian maintains that the purpose of an addiction is to defend against awareness of anxiety, but the addiction itself can evoke a defensive stance in the individual (Khantzian 2003). The addicted lifestyle has to be protected, because of the shame. This is often hidden under a cover of bravado and it may involve secrecy and complicated deception – so that the addiction can continue unhindered.

Ambivalence

Of these three narrators, Bernadette shows most clearly an awareness of her current ambivalence towards her addiction. Yet the fact that all three have had times when they had tried to cut down their drug use or stop altogether is equally evidence of their ambivalence. In the past few years, motivational interviewing has come to play an important part in the treatment of people caught up in addiction, a method designed to elicit a person's motivation for change. It is defined by William Miller and Stephen Rollnick as 'a patient-centred, directive method for enhancing intrinsic motivation to change by exploring and resolving ambivalence' (Miller and Rollnick 2002: 25).

Destructive effects of addictions

In the earlier stages of an addiction, much cognitive work can be done in treatment, for example with binge drinkers. They can become aware of triggers and can think about the advantages and disadvantages of continuing to use drugs or drink. The trouble with the chronic stage of addiction is that all rational considerations are likely to have been overturned by the importunate demands of the body and mind for more of the drug. It is a passion and a need. Common sense no longer holds sway. Fear of failure, sometimes because of previous failed attempts to stop, may also come into the picture at this stage. Most addicted people have an inkling that their sense of control is an illusion. All the narrators speak about the effects of their addictions on their employment, their finances and their social lives, as well as on their health, both physical and mental.

In his recent book on the link between Jung and AA, David Schoen draws a useful distinction between addiction and other forms of psychological disorder. Using Jung's terminology he delineates graphically how an addiction can take control of an individual. He describes the addiction/ shadow complex, which he personifies as Evil. This can only be successfully countermanded in the long term by a programme of spiritual growth such as AA's Twelve Step Programme (Schoen 2009: 94). He captures the inexorable hold addiction has on an individual, a state no longer amenable to reason. Two other American authors, Franklin Shontz and James Spotts, describe the practical application of Jung's ideas in a residential programme for heroin users in Kansas City (Shontz and Spotts 1989).

The overriding factor in the lives of people who are addicted is their relationship with the drug. This dominates their lives. It is no longer experienced as pleasure giving or life enhancing. Their predominant attitude is dissatisfaction and ambivalence towards their need for the drug. There is little evidence of a sense of confidence in being able to escape from the trap of addiction or indeed to affect what happens in any way in their lives. What has happened is that having escaped down a particular track, they now feel demoralised and imprisoned in the labyrinth. They are trapped and the addiction is tyrannical. There is a striking preoccupation with a balancing act between how much they need, how much they want, and how much they wish to jettison their addiction completely. Now their drugs are used mainly to get through the day. The narratives in the next part of the book illustrate how four former patients reached a final stopping point.

Part 2

The turning point

In this part four former patients describe the turning point at which they stopped drinking or using drugs. The first of these was addicted to heroin. He remained in hospital up to the day before he planned to stop, then discharged himself at the last minute because he wanted one last fix and then detoxified himself on his own. The second and fourth, both addicted to alcohol, stopped in hospital, while for the third of these narrators, who was addicted to both alcohol and a variety of drugs, stopping was more of a stop-start affair for many years, in and out of treatment units.

Chapter 6

I did it my way

Alfie is one of the former patients who took part in the longitudinal follow-up study of heroin users. He was originally treated at the hospital in his teens and twenties, when he was in constant trouble because of his drug use. At that time he was an active member of a group of injectors who shared their drugs. He flouted every branch of authority imaginable, with drugs and alcohol playing an ever greater part in his life. His first wife died through an overdose of heroin after she left him. Many years later his former psychiatrist is talking to him and his wife. The first person to speak is his wife, Emma. He is present, but leaves Emma to do the talking. She had to go out to work after a short time.

We've been with each other for twenty years. Obviously, in the early years there were difficulties, Alfie being involved with heroin. I knew him when he was taking heroin and abusing alcohol. It wasn't all the time. Sort of *phases* really. Sometimes he'd do[1] absolutely nothing at all and other times he'd slip back again. But that hasn't been for a long, long time.

When he slipped back, he slipped back the whole way. That is Alfie: all or nothing. Must be about thirteen years since he was into drugs. I think basically Alfie had made his mind up that he wanted to come off, and when Alfie makes up his mind to do something, he usually does it. He just needed some help to get through, you know, coming off – the rough part, but then he was so determined to do it that once he got through the initial part in the hospital, he got through it really pretty well, pretty quickly.

Once or twice a year perhaps he gets drunk nowadays. There doesn't really seem to be anything that sets him off. We drink socially and he'll have too many, but sometimes it seems Alfie doesn't know when to stop. He doesn't set out to get drunk. I don't think anything triggers him off. 'I'm gonna get drunk.' I think sometimes he'll be drinking socially and it's almost like something takes him over. And he just carries on. Before you know where you are, he's over the top. He's never been violent, physically violent. He just rambles on a bit really: more sort of irritating than anything else. Then he gets to a certain point and goes to sleep. He's OK. Myself,

I've smoked cannabis, but I've never been a regular user, just possibly, socially, you know?

Alfie continues after Emma goes out:

My first wife died twenty-two, twenty-three years ago. After that I had quite a few girlfriends. Mostly drunks. I don't think they were ever that serious, you know? Funnily enough, I met Emma in a pub. She was seventeen. She was just somehow *stable*. She was down-to-earth and content, really. I just hit it off with her, yeah? And since then there hasn't been any other girl.

My son is twenty-five. He's employed, and my daughter is twenty-seven this year. She works locally too. She lives across the road. My son smokes a bit. Practically everybody I come across either smokes or drinks. My Mum likes to have a drink, but we're talking about one drink.

I've been working at the airport for about two and a half years now. I used to do lorry driving – without a licence. I suppose I did that for over twenty years. Mainly a tipper driver. I did get caught a few times, but if I was challenged I always just talked in a foreign accent. I couldn't be bothered with it now though. It got to a stage where I just wanted to be normal, sort of.

The thing that made me do it, what made me give up junk, you know – I was registered[2] with a private doctor in London for two years, I think, two and a half years. I think I used to pay him about £20 a week, and another twenty added to get the script out of the chemist. I used to sit in the armchair in that flat and if I was lucky I might nod off for ten seconds, but whenever I did that I always used to think of my kid, my Jason. He would walk in the door, and I wouldn't be awake. And that's it. I couldn't stand the thought of him discovering me dead, you know? And that's what really got me going in the end. I just visualised him walking in, you know, a little kid, and I'd be sitting there like. . .

The one thing was that I couldn't bear that my son, who was then twelve, might one day find me dead. I think a lot of it was to do with the kids, because you know, really, I wanted a stable sort of home for them, and I wanted them to see me as stable, you know. When I was stoned, I wasn't the best of people to deal with. I'm not proud of it at all. And I was getting involved with Emma at that time. We couldn't have a proper relationship all the time that thing was about[3]. It was much more to me than a promising liaison. That sort of underestimates what was going on. She's seen me in every conceivable position and she stuck by me. It made a lot of difference. I was driving then. I used to do a couple of days here and there, just to get enough money. I lived from one day to the next.

Whenever I think of smack[4], I think of when I was first using smack. I used to have half a jack and get right down, you know? That was great. That was bliss. But that was then. It was never like that again. No matter how much you used – it was never like that, you know?

That's what I wanted then. I wanted as much heroin as I could ever get – all day, every day, for the rest of me life. But then I decided, 'No, I don't want it.' I think my attitude changed. But still, having said that, if I remember the last time I saw you, I called you all the names under the sun because you wouldn't give me a turn on[5], yeah? The next day, after we had that row, I left the hospital and I had four amps of physeptone in one hit, and that was a lot. And that was the last time I ever had a fix.

I left very angry with you, but when I had my last 'jacking', to be honest, I, when I look back on it now, I find it very embarrassing that I should feel like that at that time. Looking back now I think you were right in refusing me. I respect you for that, you know? I think it might have been a bit of a challenge for me – 'I'm going to get a turn on out of you, if it's the last thing I do.' I was determined to have another fix. I just wanted one more, one more fix and I was prepared to call it a day after that. The last time I had any opiates was the last time I saw you. The day afterwards, I had the physeptone and that was it.

I locked myself away for ten days after that in the flat over the road. I went through it all right. I didn't sleep for over a week and what with the legs jumping about, and my nose running all the time – it was dire. I had a book Emma's mother gave me about yoga. I just kept reading it, reading it and trying to get the yoga positions and it worked. You could see a way through, sort of thing. But it took about ten days till I could actually walk properly and sort of function, really. I didn't eat much. I couldn't eat. I didn't want to eat at all. Emma used to come a few times, but it was a waste of time. She couldn't do anything at all. I just wanted to be on my own and get through it. The people I was involved with then, I mean, all they wanted me for was a bit of my script or whatever, you know? You don't have *friends*.

I didn't really get any urge to use afterwards. Occasionally I'd dream that I was actually going to have a fix. I'd wake up in a cold sweat, you know, and thank God that I hadn't actually done it, you know? I used to think more about if it was actually offered to me. Would I be able to handle it? And in the end, you know, I didn't want anything to do with it whatsoever. That was it, you know? I haven't even had this bad dream for a long time now.

I just did it on my own. And now I keep away from everybody. I live a different life now. And I can say with no hesitation whatsoever that I just would not want to go back on heroin. I get embarrassed when I think about it. I had a roaring affair with heroin. It's like a mistress. It's far more than fun – it's serious. I paid a heavy price for it of every kind. I mean, my self-respect. After all, when you're living to get stoned, what sort of life's that?

I don't ever come across any other drug users from that time. I don't ever go to the town centre for that reason. I don't go to the pub, because I can't stand seeing the people who, if I did see them, would be exactly the same as if it was twenty years ago, you know? Now, if I saw Spider walking down the road, I'd have to cross the road, or go the other way, because I don't want to be involved. No. And it seems you've only got to sort of raise an eyebrow to someone that I was like and that's it, you're involved.

I'm solvent now, just about. The last time I had a brush with the law was when I went to Glastonbury about six years ago. They found a bit of dope in the car and I was driving the car so I put my hand up to it. And they gave me a caution. I do drink maybe two or three glasses of wine. So I drink about three bottles of wine a week on your own, but nowhere near as much as I used to drink. I think I was an alcoholic at one time. I'd like to think that I was not like that now. Sometimes I get home quite late and I don't get round to having a drink. It doesn't really bother me that much. As I say, I very rarely go into a pub, and if I do, I go up to London to a club. I only go up there to see a few friends, and a band or something. This is a Sunday lunch time, and I have a few drinks and I go to their house and have some dinner, and maybe a few more drinks and then I come home.

Holidays, I like. I go to Greece a lot. I found a little island in Greece and whenever I go there it's like I'm the long lost cousin, you know. I have some good friends there and it's a beautiful place. In fact I'm going there next week for eleven days this time.

I don't think things do upset me. No. I take most things with a pinch of salt, you know. Whatever's going down, you know? I think I accept things a lot better. At one time, everything was against me personally, or it seemed to be, but now I know it's not just me. Everybody's getting it.

Here we have a picture of a young man who in a former age would most likely have been a warrior. His life seems to have offered little scope for fulfillment. Adventurous, with a strong survival mechanism, thriving on taking risks, his activities frequently landed him on the wrong side of the law. Alfie put himself well outside the protective wall of human community, as Jung calls it, if by human community we mean conventional society. Alfie needed the challenge of initiatory experiences, which in some societies have traditionally been accompanied by elaborate rituals, adventures that would promote his path into a full adult life in all its potential richness. Luigi Zoja, writing about a young man who became addicted to stimulants, highlights this aspect of the shortcomings of modern Western society in providing opportunities for meaningful initiation into adult life (Zoja 1989). Alfie found an alternative for himself – heroin, and a group of heroin-using friends of which he was a ringleader. Yet he possessed another characteristic of the archetypal warrior – a longing to protect his family. His first wife had left him, only to die of a drug overdose herself later. His son was about twelve years old by the time all this occurred. The knowledge that if he himself died of an overdose, his two children would become orphans led him to enter treatment.

No therapist can predict accurately how his or her words will be received. There was a surprising outcome to the acrimonious row in the hospital ward. Alfie had a need to assert his independence and to put his stamp on the ending of his addiction. His therapist was the psychiatrist in whose hands lay decisions about treatment. It seems that his therapist's refusal to permit him 'one last fix', the cause of their row, acted as a goad in strengthening his resolve to succeed on his own. His therapist had battled long and hard with Alfie's intransigence in the face of reason. It took time and other influences to bring him to a point of wanting to quit. That in no way minimised the influence of his therapist, with whom he can joke so many years later, and for whom he shows good feelings. I think from what each of them has said, that they regarded one another as equally full of vivacity and imagination, but at that early stage, on different sides of the fence.

In the event, as his therapist has said, a leopard doesn't change its spots, and Alfie rebelled again against all the advice and took his own discharge from hospital, determined to show that he could do it 'his way'. He had confidence in his decision. After his final injection, he took himself right away from any temptation to obtain more drugs, and away from his erstwhile associates. He was even independent of Emma for that crucial time. The distressing withdrawals he experienced were counterbalanced by his determination to succeed in stopping and his concentration on yoga. If someone has decided they want to stop injecting heroin, it is perfectly possible to achieve this without medical supervision. It is commonly supposed that a great deal of outside help and effort is needed for a successful detox. Alfie's experience shows that someone with ego strength and determination can achieve it on their own. Not everyone is like Alfie, of course. But what this does show is how vital the personal decision is. Detox was difficult for him, but was bearable because of his decision to stop.

Even after all these years, Alfie has a fear of being dragged back into the world of heroin again, so he avoids any chance of coming across his former companions in the drug-using circle he once belonged to. It is strange to hear him say fourteen years later that he will not go into certain pubs or into the centre of town. This really shows how powerful he regards the influence of peer pressure.

One of his dreams shows how far he has come since his drug-using days. In a chapter near the end of his book about Jung's attitude towards the phenomenon of addiction, David Schoen presents dreams of people who have stopped drinking, and he illustrates how the dreamer's waking attitude towards the dream offers a clear picture of how successful he or she is in having left alcohol behind (Schoen 2009: 127–148). The dreamer's attitude may indicate either a longing for the long-lost drug, ambivalent feelings over its loss, or, on the other hand, relief at having escaped from the addicted life. In this case, Alfie is horrified to find himself dreaming of having a fix.

Alfie's relationship with Emma shows that he was looking for a stable person who could help him to keep his feet on the ground, and being himself a leader, he needed a partner with an equally strong personality. Meeting them now, the rapport between the two is immediately apparent. They speak highly of one another, and with understanding. When Alfie first met her, Emma represented something very powerful for him – a chance to come back from lawlessness into conventional society. As he says, the relationship couldn't flourish while heroin was around. Emma didn't stop him using heroin, but what he saw in her led him into a different way of thinking about the possibilities for his life.

In his letter to William Wilson, Jung writes about addiction representing a search for wholeness (Jung 1976: 624). The confines of his environment restricted Alfie as a young man. He started using drugs while he was still at school and at a time when he could not actually leave home. Instead he found excitement in bucking the system and taking the lead in escapades. Drug using was part of the alternative culture. Nothing otherwise in his everyday life, it seems, could provide enough excitement or enough stimulus for him at that stage of his growing up. The adventurous hero in him badly needed an outlet while he was growing into a man. This was what was lacking from 'wholeness' for him at that stage. Joseph Redfearn's description of the subpersonalities within the individual illustrates powerfully the concept of how we are all made up of so many contrasting and often confusing parts (Redfearn 1985: 50–57). When Jung talks about a search for wholeness, he is touching on how the personality can become enhanced when divergent aspects within ourselves can be better integrated. Jung regarded this as a lifelong challenge. Much of what Alfie got up to in his drug-using days could be termed 'shadow' behaviour in regard to mainstream culture. He was acting out the darker part of life.

What does the little island in Greece mean to Alfie? He identifies with the islanders. If we think about drug using as a search for a different take on life, it makes sense that just because someone stops using drugs, it doesn't mean that they lose their curiosity and longings. For Alfie, since he has drawn back from his adventurous deviant days of flouting authority, the excitement of illegal drug-fuelled escapades has been replaced by exploration of living in a completely different culture and climate. Now he is older, instead of taking the short cut to thrills chemically, he gets on a plane. He needs a wide horizon. Again, this is an example of one pattern transforming itself into another. The horizons are wider now. His story shows just how much stimulus and opportunity adolescents need to thrive. He found it, but in a way that was far too costly in the dangers it carried. Luckily, unlike his first wife, he survived and had a second chance. Although he still lives in the same town as he did as a child, to his hosts on the Greek island he loves, Alfie is the long-lost cousin. He has extended his horizons as well as holding together a warm, welcoming home.

In conclusion

Adolescent rebellion

While people are growing up they need to take risks and meet challenges and they will find them at any cost. Not all rebellious teenagers become deviant, but most go through a stage of kicking against authority and finding their own way into adult life. Because the use of drugs such as heroin is controlled by legal constraints, obtaining it and using it often represents the thrill of the illicit, quite apart from its actual effect on the body and mind. It will always be the case that some adolescents are more adventurous than the norm and seek risks, especially when it is hard for them to find outlets in a more conventional and acceptable way.

The therapist's contribution

Therapists should never underestimate the effects their approach and their personality have, even if there is little or no evidence of their having any influence at all at the time. All the people we talked to valued two things: the understanding and interest they were shown in regard to why they used drugs, and the integrity of their therapists, in equal measure. Patients know quite well how much their therapists care about their welfare. Alfie's therapist understood that adolescents need to throw over the traces, and at the same time, as a psychiatrist, he was prepared to stand his ground on treatment decisions. This is an example of the paradoxical effect of what AA calls 'tough love' on the part of the therapist.

Growing up and leaving addiction behind

Alfie now leads a full and satisfying life. Some young people do come to a point where they are ready to leave their addictions behind. Charles Winick (1962) postulated the theory that people could mature out of addiction, and though his view has been criticised, here is a case where it applies. The trouble is the extent of the casualties and the damage caused along the way. Not every story has an ending like Alfie's.

Detoxification with or without treatment

If someone wants to stop using heroin, the withdrawal symptoms can be survived without medical intervention. The teenagers in Alfie's group of friends knew a great deal about the effects of stopping, by experiencing it themselves or by observing the effects on one another. Withdrawal from alcohol is more dangerous, because there is a risk of death through fits, as well as the frightening experience of hallucinations. Vast amounts of money and therapeutic effort are wasted when people are rushed into detoxifying without having come to a personal decision to stop using drugs or alcohol. It is the personal decision which makes the difference. What should also be taken into account is that not everyone is as strong as Alfie. Some people may need far more support to keep on track once they have actually stopped, both at the start and in the longer term.

Notes

1 By saying he'd *do* nothing, she means that he would use no drugs.
2 At that time, some doctors in the UK were registered to prescribe heroin and other controlled drugs to patients on a private basis. This is colloquially referred to as a *script*.
3 By *that thing*, he is referring to his drug habit.
4 *Smack* is a colloquial term for heroin.
5 *Turn on* is a colloquial term for the result of a dose of drugs.

Chapter 7

Time to stop drinking with the boys

Hugo was admitted to inpatient care at the hospital three times in his early thirties for alcohol detoxification. In his first narrative he speaks about these experiences and their outcome. He had had continuing contact with the hospital in the form of six-monthly appointments. At that time he was thirty-eight years old. More recently, in his second narrative, he has added highly significant details about the crisis on the night he finally decided to stop drinking. He is extremely intelligent and is largely self-educated. He has played a prominent role in his local community.

It's a funny thing. My problem wasn't so much drinking, as trying to stop. Once I started drinking, it progressed to the point where I couldn't stop. Like the chap who jumped out of the third-floor window, it wasn't the fall that killed him, it was hitting the pavement. I mean, the drink itself didn't bother me too much, if I'd been able to stop I'd have been all right. When I was going out with a girl five years ago, things got really bad, and business-wise things got bad, and I'd always enjoyed a drink, all my life, and I was going pretty haywire. Right over the top. Things progressed to the point where I was going to the pub at ten o'clock in the morning and going home and sleeping in the afternoon, and going up the pub at opening time in the evening – and I kept this up for a little while. Then I used to stay in bed till lunch time and go up the pub and take a bottle home with me to save money, and it gradually went to the point where I just wasn't getting out of bed. I'd get out of bed about ten o'clock at night, go up the pub and go to bed with a bottle of scotch. And after a few days of that my parents dragged the doctors in and they whisked me off to hospital.

I started off as a social drinker, enjoying a drink. Right from my teens, I suppose. I used to get hangovers occasionally and minor problems, but I can't say it was a real problem in my life. I probably was aware, although I probably wouldn't have admitted it, that I was drinking more than I should be. But on the other hand, a lot of people do that. A lot of my friends were doing the same. And you think, 'They can do it. It's all right.' I suppose my girlfriend drew attention to it. But by that time things had got so bad that I didn't care, you know. Perhaps in a way I was trying to punish her as well, for driving me to it, making her feel guilty, I don't know.

The worst thing that happened was when – I was really at a low ebb. I went up to the pub one evening and I just couldn't stay awake. I was exhausted, physically and mentally as well, and I never quite made it. I sort of collapsed outside the pub, and somebody took me home, and I said, 'Oh, I'll be all right now.' It was only a few feet to the front door, but I never made it. I just fell down in the street. It was about half past nine at night, I think. My father came along and took me indoors, and put me to bed, but about two o'clock in the morning I woke up, like that, you know – 'Where am I?' I was getting pretty bad withdrawals. It was absolutely terrifying what I went through that night. I was lying there from two o'clock in the morning. There wasn't a drink in the house. I didn't have anything until the off licence opened at half past eight. And I could feel my whole spine was arching over backwards. I was bending over like this and I was shaking. I couldn't do anything else. But somehow I survived the night; it seemed an eternity. I went up the off licence at half past eight and had a quarter bottle of vodka for breakfast and I was all right then.

At that point the GP was giving me tranquillisers as well. It was starting to dawn on me that perhaps I had a bit of a problem. Very reluctant to admit it! But GPs, I find them very, very difficult to approach. I couldn't really say what I wanted to say, I was sort of skirting round the subject, you know? And he was saying, 'More than three drinks a day and you're in trouble.' 'Well,' I thought, 'You must be joking. I had three drinks before I came here.' This is what you expect from doctors really. You expect them to say, 'Cut down on the drink! Smoke less!' I thought, 'This isn't really getting anywhere.' I knew it wouldn't do any good. He gave me tranquillisers. I thought, 'These are nice. They go well with a lager.' It really made the problem worse. I regarded the doctor's advice as being a counsel of perfection. Doctors are always advising people to drink less, smoke less and lose weight etc., so it is OK to take their advice with a pinch of salt, isn't it? Especially when I had been dealing with GPs who appeared totally clueless about my problems.

I know when things really took a nosedive. I got breathalysed at eight o'clock in the morning. I just gave up then. I crawled into my shell and just carried on drinking for three months. In the January my parents dragged me off to hospital. Life in the hospital was terrible. It was a terrible shock. Well, for one thing, any mental hospital is a shock. Ending up, for someone that's been having a life in the outside world, ending up in a psychiatric hospital is a shock to the system – you know, surrounded by disturbed people. I thought the doctors might do something, but all they did was give me tranquillisers. I was expecting some sort of magic cure, you know. Then, a few weeks later, they booted me out into the outside world, and at that time my thinking was, 'Well, this has been a very bad period that I've just gone through business-wise, and my relationship with this girl,' and I remember the psychiatrist said to me that I'd got to stop drinking, and again I thought, 'This is what you expect a doctor to say.' I gave it some thought, but I thought to myself, 'I can't really stop. I don't want to stop. Once things get back to normal, I'll be able to revert to my normal sort of drinking and enjoy it.'

I did try controlling my drink for a while during that period. It worked to a degree, but it's an awful struggle. You only fail once, like I did, and you're right back all the way down. I did actually give up for a few weeks but one night, I had a Guinness. St. Patrick's Day it was. I thought, 'I'll just have two,' and I had three. Then the next night I thought, 'I had three last night, so I'll have three tonight.'

I had a lot of business worries too. It's a job to tell how many of these things were coincidental, how many things just happened to go wrong at the same time, or how many of them were due to other problems. For instance, if I hadn't thought, 'Oh help, here comes another problem, let's go up the pub and retreat from it,' perhaps I could have dealt with it. I think that's quite possibly the case, you know, problems that you wouldn't think much about, once you start drinking to escape from them, once the drink wears off, the problems are still there, only bigger. Anyway, my business is quite all right now.

I come from Sussex. My parents are retired now. My father was a farmer, a farm worker. I sometimes wonder whether there was anything in childhood or in my upbringing which might make me more vulnerable to excessive drinking. I was allowed to have things I wanted, I think, yes, possibly to excess. But whether that made any difference, I don't know. I think you're either susceptible to these things or you're not. But the trouble is, by the time you realise you're susceptible to them, you're trapped. Like a lobster in a pot, it doesn't realise it's trapped. You would never think beforehand, 'Oh, I'm heading towards a drink problem situation.' You just can't envisage that. It can't happen to you. I did hear tales about my grandfather coming home drunk in a horse and cart, but whether that was normal or whether that was considered excessive I don't know. My father was the absolute picture of a moderate drinker. Just the odd glass of wine.

It's a complete blur that period. I had to go back into hospital. I phoned up the GP and said, 'I must go back, I just can't do this on my own.' And that was after having discharged myself, to have to be readmitted again, that was when it hit me with a bang, especially as they took me off the Ativan[1], and put me on Librium[1] – bloody horrible things! Like being hit over the head with a sledgehammer, and I felt this horrible kind of despair, you know, because I had tried my hardest since I'd discharged myself from the hospital, I'd tried my hardest to control this problem – I was beginning to admit that it was a problem – and I'd only lasted a matter of weeks. And I thought, 'I've done all I can. The doctors have done all they can,' feeling a complete and utter desolation and despair.

Well, I was another six weeks in hospital, and do you know, since then, since I faced up to it in that light, since I've come out, I've never even been tempted to have a drink. I used to go to occupational therapy while I was in hospital and I'd break out in a cold sweat, and I'd think, 'God, how am I ever going to go back into the outside world and be able to not have a drink and survive, for any length of time?' I thought, 'A few weeks and I'll be back in again.' But it never happened. Once I'd shut my mind to it like that, I got myself to think, 'Under no circumstances can you have a drink, otherwise this is going to happen again, and again and again.' Once you've learned that lesson, then if you feel like a drink – I feel like a drink now in the same way that you feel like a cup of tea or an ice cream, whereas if you feel like a cup of tea, you might go and get yourself one, if I start thinking, 'I could do with a lager and lime in this hot weather' – the answer is no. You don't even entertain the notion, because you know it's – you just cannot entertain the idea for a minute. So you don't think about it. So there's no problem.

I have an appointment at the hospital about every six months now. It has got less frequent. That is going on from three years ago. That, I must say, that is probably a very valuable thing. That I have got to come back every so often and 'report' as it were. I think, if I'd just been thrown out to the outside world and forgotten – it acts a reminder. I know that if – I will – be tempted. And if I am tempted, I've got to account for it afterwards. And also I had Antabuse[2] – I had those in hospital, but by the time I came out, I'd stopped taking them. I thought, 'No, I'm not going to be dependent on pills for this. If I'm going to stop drinking, I'm going to stop. Full stop. It's got to be from *within*. You can't have pills to stop you drinking. I've still got those three pills, I think. But, they are valuable though, because they are – it means I've always got something in reserve. If I find the going is very tough, I could always resort to those, as a kind of a prop, if need be.

I don't think I'll ever drink again. But, I mean, it's very unwise to go around proclaiming, 'I'm never going to touch another drop for the rest of my life.' It's like a little child who says he's never to tell a lie again. It's too easy to break. It could happen. I mean, you have to face the possibility in life. If I carry on thinking as I am, I don't think it's very likely. I don't think about it at all in fact.

As a footnote, I remember the last thing Dr Rathod said to me as I left hospital for the last time just before Christmas, clutching a bottle of Antabuse he had given me while protesting that I didn't want to take them as I didn't feel I needed them – 'Take them – you'll never make it through Christmas without,' he said. Well of course that was a red rag to a bull. 'I'll prove him wrong,' I thought. And I did.

Everybody says the Christmas period is a difficult time. Like I say, it's something that, once you've made up your mind within yourself, once you've faced the facts, faced the truth of the matter, you accept that you can't go out and enjoy a drink like other people, then the subject is closed as far as you're concerned. I have this at weddings – people come up and thrust drinks in my hand and I walk around and give them to somebody else, you know. I go up the pub for lunch, there's a pub just up the road. They've got a case of ginger beer in. People say you shouldn't go into pubs, but it doesn't make a blind bit of difference to me – I think perhaps to other people perhaps it may.

Recently Hugo added to what he had said about addiction and stopping earlier, and wrote this to me:

There were a couple of milestones on my way down, seemingly insignificant in themselves. For a long time, probably since my late teens or early twenties, I had been suffering from a sort of withdrawal problem with alcohol, in the sense that if, for example, a drink gave me a 'high' of plus five points, once it wore off I would sink to minus ten, as it were. This was never really a problem for me (and I certainly never understood the significance of it at the time) simply because I would only drink in the evenings and then sleep it off. But then I started working with a guy who was in the habit of having a drink or two at lunchtime, nothing excessive, and I got in the habit of joining him. This presented a real problem for me because I would then need to 'top up' during the afternoon before going out for a drink in the evening. By this time, and I am probably talking about weeks rather than months, this habit had become so entrenched that I was unable to break free from it. In fact I would say, and this is true of every step along my path to addiction, that what started as a habit quickly became a dependence before escalating into a full-blown addiction. And by the time I realised what was happening to me it was too late – I was trapped in this cycle.

The second thing was when I learned that the best – indeed the only – cure for a hangover was another drink. That was almost literally fatal to me. And again, the big problem was that once learned, this lesson could not be un-learned. What I later (too late!) learned from this, however, was that once I had had a drink to cure a hangover, I would need to maintain alcohol in my system continuously from that point on. The body, marvellous machine that it is, had simply adapted to having alcohol in its system. Or rather I should say the brain had adapted, to the point where the mind was screaming out for alcohol while the body was literally rejecting it. I remember being given a piece of advice by a fellow alcoholic, that when you took that first sip of vodka at 8.30am in the gents' toilet, to make it a small one, as you would bring it straight up again and you didn't want to waste it. Been there, done that!

I think you have to learn to be honest. Oh yes, I mean, you can't do otherwise. I don't think anything could have been done at an earlier stage. I wouldn't have listened. I remember the first time I had to be interviewed by the psychologist, I thought he was poking his nose into my business – you know, trying to stop me drinking – people interfering like that. No. I wouldn't have wanted to face the truth. I pretended that everything was all right. I mean, you can point things out to people, but I'm sure they won't listen. It was difficult for me to accept him as an authority figure – my initial reaction was, 'Who the hell is this college kid poking his nose into my private life telling me to stop drinking.' Then, when he accurately predicted that I would be back in hospital within four to six months (it was five, actually) I began to wonder if perhaps, just possibly, he might be right and I might be wrong. It is no exaggeration at all to say that he saved my life. He has no idea how much I owe him.

I actually think it's a pity they did stop offering follow-up appointments – certainly in the initial stages it was useful for me to have to 'report back' every six months or so, both as a reminder to myself that this was an ongoing condition and to demonstrate to the psychologist that his efforts had not been wasted. As a cost-effective clinical process I have always felt a six-monthly or annual 'check-in to say I'm OK' might save a lot of money in the long term – even a five-minute phone call to remind patients that they are still receiving treatment for an incurable condition (as opposed to being spat out and told 'you're cured' – which of course is not the case) might save you having to pick up the pieces later.

I think it is worth reiterating the sense of utter surrender that was necessary before any recovery could take hold. I believe AA talk of invoking a Higher Power, and that certainly chimes with my own experience. It was as though I was in the grip of something infinitely more powerful than I was, and in order to defeat it, it was necessary to invoke a still greater power. Once I did this I was astonished at how easy the whole thing became – after years of fighting it with every power at my disposal and everything the medical profession could throw at it, ultimately all I had to do was ask, and my prayers were answered immediately. Whether this was God answering my prayers or whether the whole thing stems from within is something the philosophers and theologians may debate if they wish, but as far as I am concerned it is irrelevant – all I know is it works.

I only had one 'rock bottom experience'. That was on my third and final admission to hospital. Something very strange happened that evening. I should start by pointing out that I have never experienced any form of hallucination in my life, either while extremely drunk or while suffering withdrawals. But on that evening all the clocks – and indeed the passage of time itself – slowed right down. I noticed it when I dozed off on the bed at about 7.30pm. After a snooze I awoke, thinking I had been asleep for half an hour or so. I looked at the clock and it said 7.38. Thinking the clock had stopped, I checked the others – they all said the same. Time had just literally slowed down. I don't mean my sense of the passing of time had slowed, or that time was dragging – I mean the clocks had slowed down. I eventually went to bed at about 10pm, and awoke abruptly at 1am. I spent the rest of the night watching the second hand on the clock moving at about one third normal speed – every second lasted three seconds. Weird. Everything else was moving at perfectly normal speed – it was just the clocks that were affected. Make of it what you will, but it was literally the longest night of my life! Eventually, next morning I think, everything gradually returned to normal. Bear in mind that, unlike my first admission, when I was days away from death and pretty much 'out of it', I was in reasonably good shape this time, both physically and mentally. I was perfectly rational and my perceptions were unaffected in any other way whatever.

During this extended evening I had time to reflect on the fact that I had now been admitted three times in the past year and my life had turned into *Groundhog Day* (except I don't think the film had been made yet!). I thought to myself, 'I have tried everything in my power to stop drinking and failed completely. The doctors have tried everything in their power to stop me drinking and have failed completely.' Words cannot convey the sense of utter despair which washed over me at this point, and which, with hindsight, I regard as an essential part of my recovery. 'The only person who can help me now,' I thought, 'is God.' And I got on my knees and I prayed and I prayed and I prayed, for the one and only time in my life.

Make of it what you will, but from that point on I have never, not once, felt the urge to drink. It might be the power of prayer, or it might be a rational approach and change of perspective; I had begun by feeling that it was most unfair that others could enjoy a drink but I could not. So I thought, 'OK, life's unfair, so who am I going to sue – God?' Then I reasoned that here I was, suffering from an incurable and potentially fatal condition, but all I had to do to lead a perfectly normal life was not touch alcohol, whereas the hospitals were full of people with incurable and fatal conditions who had no such easy option – they were going to die. I felt faintly ashamed, and life didn't seem so unfair after all.

I am not convinced that reason alone can account for this apparently magical transformation in my life. At first it seemed odd to go to bed sober; it seemed strange to go out for a meal without a bottle of wine, and so on. But these were minor adjustments – the desperate craving which had tormented me for years had left me, and has never returned.

There was another aspect to my experience which I have not heard other sufferers describe. When I was drinking, or at least toward the end of that period, I felt very much as though I were in the grip of something unspeakably evil. My biggest fear was not that I might die, but that if I did die this evil would stay with me as I crossed the threshold. That is a truly terrifying prospect, but it certainly acts as a disincentive (if one were needed) against drinking!

At no point prior to the final addiction will a person accept the possibility that he will become an addict, certainly if my experience is anything to go by. Even then, you would not believe how difficult it was for me to utter the phrase (even to myself) 'I am an alcoholic', which of course must act as the precursor to any recovery. Even now at this late stage I still feel my biggest danger is complacency – you think to yourself everything is OK now and I'll be able to handle it, and you need to remind yourself that one drink will be enough to destroy everything you have.

Hugo asks himself whether there is something unique about him that makes him susceptible to drinking more and more heavily. He feels that alcohol was just a part of the scene, and, as he says, many of his friends drank heavily too. I think there are a few clues in what Hugo says about why he drank so heavily at that time which relate to his stage of life. He was into his thirties and he had yet to achieve independence from his parents. Things had not worked out with earlier girlfriends, but after he stopped drinking, he quite soon met and settled down with his long-term partner. Maybe the other girlfriends got fed up with his drinking so much and spending so much time in the pub with his mates, or maybe he invested more libido in his drinking than in his love life. His drink problem was an episode in his growing up. He identified with his male friends, as part of his growing up, and he drank with them as part of the cultural norm: 'Everybody does it.'

Of the staff at the hospital who were most closely involved with Hugo's treatment, one was the psychiatrist and the other a psychologist. Both these people could be extremely challenging and outspoken, and were both hard taskmasters when they thought it necessary. At first, Hugo appears to have regarded the psychiatrist's warnings rather in the same vein as the doctor's. 'Just what you'd expect a doctor to say,' that is, as unrealistic clichés. Patients may appear compliant, but go their own way regardless. I suspect that, as with many things in life, Hugo had to find out for himself, and had to follow his own inclinations. It may be that he had a problem with authority figures. Both of these men actually saw Hugo as a person with unfulfilled potential. There is no doubt that they regarded him as a real man, and a resourceful, clever man at that. If my supposition is correct, that Hugo was searching for his own unique way of becoming an independent man in his own right, then his contact with these two people had much more significance than simply being the people he saw for appointments at the hospital to help him with his alcoholism.

In conclusion

Falling into the grip of addiction

Hugo's story has elements of the classic search for manhood. He drank to make him feel more of a man. Being treated and respected by his therapists promoted his recovery. His drinking was a misguided search, as Jung would have described it, which came at a high price, but, fortunately, it was a stage of life which led to his greater maturity. He is one of the narrators who fell prey to an addiction without having had other serious difficulties in his past or current life: he was neither psychologically damaged nor weak in the first place. His drinking was associated with a definable stage of his development. The difficulties he faced were largely brought about by the addiction itself. This is by no means uncommon. He became addicted almost without noticing the fact. He had absolutely no idea how difficult it would be to stop. His words illustrate how drinking sociably with friends in the pub can escalate into something malign. The harm that alcohol causes may be imperceptible to the person drinking for a long, long time. Alcohol-linked problems can mount in a frightening crescendo.

'Controlled' drinking

After his first detox in hospital, Hugo believed he could keep control of his drinking and return to a more moderate pattern when he so wished. He believed at that stage that those advising him were being unnecessarily alarmist and perfectionist. What he discovered was how flimsy his intention proved to be once he was back in his old haunts. Controlled drinking may work for someone who has not become 'addicted', but for anyone who has crossed that invisible line, it can turn out to be simply impossible. His failure to make his plan succeed actually led him to new depths of despair.

Surrender

Hugo says of his addiction, 'I was in the grip of something infinitely more powerful than I was,' and that this was something 'unspeakably evil' which could possess him to the point of death and beyond. These highly charged phrases offer a dramatic glimpse of what addicted people actually feel, and indicate the pain of surrendering, against one's will, to something more powerful than oneself. The point of surrender for Hugo had little to do with rationality. It was an overwhelmingly emotional experience which he views as an essential part of his recovery.

Hugo did not become a member of AA. Yet, the fascinating thing is that in his story there is an example of an existential crisis, the 'ego collapse at depth' as Jung called it, similar to that of one of the founder members of AA, William Wilson, who has written vividly about his experience in hospital (Alcoholics Anonymous 1976: 13). Wilson reached a point where he felt completely hopeless. It was not until he reached this point that he made any headway in solving his problems. He had to come to his own decision. He recognised at that point that he was powerless over alcohol, the first of the Twelve Steps of AA.

The value of the continuing offer of support

After that Hugo did start to listen to advice, and valued continuing support, in the form of the offer of appointments every few months at the hospital, which he could attend or not, as he felt the need. Sometimes he phoned to say that everything was fine, and that he wouldn't be coming. But the knowledge of that support, if the need arose, was important to him. This shows how valuable it is for people to be able to come back to staff they know and trust. The importance of continuing support after stopping in preventing relapse has been found in several longitudinal studies (Broom *et al.* 2002, Moos and Moos 2006).

Notes

1 Ativan and Librium are both benzodiazepine drugs, usually prescribed to alleviate anxiety.
2 Antabuse is the brand name for the drug disulfiram. It has no effect if there is no alcohol in the blood, but when alcohol is present, it causes acetaldehyde, a breakdown product of alcohol, to accumulate in the blood, resulting in a variety of most unpleasant experiences. Its use is based on the principle of aversion.

Chapter 8

I was able just to be me

Isabel always lived locally but in her adolescent years she did not primarily have treatment at our hospital, although she had one detoxification and some contact. At that time she was obtaining methadone and tranquillisers on prescription from London drug clinics and from doctors who were permitted to prescribe controlled drugs privately, as well as heroin and other drugs which she obtained from illicit sources. During that period she was an inpatient for detoxification three times at London hospitals, twice with her partner and once on her own. Many people, like Isabel, go on a merry-go-round of stopping and starting again. In this narrative, several years after she stopped drinking and using drugs, she describes her life at that time and the treatment that proved effective for her. This involved addressing psychological aspects of her addiction. She is a feisty woman who loves a challenge. As she says, 'I love coming back from behind.'

I was on my own, following my partner's death, with my two children. I was attempting to detox. I think I'd been driven along by other people's motivation for me. Because my partner had died, this was a time in my life when I *should* do something, but I actually feel that on an emotional level I wasn't ready to do anything about it. There were lots of parts of my drug use that had become uncomfortable in terms of there never really being enough drugs for me and the fact that I wasn't finding methadone particularly satisfying. I had quite a lot of physical problems at the time, with abscesses and not being able to get veins[1] and things, but I think most of the rationale for my decision was my need to please other people. It obviously was a pretty traumatic time for me because he had just died and I needed the security of people around me – those people kept saying, 'This is what you should do.' I was injecting methadone amps. I was registered at this clinic in London. I was also using a variety of other drugs, sleeping pills, temazepam, all those other things, some prescribed, and some bought illicitly. I was still part of a circle of friends who were using drugs. I could get hold of stuff, so long as I had the money. I had bargaining power, because I would get a prescription in a few days' time and I was sharing mine as well. So that was the run up to that detox.

I went into hospital here to detox and I just remember it as being a something and nothing affair. I guess because my heart wasn't in it. There were lots of attempts to try and link me up with a social support network, but I think I just wasn't ready. I remember the day I left the hospital going straight to somebody who'd picked up[2] that day and I remember having a hit of heroin and methadone and instantly being sick and thinking, 'At least now I can *feel* my drugs for a bit longer[3].' I was back to a situation where I actually could be aware of the effects and enjoy it, which was a bonus. I was still on the merry-go-round, but it becomes more complicated because of course you can't verbalise that to people. It's when it becomes a whole load of lies. You're sitting there and the counsellor is thinking you haven't used, and you *have* used. Because with me there was always a part of me that didn't want people to give up on me. And yet when I felt they had given up on me, that's when I actually did something about it.

So after that I found another partner. He was originally a drinker. I found him because he was a volunteer at an agency. I linked up with him, and what happened is that, on some level, he wanted to use drugs. What we did was *swap* addictions. I had never really had an alcohol problem, but I did drink socially. It hadn't crossed over into being an addiction in terms of drinking morning, noon and night. We got into a partnership very quickly. In that phase of my life we didn't drink tea or coffee, we just had vodka in the fridge, and I gave him a methadone problem. He'd used amphetamines, but he had never used opiates. So then we had this crazy situation where for a couple of years there was a period of what other people would see as progress, because I was drinking more but using less. I was not buying as much stuff on top. I was losing a little bit of weight. I was actually more together *initially*, and he was not going on benders that were lasting for days on end. He was actually able to go out and function and go to work because he'd got methadone inside him most of the time.

But of course with anything like that, it doesn't last. From a period of it being OK, it blows big time. And that's what happened. It was also at that period of my life that I had entered the last phase of my using. I was aware by now that I wasn't living as I wanted to, but I felt incapable of doing anything about it. The alcohol, when I was drunk, made me incredibly angry, so I entered a quite schizophrenic phase of my life. Always before in all my using I had been a passive person, *butter wouldn't melt*; always the sort of person drug workers would describe as intelligent, articulate, sensitive. Suddenly I entered this phase in my life where I had this real 'alter ego', particularly with this guy. As soon as I'd had a few drinks, I'd start going 'on one', basically. My children were with me. Things blew up, and everything was getting to a ridiculous phase, you know, I'd always be calling the police. It would settle down and then start up again.

What happened at that time was that we decided to go into treatment together, as a couple. He'd been to a place in London that runs a detox, and we'd got in touch with them and they'd agreed that we could go in as a couple. The primary purpose – it was like a game. The agenda that we told them was that, 'Yes, we definitely wanted to come off,' but my agenda was to stop drinking. What was interesting was that we got there and I actually decided that I quite liked this whole idea of getting totally clean.

For the first time I had gone in as one of a couple and of course the dynamics of the couple came into play. Initially we'd gone in and all the feedback we were getting was that I was really passive and quiet, pathetic almost, and that I was putting too much pressure on him. So I thought, 'Well, I'm not having this, because this isn't the case. I actually am the one who keeps everything together, I organise everything.' So, I basically let that side of me show in this place.

I started to think, 'This is really quite good. I can do this. I can do these peer evaluations,' and what happened was then there became an incredible conflict between the two of us, and we couldn't assimilate the change in the state that we were in. I think we were both competitive and that's still an issue today. But the difficulty is that he's not a self-aware person on any level, so he just acts out, you know. And the difficulty as well was that the people in the treatment centre were going faster than we were. They were really encouraging me, and he thought they were encouraging me and slighting him. I was the more gratifying patient. I was really a patient that *I* would like to have: I said all the right things, totally amiable. Then there was the added dimension in this that he absolutely hated my key worker with a passion, and she hated him with a passion. So there was then this dynamic that he was calling her all the rude names under the sun; I was going, 'Please don't do this. This is awful.' And when we got to six weeks, we happened to receive this big cheque, and – a kind of spur of the moment thing – we decided to leave. But you know there was a part of me that thought at the time that I'd be back very soon on my own. I thought, 'I actually quite like this, but it's not going to work now. This isn't the right time.' Because they were saying, 'Well, you don't have to be with him. You can move somewhere on your own.' And I was thinking, 'What about him? I can't just drop him off the side.' It was all too fast really. So I left the treatment then with the idea that I'd be back within the year. But I kept that bit to myself.

We came back home, and we picked up exactly where we left off, except we'd gained something from our six weeks away. We'd gained a knowledge that we didn't need to drink. We just used. We replaced the drinking with benzodiazepines[4]. So we then had the situation where I conned every doctor virtually in the county. I know every health centre. I'd go in and say, 'Funnily enough, I'm down here for this, that or the other.' I'd use ideas of where my sisters lived, so if a doctor wanted to check out my knowledge of the area, I could come up with it. So I wouldn't be thrown out.

In the end, we were using tremendous amounts of whatever we could get hold of. But we preferred temazepam and 10ml Valium alongside the methadone. We were coping with it at that point. Then what happened was my father died. My mother had died when I was eleven. He died in bed at home of a heart attack. Our relationship had always been kind of difficult; and I now know that he had another life with another woman and another family. She didn't know about us. She thought that he had one child, so there was a lot of kind of intrigue, really. He'd always been a bit of an absent father, but he left me quite a lot of money. In fact, his style was so covert that this woman phoned up on the morning of his death. I don't know what she was thinking about, because he hadn't rung her. She asked to speak to my mother, believing my mother was still alive, and my eldest sister, whom my father lived with, said to her, 'She's been dead for twenty years.' So he didn't want to have to marry her. He had two lives, two families, the lot.

There was this big cheque, and the result then was that I had this money, a raving habit and a feeling of desperation and of course at the time there were private doctors in London who would do you the most wonderful combinations if you had the money – and I had the money. So then I entered the final phase of my using because now I had all this money, which meant that we could go anywhere for these drugs. We were so good at saying one thing and meaning another.

Physically we didn't look wonderful. I looked obesely fat. We'd tell this wonderful story, that if they just gave us what we needed, then we could be the most wonderful parents. We both ended up with these enormously great big scripts and it didn't stop there – I was trying everybody else's big scripts as well. My existence was literally getting all these scripts, and still we couldn't get enough benzodiazepines, so I was still doing all these private doctors, and the NHS doctors – I gave false names as a temporary patient, and that required some organisation, I can tell you, for somebody whose mind was befuddled. When I went into treatment, I was a pound over twenty stone. I could hardly walk. It was terrible. They'd now devised this methadone in 50mg form, so I was injecting into myself something like 30 amps a day. I had all these sores and abscesses all over my legs, and slowly the money started to dwindle. The methadone was so concentrated, it used to create these burns which would get infected, plus I was picking them and doing sort of 'minor surgery'.

I realised we weren't going to get clean together. I do love this man, but. . . The real underpinning, the thing that was preying on my mind, was that my daughter was about to be ten, and I was really scared that I would die and she'd end up without a mum – like I had. So I asked him if he'd move back to his own flat and then I decided that I wanted to go into treatment. And at this point I picked up alcohol again. By this time my family were against me trying to stop, because in all my previous attempts I'd ended up worse than I was the time before. I can even remember coming to this hospital because the money was drying up. I'd spoken to Alan[5] in my early twenties, and he'd said to me, 'Oh Isabel, you're so intelligent.' Even in those times I'd wanted to become a social worker. I'd done so much people watching, watching my mother sort out everybody else's problems. This time when I came to the hospital, there was no, 'Oh Isabel, you could be so much more.' That had gone out the window many years before. I felt I was never going to be any good. Alan was so different this time. He was saying, 'Please don't let's go down this road, because it never leads anywhere.' I picked up alcohol again because I thought, 'I'm going to show you how desperate I am,' and there were lots of suicide attempts. I really did feel everyone thought they'd had enough. So I went into hospital in London. I felt I'd really got to do it. I'd really lost myself. I can't begin to describe – I'd gone from, in my early twenties, this person that everybody had so much hope in, the good person, the star, the amiable one, the problem solver.

At the hospital in London they said to me, 'Oh, you're doing so well. You can go on to the next phase.' This was the thing: I went to the next phase but I wasn't ready. I was in all these groups, but I'd been cut off from my feelings for so long. I felt totally isolated. I started getting quite a lot of stick from them, which I wasn't very happy with. I only showed people how I felt by how I acted out – I went home and used. I felt it physically, but mentally, I didn't feel it at all. It didn't take the rough edges off life. All I could think was, 'What have you done now? You've done what everybody expected you to do.' I was taken back but I'd changed from being the model pupil. Their star pupil had now gone to being totally out of order. So something changed within me. I stopped playing the role of being the good girl, if you like. I think I've got a dependent nature, while other people are carrying me on, I go with it.

But this time I had a really good key worker, which I think was good for me, because I felt in disgrace. She had worked with me originally, and then passed me to somebody else, as they do. I was sort of relegated. She did see something in me, and I felt that was really positive. But the other very good thing about her was that she kind of explained things to me. In the past, people made off the cuff remarks but nobody explained to me that broken attachments earlier in my life affected how I operated today. So I might have feelings of loss now that would be magnified because of feelings of loss earlier. Nobody had ever done that. Previously, I had got attached to workers but it didn't affect my behaviour in any way. But in this relationship it was strange because I was very aware of that not happening. I was aware of wanting to be independent. Key workers before had said, 'Do this, do that,' and I would tend to play the game. I would be the perfect patient. But now I was able to show the other side of me, that isn't the lovely, easygoing, compliant person. I was able just to be me.

Previously, in groups, I would think I was doing the worker's role. I could be wonderful with everybody else's problems. This time, I was genuine. So I came back here. I completed the detox and the rehab and found it really difficult to come back. My daughter had been used to totally coping and doing things for herself – suddenly, I was there, not as this passive person. She was worried that I would slip up. I'd changed and moved on, and people were angry about it. It was like, 'She goes up there and she floats in here now with all these plans, and we're on the floor.' Twenty years of this chaos, but my family would never talk to me. This was part of my problem in the first place, no one had ever been as upfront as to say that. That's what I realise now.

I love coming back from behind, and things really helped me then. I came and saw Alan, and I'm really indebted to him because the first two years that I was home he was really good. I thought it was a wonderful time. I walked into the street agency. . . My life slotted into place. A job came up at the Drugs Advice Centre and I took that job on. It was an incredibly vulnerable time, because all these people were social drinkers, all these drugs workers, and I'd kind of fallen in love with being the big hit drugs worker, from being the drop out drug addict, now, and I'm always the one for a roll. I worked hard and played hard. I learned a lot, but Alan questioned why it was so important for me to be part of the crowd.

My sanity was the fact that, no matter what, I could still study; I could still do my job. You know, apart from my partner. I could do my job and I do it well. And, I had a lovely practice teacher. Wherever I go, I carve out a mother. It's obviously unconscious transference, but I do. It's not a conscious thing. I had this wonderful relationship with this practice teacher, who was just like another mum. So I enjoyed that. They were the kind of things that kept me sane through that period.

In my own treatment I had to go from being a good girl to getting honest about me as a person, and I then had to go from being the one who was so politically correct in NA to suddenly – I'd lived with somebody who was using. It wasn't all this hearts and flowers stuff. I had a different message, I feel, because by then, I'd thought that in NA, when any kind of problem happened, I'd have this support network – it did catch me, but, for example, we moved and I thought they would physically help me to do things, and that didn't happen. But what it did mean was that by doing the things that were suggested, it built the reserves within me. So, you know, people don't have to agree with me all the time in what I'm doing; I don't have to have everybody's approval, but by doing certain things that were suggested, I'm able to live by the way I feel.

When you've been in these situations, you do really gain such a lot in understanding how it is for people. As long as you don't pick up, as long as you do actively recognise that using isn't an option, and you have a really solid foundation. For me, I just know there's no way I'd pick up, I've got no reason to believe it would be any different from the other times. The whole thing just isn't attractive at all, and I just think that for me – my values are that I don't feel it would be OK to drink or use recreational drugs, like so many drugs workers do. To me, it wouldn't be OK when I'm working alongside someone who's trying to do something about their problem.

The death of a key figure played a vital part in Isabel's development. Her mother, a strong figure, died at the very brink of Isabel's adolescence, and even preceding this tragedy, there was a secret at the heart of the family, namely the duplicitous relationship of her father with a second, hidden family. This cannot fail to have had an effect on everyone concerned right from the beginning, but for this to come out into the open on the day her father died was a bitter blow. This background set the scene for Isabel's riotous years, when she was known in the town as 'Mother Drugs'.

Isabel says nothing here about the effect of her addicted lifestyle on her own children up to the point where she herself stopped, although the spur to change eventually came when she imagined how her own ten-year-old daughter would suffer if she herself were to die. She does, however, speak about the effect of stopping on members of her family, who had to adapt to a completely new situation. Up to that point, the efforts of the family were focused on surviving or coping with the difficulties of living with someone who is addicted. Suddenly that situation was completely changed. Therapeutic input was centred on Isabel, so, yet again, she was the centre of attention. For members of the family of someone who stops drinking or using drugs, as well as a sense of relief that something has changed from the days of active addiction, strong feelings of resentment over the years of hurt and damage can emerge. This is the counterpart to the crushing sense of guilt which so often overwhelms the person who has just stopped. The result of all this is that there is a great deal of emotional turmoil for everyone to work through and people may need help at this stage to readjust. Each individual may need to belong to a group or see someone, maybe a therapist, who can allow them to voice and explore their feelings. Self-help groups, such as Al-Anon and Families Anonymous, exist because there are often problems that are not easy to resolve. Family members can play such an influential part for good or ill after someone leaves addiction behind, the crucial challenge being one of trust. Can we forgive, while not forgetting?

Isabel feels that NA helped her not simply to rely on others for help, but to discover and use her own inner resources. This is a factor commonly overlooked by critics of self-help groups, as is the ongoing nature of the need for people who have stopped to face complicated problems and emotions lingering from their addicted days. Like all of us at times, Isabel felt a need to rely on others. If there was someone to depend on, she would happily do so, though not always wisely. When there was no one to rely on or when she was challenged, a wonderful independent streak emerged. Then she could realise her own strength.

Working the Twelve Steps, the spiritual path of AA and NA, is an example of help in facing the issue of self-destructive guilt, putting in its place the possibility of making reparation, provided that doing so does not make the situation worse (See Steps 8 and 9 in Appendix 4). In the longer term Isabel found her way into the role of wounded healer as a social worker with an important role in drug treatment. By doing this she has been able to identify with and take on the mantle of her mother, whom she says was regarded by all who knew her as a tower of strength in times of trouble.

Partly because she is a therapist herself now, Isabel has reflected on what did and didn't work for her in treatment. She was unable to benefit much from therapeutic input for a long time. While she had money available, she went her own way. Her drug using led her into behaving in ways that made her a pretty challenging proposition for any therapist, since hoodwinking therapists and pharmacists was part of her daily existence. Yet she despised those who believed her lies. In some of her detoxifications, hospital staff, she felt, went too fast. They were too keen to see progress where there was none. Perhaps the therapists became too competitive with one another or were blinded to the reality by their own narcissistic need to 'succeed'. Were they fully aware of the delicate juggling of alcohol and drugs by this couple?

Another therapeutic error seems to have been a failure to appreciate how bound up with one another Isabel and her partner were, and a tendency to see one of the couple as 'the good one'. These failings are magnified greatly when patients are passed from one key worker to another at different stages of treatment. The result for Isabel was that her family thought that each time she went into treatment, she simply came out worse than before.

Isabel makes the surprising observation that in her early contacts with treatment services, she cannot recall any therapist making links between her current behaviour and her past life. She cannot remember anyone sensing the distress lying behind her outrageous ways. If they did so, it failed to get through to her. The breakthrough came when a therapist in a rehabilitation centre saw through her attempts to please others. Isabel's experiences have much to teach therapists. How often are we misled into looking only at the outward presentation of a person? At the height of her addiction, she weighed nearly twenty stone and had serious health problems, as well as a chaotic lifestyle. Now, no one would guess that she had ever looked like that, and she has become one of the most highly skilled and respected drugs workers in the area, yet it took her many years to get off the merry-go-round of stopping and starting again.

It is vital for therapists to be alert and sensitive to what may lie behind their patients' evasions. AA calls alcoholism the disease of denial. There are various different forms this takes. It can be unconscious denial, or the person may know that things are going wrong, but pretend otherwise. If they can keep the voice of conscience muffled, then no decisions have to be made, no self-recriminations faced head on, no responsibility accepted. The therapist's task in the face of these waves of confusing signals in people who really don't know which way to turn is to enable them to reflect on the true situation.

Just as her father had kept his secrets until the day he died, so Isabel herself was difficult to read. Therapists failed to see that her need to please at the expense of her own longer-term well-being resulted from her longing to find a strong parental figure. Therapists were impressed by her potential, but it appears to have blinded them to the true extent of her vulnerability. She was never an abject figure, and was hard to understand because her persona was so confusing. She lived behind a smokescreen of activity, much of it self-destructive in the extreme, which hid her confusion and pain – at the same time as increasing it. Having addicted partners didn't help matters. Crucial to her was what she describes as becoming honest. A key worker whom she was unable to hoodwink, as she had done so many professionals previously, showed her the links between her drug using and broken attachments in her past. It was an enlightenment for her that she could stop needing to please people and could start to think about her own life.

Isabel eventually disentangled herself from her drug-using life. She became gradually able to seek out and benefit from relationships with parental figures and she forged new bonds with her own children. Eventually, after university, she ran a family centre for families overshadowed by addiction. She is a striking example of someone whom we may call a wounded healer. She began to realise her true potential, and to develop her own skills as a therapist to others.

In conclusion

Stopping

The challenge of leaving addiction behind is particularly complicated when both partners of a couple are addicted. It is as if each person always has a tiny glance ready to fall on 'how the other is doing'. There is also the temptation for each partner to try to exonerate him or herself at the expense of the other by apportioning blame. This only starts fresh uproar. Many partnerships fall apart at this stage. In a later narrative, Chapter 18, we have a closer view of how such difficulties can be faced.

Detoxification as a stand-alone treatment

However available and effective detoxification programmes may be, they are only the beginning. Isabel's words demonstrate how her own personal development, as well as her relationships with her friends, family and partner, affected the outcome keenly. Her statement that she was not living as she wanted to, but felt incapable of doing anything about it, captures the flavour of the trap of addiction.

What's the past got to do with it?

Because she has trained as a professional therapist after leaving her addiction behind, Isabel has looked back at the treatment she herself received with a thoughtful eye. Like many who are addicted, she was unable to make radical changes until a therapist suggested some links between her present and past life, making it possible for her to gain insight into the roots of her chaotic lifestyle. This highlights the limitations of any treatment based too exclusively on a behavioural approach. However perverse a person's actions may appear, they are *symptoms*, and as Jung said, symptoms also point the way forward. They also give us clues as to what is amiss.

The wounded healer

Isabel demonstrated her aspirations in therapeutic groups early on in the treatment in which she was a participant by assuming the role of leader – a common role reversal which can be interpreted in a negative way as avoidance. She herself came to recognise this as a 'false dawn' and first of all she tackled her own addictions and secondly, she trained as a professional. She is aware that some of the drugs therapists she has come across are vulnerable because they have not taken those two steps. Simply being wounded does not make anyone a wounded healer – the path towards meriting that description is one of personal growth and apprenticeship.

Notes

1 By *getting veins* she means finding a vein into which she could inject her drugs. Over time, the veins become unusable.

2 By *picked up* she means picked up a prescription for opiate drugs from a pharmacy.

3 She could feel the effects of her drugs for a longer period because her tolerance had reduced following her detoxification. This reduction in tolerance is potentially extremely dangerous. Another of our patients died the day after he was released from prison, where he had not had access to drugs, because he injected the same amount of heroin as he had been used to injecting before he went to prison and was presumably unaware of the disastrous effect this would have on his body.

4 Benzodiazepines are the class of tranquillising drugs such as Valium, Mogadon, temazepam, etc. which are prescribed for persistent acute anxiety states and sleeplessness. They have a high dependence potential and are difficult to cut down or stop.

5 One of the facilitators of the relapse prevention group was Isabel's therapist.

Chapter 9

The prize fighter

This is a story of survival against the odds. Though his early days demonstrate Jim's resilience of spirit, little of that was on show when he first appeared at the hospital in the worst stage of his drinking. Whether he would survive at all was in doubt because he was maintaining vigorous denial of his drink problems with bravado. His story, told several years later, illustrates what eventually brought him to the point of stopping when even an accident in which he had broken his neck had failed to do so.

My childhood was very poor. We were poverty stricken and I spent my early days in a children's home. But, I don't believe my early days, my school days, are anything at all to do with alcoholism. Alcohol brought that on. That's my belief and any opinion I express here is *my* opinion. I want you to understand that. And, sometimes I may refer to 'I', 'we', 'us', – I'm referring to me, Jim.

So, I left school at an early age, a primary school education. Full of mischief at school, but academically quite good. I was the teacher's blue-eyed boy, but I was also the ring leader of anything that went on at school. I could get away with murder, because I was quite good in class, and afterwards, he would say to me, 'You of all people, Jim – you should know better.' This was a bit of my character – the search for adventure and excitement, all the time.

Anyway, I left school, grew up, had many jobs. When I left the children's home, I was very naive, but I'd travelled quite a bit before I was called up for national service. Now, in my early days, I'd done very little drinking. The first thing I'd tasted was sherry when I was about fourteen to fifteen. I had a sip – that was quite nice; tasted whisky – I didn't like that. I think I was about seventeen when I had my first pint of bitter. I thought it was vile, vile stuff, but I drank it because I wanted to be one of the chaps. I was seventeen years old, and I wanted to be part of the crowd, you know. Didn't use pubs a great deal, not as youngsters use them today, because we had our coffee bars and so on, dance halls. Called up for national service, went abroad – Egypt. And started drinking over there, because it was a bit of a boring life. By the time I completed my national service, I could consume quite a bit of alcohol without getting drunk. So I became, not a heavy drinker, but when I did drink I could consume quite a lot, your original 'hollow legs', you know, but I could take it or leave it. I despised the people who got drunk, I referred to them as 'piss artists', and I had nothing but contempt for them, nothing but contempt for these people, who fell around drunk, who were incoherent when they spoke.

While I was in the forces I tried to educate myself. Any education I have now is mainly self-education. I had no further education since I was thirteen years of age. I used to read *Readers Digest, Improve Your Word Power*, I read Dale Carnegie – *How to Win Friends and Influence People*. I tried a lot of that! Anyway, I went into business on my own accord and I was quite successful. I got married and my first wife, as I know today, she was alcoholic. I accept that I am alcoholic, but I didn't know then that she was alcoholic because I didn't know anything at all about alcoholism. I couldn't understand why she got drunk quite a lot. She would go for weeks, months, be a beautiful person. Then she got drunk and she'd go on a bender for two or three days. She'd go home to her parents. We stayed married for about thirteen years. And, during this time, I never drank during the day, didn't drink during business hours, I drank in the evening socially. My wife would get drunk and the things she did were unbelievable. She didn't go to bed with other guys – I checked on that. But she would go off to her mother, get drunk, buy drinks for friends and at the end of the day, I decided I couldn't take any more of this. At the time, I had a beautiful detached house, all the trimmings that anyone could want. Materially I had everything, but inwardly, really, I had nothing, because I think I was very lonely. In retrospect, looking back, I was lonely all my life because I couldn't share with people. I didn't want to share anything. I had this barrier. And, when I went into a pub I tended to be very aloof. I didn't want these people getting inside me – I don't know what I was trying to hide – maybe it was my childhood, because it was different to normal people's. I didn't have a home, but that didn't make me an alcoholic. That's my opinion. You can become aware of your character. I'm aware of my character today, due to looking at myself.

So anyway, I started drinking socially, heavily in the evenings when I found myself in the pub. The company was great. In there I found a kick. I liked the people who were the heavy drinkers. I didn't have much time for the 'half of bitter', 'pint of beer' merchants. I liked the guys with the large whisky, the large brandy, anything went, then I'd go home. Never drank during the day. That was part of my set up. But in the evening I felt free to drink, and I drank and invited people back to my home, and at the time I had a prosperous business in the West End. Unfortunately I had a partner who decided he wanted to be a big time gambler in the West End, and the partnership broke up and I lost quite a lot of money. Then my drinking started heavily, because I think I was trying to escape, you know, I was trying to escape from my losses, and the self-pity was in me. And, I drank a lot. Then I started drinking in the lunch hour, I'd sit and drink in the mornings, and I didn't think I had a drinking problem. Now, with smoking, I stopped once, started again, then I stopped and I knew that the first time that I started smoking was the last cigarette that I would have. So I didn't smoke any more. Quite a strong character, you see, I told myself. Everyone told me I was a strong character. The arrogance is still there, but now I'm aware of it, you know?

Because my business was going down the drain I decided to buy a pub in this part of the world. I thought I might be too frightened to drink in case I became an alcoholic, not realising that I *was* one. I was going to work so hard that I wouldn't have time to drink. But all I achieved was a 'geographical'. I started drinking more at home. I was treated for jaundice in my local hospital – the first indication that drink had affected my health. At that time, I was warned not to drink any more, and fully intended not to. I felt great for two months, then started drinking again, and the GP asked the psychiatrist to visit me. I did feel guilty about the quantity I was consuming and I denied having a problem. When he came to see me, I had a drink hidden beside my chair. I went into hospital, mainly to please other people, especially my wife, to keep her happy. I was convinced I was cured and could stay off. 'If I wanted to climb Everest, I could do it!'

After a further two months, I started drinking more heavily than ever. All my waking hours, I had a drink in my hand. This to me became a nightmare. I now had to have a drink from the time I woke up. If I woke up in the night, I'd have a drink. It didn't matter what it was, as long as it was alcohol. My psychiatrist at the hospital told me I had to come to terms with reality, with life as it was today, because I was drinking to escape the reality. I couldn't accept what I had become. I couldn't accept that I was the small business man that I am now today, as the drop-down from where I was. I wouldn't accept that it was because of alcohol that business was going down.

At that stage, I was again warned that my drinking would have disastrous consequences and that got through to me. Dr Rathod said to me, 'Jim, if you carry on the way you are, drinking, you will lose your wife, you will lose your children, you will lose your home and whatever business you go into you will be a total failure, an absolute and total failure, whatever you do.' This is one thing that came across to me. I left the hospital and I wanted to stop drinking, but two months later – the physical desire to have a drink goes, but the mental desire carries on, yeah? It can happen at any moment. It can happen in ten minutes' time. I don't know why, but it can happen. I can't see into the future. I don't try – I haven't stopped drinking for the rest of my life, is how I go about today. I don't know if I'll drink again. I may drink tomorrow. I don't know. But, I will not drink today. Today is the important day to me. I make my plans for tomorrow, but I don't anticipate what's going to happen. So I live my life a day at a time. That's how I live.

My wife didn't leave me. That's good. But I had a few accidents at home – I fell downstairs and broke my neck. And I gave her a hell of a time, not physical violence, but mental violence. I was not aware of it at the time. I didn't really want to know about it. I also went through a phase of great annoyance. Do you remember me coming to the hospital, and tearing a strip off the staff? I put them in their place.

But then something happened. I had a Doberman dog and he got killed. I couldn't handle the situation. I turned to drink. I'd been six months out of hospital. I couldn't handle the stress. I didn't want to drink. I had this dog I adored. He got killed on the Saturday morning. For an hour my instinct was to get a bottle and have a drink. I resisted that for an hour, and after that I didn't give a damn. I just got drunk for two days. That was one way of coping, that instead of experiencing marked sorrow and anger that he had been killed, I just drowned it, then I took it out on myself and on others.

The turning point came when I thought, 'I'm not going to drink today – they told me in hospital that I mustn't drink for the rest of my life – the turning point actually was when I phoned up a man, not in the caring profession, but a man in AA. I thought I was going to drink again. I had planned to have a drink again, because I still thought I could handle it. Cut down. Just have one or two drinks, like a normal person. I phoned this man up, and I said, 'I want to beat this thing, you know.' And he said, 'Pal, you won't beat it. It will beat *you* into the ground. Nobody has beaten it yet. A chemical will beat any human being. Alcohol is a chemical. It will beat you into the ground. You have to accept defeat. Accept that alcohol has beaten you.' He said, 'You're like a picture of a prize fighter who has been the champion. It's like you're the champion of the pub – the raconteur, the story teller. Great adulation. "Jim, lovely to see you again. Terrific, great," like a prize fighter who was the champion. He's been around some time, and gradually he's taken a few hits, and he doesn't win. He loses. But he's going to make a comeback. So he goes back in the ring again. They say, "Lovely. Great to see you back." So you go back in the pub. The guy goes back in the ring and gets knocked down. You suffer. You go in the pub. You have a drink. It'll last a little while, maybe a few days, maybe a few weeks. You'll be sick again. You think, "The hell with that." So you pack up. But at the back of your mind, you're going to make a comeback. You're going to try it again, you know? And you try it again. The prizefighter goes in again. Great. The spot lights up. But this time he gets a bigger hiding than ever. So he still comes out again and he goes in the pub. You're welcome again. "Lovely to see you; like old times." And somehow at the end of the day,' this guy told me, 'you've got three choices. You can die in the ring, or you can die from alcohol. You can finish up punch drunk, incoherent, don't know what you're doing half the time. You can finish up with a wet brain [as he called it] in a psychiatric hospital – somebody feeding you with a spoon and you're saying, "Good pud!" *Or* you can recover. So if the prizefighter wants to recover, wants to stay good – keep out of the ring. Your choice is to stay away from alcohol and you can recover.' 'The rest of my life?' 'No,' he said, 'Just one day.'

After I gave up drink I got another Doberman, and three months later he attacked my thirteen-year-old daughter in a rough game. He had to be destroyed the next day. When I handed over that job to my wife I felt a real Judas, but the important thing was, I didn't drink. I wanted to, badly, especially a few months later, but I handled that situation.

At the time, I thought the children didn't know about my problems, but they went into a huddle with their mother. This made me very paranoid. Now my son trusts me, my wife trusts me more than I trust myself. My daughter asked me anxiously if I would drink when I went to Spain recently, but my wife then told her, 'Dad won't drink.'

Jim says nothing about what it was like for him to be left by his parents in the children's home, but he learned how to look after himself early on. At school he was a bright spark, a leader, a resourceful boy, able to engage and impress his teachers. Leaving school at thirteen he survived the hard transition from children's home to the outside world and he is rightly proud of being self-educated and self-reliant. Yet in his adult life maybe the feeling of being a 'big man' in the pub made him feel good as a compensation for a hidden, disowned sense of vulnerability.

In Jim's early adulthood, the environment played an understated but crucial part in the picture, as did the way alcohol interacts with the body and mind in ways that, at the beginning, are not at all obvious to the drinker. It is a macho thing to be able to drink others under the table, and the less experienced drinker who gets legless is the one who doesn't come up to the mark in the eyes of his more hardened companions. Jim's first wife turned out to have serious problems with alcohol, and this no doubt played a part in the picture, but of course, she may have been indirectly influenced by Jim's drinking too. As Jim's drinking became heavier, he notes that it was 'part of his set up'; again, here is the picture of a lifestyle increasingly coloured by the patterns and customs of drinking. In time, his drinking started to have an adverse affect on his business, and he drank to hide from that fact as well as to avoid withdrawal symptoms. It becomes a complex network of cause and effect.

Most people would think that breaking one's neck having fallen downstairs drunk would be a pretty powerful incentive to stop drinking. Yet this did not lead Jim to stop. Trouble, in the form of drinking to drown his sorrows when his fortunes took a dive, had escalated because his drinking no longer meant having a good time and being the leader of the gang, but the very opposite. Alcohol had once enhanced his life, but now fulfilled a quite different purpose. It helped him to hide from the harsh reality of what was going on. He was most likely aware, but turning a blind eye to it, sure that his willpower could come to his rescue when his back was really to the wall, in just the same way as he had done with cigarettes. Yet each time he detoxified in hospital and vowed not to drink again, he found himself breaking that vow within weeks of leaving the hospital.

It seems that some people have several rock bottoms, none of which is definitive. However, this may be useful to people looking back on their addicted lives in that it may help them to explain to themselves why they didn't stop drinking or using drugs sooner. In retrospect, they can make sense of their addictions as having been accompanied by a crescendo of harmful effects which eventually led to the lowest point.

People did attempt to show Jim that he needed to stop drinking if he hoped to survive, yet to no avail. The circumstances when he actually did stop were different in several ways. He admits that by that time he was actually afraid he would die. He also says that he came into hospital *for his own sake*, as he puts it, not at anyone else's behest. Finally, when he contacted AA from the hospital, the AA member who spoke to him used one of the most engaging means of persuasion – a parable. The words had a magical quality for Jim. He himself was metaphorically a 'prize-fighter', left in an orphanage at an early age with his brother because of parental destitution, and in some intuitive way, his AA phone respondent tuned in to this. The juxtaposition of a fighter, lord of the battle in the ring, with the Korsakoff's syndrome sufferer with a 'wet brain', totally abject and childishly helpless (see Appendix 1), is a dramatic tour de force. The AA member used an intuitive empathy to bring Jim in touch with his own vulnerability. Jim had had a long affair with the mistress, alcohol, and was loath to let go, but in the end, the story of the prize fighter spoke to him. It tuned in to the terror he had felt that he was going to die. Perhaps the thought of being dependent for even the basic necessities of life, such as eating, terrified him even more.

The AA member showed Jim that his drinking companions were fair weather friends, all too ready to welcome back a fighter who reinforced their own drinking habits, and brought them entertainment, too. The dramatic way Jim tells the tale of this phone call captures the emotional impact it had on him. The hard man, Jim, was touched by the tale of the prizefighter. It spoke to him.

The idea that alcohol is a chemical and that no one can beat a chemical gave Jim permission to give up fighting battles with his addiction. Until then, he had needed to prove that he could use his willpower to overcome any problem: 'I can climb Everest if I need to.' Maybe Jim could listen to a member of AA because he spoke as a member of a group, rather than as an individual. Jim himself had survived life in children's homes and he had done well at school and in the army.

In the AA tradition, he distanced himself from damaging self-reproaches by saying simply that it was alcohol itself that caused his alcoholism. He acknowledges the harm he caused members of his family, particularly his 'mental violence' towards them. He has taken on board some of the key ideas of AA, though he doesn't speak about the Twelve Steps or about having a sponsor. These ideas include acknowledging the folly of thinking, as he did when he moved to the country, that a move of geographical location is the same thing as a psychological move into a different way of functioning. Now he has developed a healthy respect for the powerful lure of alcohol, and doesn't trust himself, but says that his wife has more trust in him. He has an awareness of the hazards around him and an awareness of his own weak points.

In his life, Jim has experienced many extremes of fortune and many paradoxes too. At the time when he was being fiercely determined to be independent of help and advice, something was hiding in the shadows. He was trapped in his slavery to the bottle. But out of the rubble of his desperation was born a richer life. He accepted the challenge of making a radical change. Jung himself found that from the rubble of his desolate years after his break with Freud, years which lasted throughout and beyond the First World War, came a fertile period of work and study. He allowed himself to experience fully the desolation and explore it (Jung 1963: 194–225). This brought new discoveries of what he could accomplish. He came to see that many people come to a point in midlife when they find no satisfaction in the way they have been living. Often this relates to the consequences of having put so much investment into forming a successful career and family that the inner life is forgotten. The harm caused by heavy drinking brings many drinkers to the brink of destruction in midlife, and it is only when they are at this point that they draw back. This is what Jung was referring to when he talks about 'nothing less that a complete conversion', which he believed was necessary for his former patient, Roland Hazard, if he was to have any chance of stopping drinking again, after he had relapsed.

In conclusion

Sacrifice in the interest of survival

In his story of the prize fighter, the AA member told Jim that he should know when to retire gracefully from the ring, because, 'You yourself are more important than your audience's entertainment. Don't destroy your life.' Just as Jim's parents gave him and his brother up for the sake of their survival in the face of destitution, so he has given up something he loved – alcohol – so that he can survive and flourish.

Not stopping

Whatever nightmare life has become due to the negative consequences of addiction, this may fail to persuade the individual to stop. This, above all, demonstrates the power of addiction. It is beyond reason.

Synchronicity in relation to stopping

Timing plays a crucial part. The synchronicity involves the impact of an event or experience coinciding with some readiness to respond in the addicted person.

Enantiodromia

Jim's life story at this point illustrates an example of what Jung called enantiodromia – turning round and going back in the opposite direction

(Samuels, Shorter and Plaut 1986: 53). From being put into a children's home by his parents, he had pulled himself up to lead an exciting and challenging life as a young man. This is paralleled later by his turning around from the road to disaster by becoming able to listen and to accept and act on advice from another alcoholic who recognised his omnipotence. When he describes at the end of his narrative what life is like for him now, there is no talk of business or social successes, but rather, he speaks with feeling about his wife's trust in him.

Chapter 10

The turning point

A talisman of hope

Just how important in the longer term is the act of stopping? Stopping is just the start. Everyone who has had the experience of being addicted will tell you that it's not the stopping, it's 'staying stopped' that's difficult – and crucial. Yet the narrators recall their experiences of the particular act of stopping which started their long-term abstinence in vivid detail, however many years ago it happened. Their descriptions tend to resemble those of survivors of wars speaking about battles and personal escapes which colour their perception of the world for ever after. The experience has great significance in the flow of their lives, and it may well be that recounting it helps the person to maintain their abstinence. The recollection and retelling of the story acts as a talisman of hope, an intrinsic part of a new identity as a non-drinker or non-user.

In thrall to the addiction

All the narrators spoke about an escalation of the adverse effects of drug misuse over a prolonged period which had not prompted anything more than a temporary desire for change. Up until then, even after crises, they wanted to carry on as before, once the unpleasant effects of their drug use had been dealt with or receded. Over the years people who are addicted begin to find that their drinking or drug use no longer brings them the pleasure or rewards they experienced in former days. Instead they can only visualise disappointment, harm and losing control, for they cannot stop themselves from returning to the drug. There may be many unsuccessful or abandoned attempts at stopping, which add to the distress. While an addiction is sustainable or still pleasurable, there is little reason for stopping unless supplies of the drug are completely cut off. For our narrators, the love affair with the drug may have had more and more inconvenient aspects as time went by, but they had pushed these thoughts aside for a long, long time. Even when there was strong pressure from the external world to make changes, they overrode this pressure.

Attempts at controlled drinking

Some people hoped to control their drinking, rather than stopping completely. Hugo tried to control his drinking, and failed spectacularly. For some drinkers who have gone far down the line of being dependent on alcohol, controlled drinking is quite simply a form of torture. They expend a great amount of energy working out plans, counting up units and generally trying to keep an eye on their own behaviour in the face of the disinhibiting effects of alcohol, and in the end, it often all becomes too much and they ditch their good intentions, usually dramatically. St. Patrick's Day was the day for Hugo. Controlled drinking can work well for some people, but mostly for those who are at a less addicted stage. For heavily dependent drinkers it is not a practical option. Alcohol has a funny way of coming back and slapping them in the face. It's simply too satisfying to accept that drink – and the many after that.

Coming to the point of stopping

Prior to stopping, an escalating series of physical and emotional traumata had caused people to plummet into ever worsening situations in their lives. They all experienced severe adverse physical effects of their addictions, including severe withdrawal symptoms when they couldn't top up sufficiently. Some experienced reverse tolerance, where they were simply unable to drink or use as much of the drug as before without feeling seriously ill. Others had accidents of one sort or another. In the USA, a longitudinal study has been conducted in the settings of ninety-six treatment programmes called DATOS (Drug Abuse Treatment Outcome Studies). From the information gathered many studies have been conducted, including one which found that problems with the drug itself were the strongest predictor of readiness for treatment in both adolescents and adults (Handelsman, Stein and Grella 2005).

Quite apart from the physical effects, the emotional effects of the narrators' addictions were horrific. Acute disappointment at their repeated inability to succeed in cutting down or stopping, especially in people who like to see themselves as self-sufficient in life, erodes morale deeply. People spoke about a sense of powerlessness which they found overwhelming. They were disgusted with themselves. They were also very afraid: fears of death, fears of what they were doing to those around them, particularly poignant fears of what they were doing to their children. They all knew other people who had died through drink or drugs, and were having to find a way of living with that knowledge, even if their way was rigorous denial that it could ever happen to them. Some had come to hate being so dependent on the drug – yet they had carried on in just the same old way. Others said that they had bitter regrets about the life they had lost through their addictions, and though they felt trapped, they were longing to be able to be open and honest again. Therapists need to be alert to how very ashamed patients may be feeling at this stage, even when they can mask it from the gaze of others. The therapist should be able to sense the shame and encourage the patient to give it expression. Only by opening up to someone trusted can they begin to own and face guilty feelings.

Patterns of arriving at the point of stopping

The reader will see that there is no one pattern of stopping. Many studies have traced the path of people who stop without treatment, notably Patrick Biernacki who wrote about 100 heroin users (Biernacki 1986). It is well known that the great majority of US army war veterans who had used heroin in Vietnam were able to resume their lives at home without any drugs or treatment because heroin was no longer quite so easy to come by (Robins et al. 1977). More recent studies in this area, as well as the earlier studies, are reviewed and examined critically, reporting on research on recovery from both drug and alcohol addiction, in a book edited by Harald Klingemann and Linda Carter Sobell (Klingemann and Sobell 2007). One or two of the narrators we spoke to stopped without help. Most of the narrators made more than one attempt at stopping before they actually succeeded, whereas others stopped dead and never lapsed or relapsed. Ben, whose narrative comes later, injected heroin some months after stopping, but because he found the experience so disappointing and was reluctant to return to a drug-fuelled life, he never repeated it. Another former patient claimed that he was 'forced' to stop by a life-threatening accident which landed him in intensive care, whereas this sort of experience did not stop others. Breaking his neck in falling down stairs failed to stop Jim from drinking. Another pattern was like Bernadette's, where she substituted one addiction for another. Even among the four narrators in this part, there were striking differences. Alfie made an act of rebellion before stopping, but it is worth noting that he had a strong though stormy relationship with his psychiatrist, and bore him no lasting ill will. Jim was finally touched by the power of the words of an AA member. Hugo eventually decided he could do no more for himself in trying to stop. With Isabel, it was a pattern of stop-start until she began to understand what was driving her drug use.

Rock bottom

Hugo and Jim both had what AA calls a *rock bottom* experience, after long periods of resistance and uncertainty. The illusion of control and self-sufficiency no longer stood intact. When people reach this point they experience what Jung called an *ego collapse at depth* which leads to surrender. By this, he implied that willpower is utterly useless at this point. Growing ambivalence about drug use leads to a highly charged existential experience, encapsulated in William Burroughs' 'naked lunch' experience (Burroughs 1986). In psychological terms, this is defined as a cognitive and affective state of acute self-awareness – experienced without the benefit of protective defence mechanisms – of the self in a situation perceived as dangerous to the physical, psychological, or social selves. The despair is beyond thought or words at this stage, but looking back after time has passed, many narrators gave graphic descriptions of what they realised had led up to that point. It is not that the events and context were very different from those of past crises. Whatever may act as a trigger, awareness breaks through so that it is harder to deny what is going on or to deny the part they themselves are playing in it. It is as if there is a realisation that once valued parts of the self have been overwhelmed by the 'addict self'. What is without doubt is that people felt that their worlds had caved in around them. They were unable to cope at all. Many were suicidal.

Controversy surrounds the concept of rock bottom. Bernadette, for example, used the idea that she had possibly not reached her rock bottom to procrastinate over her decision to stop. How do you ever know that you have reached the very bottom? Another problem is that people commonly talk about having had several rock bottoms, but that would seem to invalidate the meaning of the term. Certainly it seems clear that people who are misusing drugs but are less far along the path of being addicted have more chance of being able to use their conscious judgment about their situation to decide to stop. In other words, they may not have to come to a dramatic point of rock bottom. In Prochaska and DiClemente's 'revolving door' model of change, developed in relation to tobacco smoking, the smoker steps from being in what the authors term the 'precontemplation' situation into that of contemplating a change (Prochaska and DiClemente 1983). Much of the time of therapists employed in treatment agencies is spent in working with patients to negotiate this transition, because it cannot be applied in a formulaic manner We each have our own value systems and needs – this is what makes us individual. It would be rash to assume that we, as therapists, can know what will inspire a wish to make changes. Something impels people to make changes. They find that they are unable or reluctant to do so, yet they must. It may be relevant that Prochaska and DiClemente were writing about tobacco, which does not produce the extremes of oblivious intoxication of some other drugs, such as alcohol or heroin. However much can be done to help someone arrive at a rational decision to stop, with chronically addicted people it does seem that they often have a life-shattering experience which leads them to the point of stopping.

Help at this stage

It becomes clear that however desperate and confused people were at the time, the response of the therapist did not go unnoticed. This applies not only to therapists in the strict sense of the term but also to people like the members of the Samaritans, or AA or NA, who made a vital contribution to the outcome of cries for help. Finding the right language in the dialogue is an art. People felt, in retrospect, that it had been a help to be with somebody knowledgeable who cared about their feelings, somebody whom they could trust. This helped to confirm for them what they already sensed. Could they really go on dealing with their problems in the way they had been attempting to do? As one former patient said years later to his psychiatrist, who was tending to decry his own part in what had gone on, 'It *did* matter that it was you who said these things to me and how you said them to me.' In the case of the four narrators in this part, they had all had ongoing contact with the staff of the hospital prior to stopping. Although they each had their different way of relating to the therapists, their previous contact formed the backdrop to what happened, rather than affecting it directly at the point of stopping. A critical review of various different models of change is given by Sobell in a book on self-change (Sobell 2007: 13–16).

Synchronicity and emotion

When these former patients spoke retrospectively of events which they believe led them to stop, they spoke with very great feeling. They tended to recall both a crescendo of events and an acceleration in their frequency. Jung's theory of synchronicity, when an event in the outside world coincides meaningfully with a psychological state of mind, is relevant here. Had such an event occurred at another time, it might have had little effect. It was the concatenation of happenings and disturbed emotions that awarded the event significance sufficient to bring about a desire for freedom from the addiction and to induce action towards that end. In speaking of a readiness for a radical shift, many people stressed the importance of their own sense of initiative. No one else could implant it until they felt ready.

Long afterwards, the narrators looked back and reflected on the time just before stopping. The sort of things they said were that you have to want to stop for your own sake, not to please someone else – no one else can do it for you. You have to realise that you are the one who has been doing the drinking or using the drugs. You have to want to join the mainstream of life again, and you have to stop procrastinating in looking for help, instead of trying to manage all on your own. For some addicted people, a significant experiential crisis, a rock bottom, marks the start of change. The memory of this rarely fades.

Part 3

The new task

The early days after stopping drug use are crucial in the life of a person who has been addicted because they either lead to further discouragement and disappointment in the form of a relapse or, alternatively, the groundwork is laid for continuing recovery. It is a time of unique vulnerability for the person who has just stopped, for they plummet into a time of radical readjustment without the familiar prop of the drug. If the pitfalls of relapse are avoided successfully, the experience of meeting the challenges successfully can form a basis for building confidence.

Four former patients recount in detail what happened to them at this stage, as a part of their life stories. The first and third narrators, whose lives had been in alcohol-fuelled chaos, recall how they tackled difficulties of daily living after they stopped drinking, while the second narrator describes facing the emotional shock of living without heroin. The fourth narrative shows how a relapse can come about seemingly without any prior warning, even years after stopping, and the narrator describes how he adopted a radically changed approach after that relapse which enabled him to get his life going along quite different tracks.

Chapter 11

Starting from scratch

Linda had contact with our service after she had actually stopped drinking. In this narrative she is looking back twenty-five years to the time when she eventually stopped and the days that followed. How do you put the pieces together if your world has come tumbling down around your ears? She came to the point where she felt there was no way forward. Her first port of call was the Samaritans, who in turn put her in touch with AA. For her, at a point where everything had fallen apart, it was a lifeline with its straightforward message and its unequivocal instructions. When every other hope had gone, this simple pathway was a way forward.

Actually, I've just had an AA birthday. I'm now in my twenty-fifth year of *a day at a time*, which is inconceivable. If somebody had said that to me when I first came in, I'd have packed my bags and run in the opposite direction. The time's absolutely flown. But, I went to AA following a suicide attempt.

I'd tried doctors, psychiatrists, hypnotists, psychotherapists, because I wanted them to stop me drinking. That wouldn't actually involve any effort on my part. There was going to be this magic wand, and in the end it was my behaviour towards my son that I just couldn't tolerate – the way I was behaving towards him. So, I sent him to his father – we were separated, no, actually we were divorced by then, and I lay down with booze and a load of pills, and I thought, 'Right, that's it. I can't cope with this any more.' And, I didn't leave any letters or anything. And I couldn't believe it, but the next day I woke up thinking, 'Oh, goodness – I can't face this.' I got on the phone to the Samaritans. They were wonderful to me. My drinking had made me incredibly depressed, because alcohol is a depressant anyway. I was friendless, because I'd drunk myself out of friends. Nobody wanted to know, and I can quite understand that. I was very isolated, desperately lonely, and the only people who listened to me without judging, I felt, anyway, were the people on the end of the phone, the Samaritans. And for the umpteenth time I picked up the phone and spoke to this lady whom I knew, and from nowhere came these words, 'I think I must be an alcoholic.' First time ever, and I don't know where these words came from. She asked me if I'd like a contact number for AA, and she actually phoned up an AA member who came round to see me that day. And I haven't had a drink since then.

It's been hard. You have to start from scratch. I've had to start from scratch. I still had a roof over my head, because my ex-husband was paying for the mortgage on the flat, and my son was still living with me. Years later I asked my husband why he had left our son with me, because I wasn't safe to have him. I couldn't look after myself, let alone a child – and his answer was, 'You had nothing else.' Well, there we are! Robert was seven. He's now thirty-two. Really, my husband should have put Robert's welfare first, but I'm glad he didn't.

I used to drink surgical spirit. I'd buy it by the gallon. I used to go into the chemist and say to the chap, 'Oh, I wash old ladies' feet. I need the economy size, a plastic container of surgical spirit.' And I got it! What else did I drink? Boots' cheap eau de cologne and their lavender water. It's not pleasant. If I didn't have the money to buy vodka, I just used to get surgical spirit. I read about surgical spirit in the *Daily Telegraph*: 'Medical students get drunk on surgical spirit and are expelled from medical school.' And you see, this is the *alcoholic* thinking. All these little bits and things that could send you off your head, you know, you store them away. And I'd stored that. And when the money dried up, there was my one and sixpence for *surg*. I mean, it sent me balmy obviously, and I remember the psychiatrist, a super chap, said to me, 'If you drink surgical spirit it will send you blind.' But it meant nothing. He could have said, 'Your arm'll drop off' and I'd still have gone on drinking. I mean, at the time I didn't know I was drinking. When anything got painful I would drink. Or, if the sun was shining, I would drink. If it was raining, I would drink. If I wanted to, I'd drink, basically.

I was sleeping around, and generally being a nuisance, and the police were involved. I wasn't what I'd term 'a quiet drunk'. I was loud, raucous, violent, very abusive, which I think now was probably the anger I felt inside. Anger at myself for my behaviour would come out, and I'd spit venom and hatred to my in-laws and anybody else. I was always blaming other people for my drinking. That anger took a long time to go. My husband had had me sectioned twice, and I was full of rage at him, because I was sectioned without two doctors being there. I felt it was unfair, unjust, and particularly in that psychiatric hospital where I was sectioned, I didn't have a voice. I was totally powerless. I'd been seized and had my elbow dislocated by staff, you know? I was full of bitterness. Rage, absolute rage. And it took years to go, because I felt it was unjust, unfair, and it took me a long time to accept – maybe my husband didn't think he had any other choice. Maybe.

Then what did I do? I had this flat, and no money, and my son. I hadn't worked for quite a while, because I'd given up. I had no self-respect. I couldn't function, and I was full of fear. Everything frightened me, especially people. I was frightened that I was going to drink. I thought this big thing would come out of the sky and point a finger at me and say, 'You drink again!' because I'd always drunk again – I used to drink in bouts.

So, there was I. I wasn't drinking. I was going to AA meetings. I was riddled with guilt, and shame, and remorse, because of my behaviour, because my drinking had been characterised with behaviour that – I wouldn't have behaved like that if I'd been sober. And I remember somebody at one of the meetings *laughing*. I thought,

'How dare they laugh. This is so serious.' But that's actually one of the attractions of AA meetings, the laughter. Because we've spent a lifetime, most of us, full of self-pity, and all doom and gloom, and I think, you know, it's nice to laugh. We've got to laugh about our past life, and some of the mad things we've done. And a member said, 'But, you know, if you don't pick up that first drink, you won't have the next one, and the next one, and you won't get drunk.' It was like something clinking in my head, and the penny dropped. And suddenly, I thought, 'I don't have to get drunk again.' I had always thought I had to get drunk. I mean, I knew I couldn't social drink. Anyway, I've stayed sober. Mm.

It was a relief to think I wouldn't have to get drunk. It was most wonderful. Like a revelation, because I thought that I always had to drink and that this was my life's destiny, to pick up a drink; drink some more; get drunk; get into dreadful trouble; suffer the awful withdrawals; be all right for two or three weeks – and then I would have to do it all over again. So when it was pointed out that I didn't have to, that I actually had a choice – those first couple of weeks were extraordinary – I felt that it was my spiritual experience, if you like. I would wake up and laughter was bubbling from my mouth, and I hadn't laughed for years. It was like a freeing of the soul. It was just a wonderful, wonderful feeling. Yes. That was my little spiritual experience.

Only twice in the whole of the time that I've stayed sober have I wanted to drink. I had a lot of problems with my mother. I found arguments between my mother and sister, both of whom drink heavily, very upsetting. I always used to drink when I visited my mother to cope with my distress, to the extent of drink driving. I was banned for a year. On this occasion I went into the kitchen where I saw a bottle of Gordon's gin. My old behaviour rushed to the bottle. I thought, 'Drink can cope with it.' And the *thinking* started up. 'I'll just have a bit and I'll be able to cope with it.' Thank God there was enough AA teaching in my head: 'You don't have to do this. Walk away. Make a phone call. Get the hell out of it.' Not to pick up a drink – and I didn't. There was only one other time when I wanted to drink, and I ran out of the house. That was then like a blackness – I *needed* a drink. But that's been it really.

Anyway, I got my life together. I went to two AA meetings a day or certainly a meeting every day for quite a long time. And that was my priority. Oh, the gratitude was just extraordinary, because I wasn't drinking. I'd got friends, people talking to me. It was nice to feel well. Still very fearful, I got a sponsor, and she said, 'Put your sobriety first, then put your son first.' I was still riddled with this awful guilt, about the way I'd treated Robert. She said, 'You're doing the best you can, you're staying sober.' And that made sense. I couldn't do anything more at that time.

I started to work again. First I taught foreign students, then I taught at a private school and then at a senior school. I did Twelve Step work in AA and later on I started to sponsor other people. For me, that was the thing that made life worthwhile. The best feeling ever – to be able to help another alcoholic, really, whether they make it or not. I know they talk about *tough love* – but I always keep a door open. I've seen no-hopers, so-called, make it. Other people have a different approach, and that's good too. They say, 'Oh well, I've spent two or three weeks, months with them and they don't want to know, so that's it. I'm moving on to the next one.' It doesn't stop me helping anybody else, but I always keep just a little door open. I've seen it work.

My worst fears were caused by financial insecurity. I'd given up washing and cooking and cleaning, so I had to start from scratch. There's a card we have in AA called the Day Card; it just says, 'Do one thing!' I couldn't read when I got sober because my eyes were bad and my concentration had gone. So I would just pick one thing on this little card, and do that. It was a plan, because I didn't know how to live. I had no discipline in my life at all. I had to make a plan: get up, get washed, get dressed – it was as basic as that. Cook egg, you know, take Robert to school, tidy up the flat, go to a meeting if there was a day-time meeting, make sure there was enough food for him for his supper, make sure there was a babysitter if I was going to a meeting. So it was very basic. There was this overriding terror, absolute terror that everything was going to cave in on me and I'd be left with nothing. My mother wouldn't help out financially.

It was a struggle up until ten years ago. It took a long time. And occasionally – I was quite nervous that you were coming today. I wouldn't talk about my drinking and recovery to anybody. I don't know why. I don't know. It's like if I go to a strange meeting, there's this little residue of fear. I think I've always suffered from lack of confidence. My mother told me I was no good, and I took all those messages on board. When I was young, you're too young really to think that your parents are wrong. So that's ingrained, I feel. My father did try, but – this is just for me, I don't know if it's true for alcoholics, it probably isn't – but if one person says to me, 'Linda, you've done so well, look at what you've achieved,' and somebody else says, 'Well you could have done a lot better,' I completely dismiss the positive and I will pick up on the negative. Um, intellectually I know that's ridiculous, that's stupid, but truthfully I'm afraid that's the way I feel.

When times were hard, I wanted to run away. I wanted somebody to make it better, somebody to tell me it wasn't happening. And I went to my doctor once and I said, 'I'm just telling you. I know I can't – but I would love something to take this pain away.' He said, 'You know I'm not going to give it to you.' 'And I'm not asking for it either, I'm just telling you how I feel.' And that was very hard. Very hard to do. It's been exhausting really. There've been lots of problems. But life isn't fair, which I didn't like anybody saying to me.

At one stage earlier in my recovery, I had a breakdown due to the many pressures. I couldn't continue teaching and was prescribed tranquillisers, which I found very hard to give up. My second husband turned out to have been a 'rat fink' with other women. I got into a state, after I left my tears behind and stopped pitying myself, when I couldn't cry. I learned that I could say no if I wanted to, without giving an explanation, and I became what I consider to be more hard and ruthless.

Last year, I looked after my grandson and a little friend. I love helping others. I do look at my life and I ask myself, 'What's being happy? What's being content?' And I know I'm at my most fulfilled, really, talking to another alcoholic. To tell them that, you know, I was incontinent. I'd done all these things, and sometimes you can see a little glimmer, and that's all right. I find that's fulfilling. I don't know whether it's a lack in me, or what.

I used to analyse everything but I don't now. That's the best thing. And I've overcome fears that let me go abroad now. I flew from the age of twelve, when I used to go to France every year, and I was fine until a few years ago – maybe it's the menopause, I don't know. But I was beset, riddled with fears – it was after my husband died. I think maybe it was the result of stress. All these things, all happening at once. And I couldn't fly. I couldn't overtake a car on the road. I couldn't go up or down a glass-sided escalator, and I certainly could not get into a glass-sided lift. But now I've achieved all these things. For me, this is what recovery is. These are things that people take for granted. But the person who's my sponsor, we have a laugh about this. So, what have we achieved this year? It's these little things. Like overcoming fear of going up the glass-sided escalator. That to me was the number one achievement last year, plus going through the Euro Tunnel, on Eurostar. That was a big achievement, and the year before that, getting on a plane.

At a meeting I went to on Tuesday a long time sober member who's been a great help to me was talking about material possessions. And at one time, because either I was greedy or I'd had so little when I was drinking, it was very important to me to have goodies, material possessions, the jewellery, the car, the clothes, the la-di-da. But I don't give a fig now. Quite early on in recovery, my definition of me being sober and having made it in AA and in recovery, I think, was that I should have a crocodile shoulder bag (which is very non-PC now!) and a new car, and a holiday. This was going to make me Mrs. AA, Mrs. I've-got-it-made. So I actually got all these things and there was still a big void and gaping hole inside. I didn't feel one jot happier at all. And now I've got lots of nice things, but I'm putting lots of stuff in to auction, Phillip's jewellery auction, because at one time, these are all old habits really, I invested quite heavily into antique jewellery, which I keep in the Bank. Well, what is the point?

I was talking with my sponsor recently and we were both agreed that failure in my life has been in personal relationships. I have chosen badly. I cannot make good choices when it comes to personal relationships. Friends are OK, but partners, no good. When I met my second husband I was nine years sober, and I thought I was OK. But, no. No. I live with it. Because – it would be lovely to know what a personal relationship's like in the normal world – it would be nice. I believe next time around, in the Buddhist thing really; I've been sent this time, I believe, to come to terms with addiction. I think in a previous life I must have been some sanctimonious preacher saying, 'Don't drink' and I've chosen to work through that. I do. And I feel I've worked through it, quite frankly, or I am working through it. I've cracked the smoking, which has been very hard. Yes, but you see, it's not like the booze, there's no guilt and shame.

I get full of self-pity sometimes, and lonely sometimes, and depressed sometimes, but I think there's a line between depression and self-pity, you know. I can hoik myself out of the self-pity, but other times depression just has to pass. And it does. It sort of lifts. But, I think perhaps most people get this, you know. It doesn't last. I think I'm extremely fortunate, because every other area of my life is absolutely fine. It's just this living alone. But I wouldn't know how to live properly, or maturely with anybody. I'm too selfish, I know. I don't want to compromise. I'm set in my ways.

Linda has great charm which derives partly from her quiet ability to listen and partly from her warmth. She has thought a great deal about the formidable challenges she has faced in her life. To have a promising start in one's adult life, with a glittering career and marriage, is one thing. To seemingly throw all this away through alcohol is a tragedy. But that is where excessive drinking can lead many bright young people, who, for whatever reason, get caught up in the moil of addiction to alcohol. When Linda surprised herself by saying, 'I think I must be an alcoholic,' her words seemed to come from nowhere – the truth came straight from her unconscious.

After stopping, anyone who has been addicted is extremely vulnerable. The addiction itself has taken a toll both physically and psychologically. They have forgotten how to deal with everyday life without the drug and they have to start learning how to cope. A radical turnaround starts with simple steps in mastering life skills, as well as filling the gap left by the absence of drug-determined activities. Meeting the practical challenge of life without the drug is symbolic of self-care in a deeper sense. Most people cannot do it without support. Compared with detoxifying in a therapeutic setting, as some of the narrators did, Linda had to cope in the community, as many people do. Picking one thing from the Day Card (an AA card entitled 'Just for Today' which gives simple tips for facing the challenges of everyday life) gave her a sense of agency in the face of circumstances she would otherwise have found overwhelming. She experienced a terror that everything would cave in on her. This suggests that her mother had failed to give her a sense of being safely contained as a baby and as a small child. Being held, as it were, in the mind of her AA sponsor helped her to progress in a modulated way, through her first steps without alcohol. AA does not only offer practical advice about how to manage the seductions of alcohol, but also offers the experience of being understood and valued by others. From this starting point, people can discover how to gather other support for themselves.

When Linda tried to kill herself, she had given up any illusion of being in control of her life in her toxic addiction. Having given up her attachment to alcohol, she was able to retreat to the cave of her own being, and was able to connect with her pre-addictive self, or possibly a self *in potentia*, prior to her experience of mother. Drinking can represent a desire for Paradise lost, where the world is just and fair.

Quite soon after stopping, she was tempted to drink as she always had when she witnessed the stinging words of quarrels between her mother and her sister. At that point, her lifeline to AA held. Instead of drinking, she made a phone call. No hospital or statutory service can provide this level of support. We sit in our rooms or groups with our patients and can only hope that they will have the strength to resist the lure of drinking or using when life gets tough and they are back in the bad old situations. We have to hope that they will be able to internalise our support enough to get them through. But there are moments when AA, because of its very nature, having no axe to grind, no funds or hierarchy to maintain, can meet the need. Much of the shame Linda felt when drinking was alleviated in the AA meetings, so that she was able to make that phone call. The backdrop of the group, her individual sponsor and her sense of belonging made her yearning to drink very different from the way she had experienced it in her confused addicted days. Every element in the kaleidoscope had shifted just a little, so that the picture was quite different.

Linda soon found that presenting an impressive persona to the world became less important as she discovered that material possessions could not cure her sense of emptiness. Gregory Bateson observed that many alcoholics feel more sane when they are drunk rather than sober because they are dissatisfied with the materialistic values of the West (Bateson 1971: 303). Linda is critical of the persona she presented in her first months in AA, wanting to be seen as 'Mrs. AA', yet from another perspective this showed her desire to identify with her new 'family' and to shine there. Maybe she had always been the pupil who did well, the student who shone. She saw a danger in this, suspecting that it covered a deeper sense of insecurity about her worth. Most likely her desire to look the part in AA was partly due to a sense of relief at having left the sordid life of her last drinking days behind her, but even more because of her pleasure at being valued for herself – something she may well have sadly lacked as a little girl. Many alcoholics despise themselves because of the plight their drinking has led them into, but with Linda, it seems more likely to have been the other way round – that her self-esteem was low in the first place because she was shown too little affirmation of her true self by either of her parents. She does not blame them for her drinking, but it seems likely that she found the disinhibiting effect of alcohol helped her in the situations she found daunting.

It comes as a shock to hear the seemingly ridiculous statement from this intelligent person that she had not realised that she didn't *have* to go on drinking. Yet that is just the kind of crazy logic that many addicted people adopt in the chronic stage of their condition. The minute someone in AA took a firm line and said, 'No, you don't have to go on drinking', she was relieved. At last someone cared enough and understood enough to put their foot down.

Time passed and out of the ruins Linda built up a life for herself again. She does not gloss over the difficulties – her fury at her ex-husband, her fear of financial insecurity, and her breakdown at the end of her second unsuccessful marriage to a faithless husband. But she kept faith with herself and her commitment not to drink. In time, she herself became a sponsor to others in AA and she worked as a volunteer in the hospital service, counselling people with drug problems. Her description of how she is able to 'hoik' herself out of depression shows that she has become able to tolerate frustration, whereas previously drinking was an attempt to repair intolerable frustration. The best thing ever, she says, is helping another alcoholic. Because she remembers what a hopeless mess her life got into before she stopped drinking, she now gives back to others the help and acceptance she once needed so desperately.

Linda may be said to be making reparation for the disruption in her son's childhood by taking an active role in looking after her grandchild now. Interestingly, her son has himself achieved a significant role in one of the helping professions. Out of the mess, chaos and despair, can come a new beginning.

In conclusion

Paradox

Immediately following stopping, paradoxical emotions start to show themselves. While Linda felt nothing less than joy at being liberated from her addiction, she was horror-struck at her vulnerability. She had lost any sense of being able to lead her life, to such an extent that she had to start with the most basic steps each day. The experience of enduring conflicting emotions is one of the hallmarks of recovery, as it is a hallmark of what is called maturity.

The wounded healer archetype

As early as July 1939, four years after the founding of AA, Dr. William Silkworth, who had treated many of the first members, presented the first medical paper written about the Fellowship. In his list of essential features of the new approach, he makes the suggestion that people 'should, if possible, attend weekly meetings of the Fellowship and actively lend a hand with alcoholic newcomers' (Alcoholics Anonymous 1957: 302–308). The two founding members had found this in itself a help. When they visited an alcoholic patient in hospital, they asked if they might speak to him *for their own sakes* (Alcoholics Anonymous 1976: 15). Harald Klingemann has studied people in Switzerland who have been addicted themselves and who later find careers in the treatment field (Klingemann 1999).

The phenomenon of the wounded healer has appeared in different cultures from the earliest times. Jung not only wrote about it as an archetype, but experienced its truth for himself. From the start of his professional life, he used memories and dreams as a bedrock of his understanding of human functioning, and an awareness of his own vulnerability enabled him to flourish. He faced desolation after he and Freud split and the years of his own 'breakdown', when he came to terms with hitherto unconscious aspects of his personality, were also the time when he blossomed as an original thinker (Jung 1963: 165–192).

Retrieving lost parts of the personality

In addiction only the *addict* part of the personality has a chance to function, while other aspects lie dormant. This is why the addiction strikes those who know or care about an addicted individual as such a wasteful tragedy. The first days after stopping are important because of the need to prevent a relapse, and because precisely at this stage there is the possibility of laying the foundations for a more ordered life in which it is possible to retrieve aspects of the self lost during the addiction. This in turn may lead to fresh growth and development. Linda blames herself now for her need to display a fine persona at the beginning of her membership of AA, but this could be interpreted in other ways. It exemplifies AA's injunction to '*Fake it to make it*', in her case, as a stepping stone to greater self-esteem. It also represents symbolically a return of aspects of the able young woman she had once been.

Chapter 12

Putting away my crutches

As an adolescent, Johnnie lived in a children's home and went to school in our town. He was referred to the hospital because his heroin injecting had come to the notice of the police. At the age of forty-five, fourteen years after he had stopped using drugs and drinking, he recounted his experiences to Dr. Rathod, who had treated him during his teens. His story should make interesting reading for those who fear that drug addicted people from difficult, disrupted backgrounds are no-hopers.

Coming to the end of the road in my addictions was a very painful, lonely experience. I'd lost everything, which is what drugs and alcohol do to you in the end if you let them. I honestly haven't found any drug as good as opium since I dropped it. I love taking heroin and speed, but they don't love me. I'm their slave.

My mum actually was the one that broke through to me. There's no love lost between us. We're not close at all. It was at the end of my using that I used to go and visit my mother, but I hadn't seen her for the last five years, from the age of twenty-seven. That's when I first met my mother and that, in a way, caused a lot of turmoil in me.

She saw me at my worst. I'd gone up there for the weekend and the weekend turned into weeks. I was drunk, staying at her place on the sofa. One night she said to me, 'If you're going out, don't come back if you are any worse than you are now. I won't let you in.' For the first time that cut home and I thought, 'Well, you've rejected me once and you're not going to reject me again.' I really felt that I had to do something for myself. I felt that bad.

I phoned the Samaritans first. I was broken. I was in tears and I didn't know which way to turn. I didn't want to drink any more, or take drugs and I didn't want to get any worse, because I was afraid of the blackouts and the craziness. So I phoned the Samaritans from a public house and spoke to them and they phoned my mother and offered to be a sort of go-between for us. I did go back home but by the next morning already the craving for alcohol was immense, so I went out and got a small bottle of brandy. The Samaritans phoned me back – thank God they did – and then I started to talk about my alcohol and drug problem. They said, 'Why don't you contact Alcoholics Anonymous?' and that's what I did. I spoke to somebody at the AA office, another recovering alcoholic, and I can't remember anything except that what she said made me feel that I wasn't hopeless. She made me believe I could make it. She said something like, 'I understand where you're coming from. I haven't had a drink today.' Up till then, I never listened, not because I wasn't speaking from the same stance as that woman was speaking from, but because I wasn't ready to listen.

As for the insult from my mother, it wasn't an insult actually. She didn't want to see a son so downgraded. My mother rejected me once by not bringing me up. I don't resent her for it. It's just plain fact. I felt she rejected me once and I wasn't going to reject myself – I didn't want to reject myself any more. I could've gone back to the drugs, to the booze, but when I went out that night it hit me in the gut and at that time I got frightened. My thought was, 'If a mother doesn't want you, who the hell wants you? I'd be rejected by everybody now.' It just emotionally hit me at a gut level that I can't explain. It was a very important thing that my mother said, 'Enough is enough, I cannot take any more of you as you are,' and that negative impact led me to the Samaritans and then to AA.

I thought I was going insane. If I drank more alcohol to drown the feelings, I'd get worse. It was frightening. I was having so many blackouts and I was ending up in strange places and being arrested and sometimes ending up in a police cell and I could have been done for murder or anything. I just blacked out. I was frightened actually of the results of the drugs I was taking and also frightened of my own insecurity. I didn't take an overdose because I was scared. I didn't have the guts and I didn't do that for some reason that I can't explain. I knew that if I wanted to I could make it, as frightening as it was.

The most important thing that led me to abstinence was AA. I went to that meeting. Then I spent a week coming off those drugs and alcohol. To begin with, when I stopped, it was very painful. It was a learning process, all a new learning process. About a month later I had a drink. I can't really remember too much because, remember, for many years I'd been living rough, taking drugs and alcohol, so I wasn't too tightly wrapped. I wasn't tuned into things. I went to this self-help group, Alcoholics Anonymous, and it's the best thing I've ever done in my life. They helped me to help myself.

That drink was just me kicking like a kid. I was resentful. I was at a meeting and I was listening to people saying, 'I'm glad to be sober' and there were people in that room lying through their teeth, you know, they're full of bullshit, and I see that and I see my own bullshit. I couldn't let go of that – I had to focus in on that and so what I did was, I said, 'To hell with you lot,' and walked out. Thank God nobody followed me out. I went and had a drink and it was then that I realised what I was doing to myself whilst I was drinking. And from that day on I was gradually coming to terms with a very angry child.

I didn't *want* to use [heroin] any more but after a few weeks I did use because I wasn't quite ready to stop, and it was when I was using that night that I said to myself, 'For the last few weeks I have found freedom, self-respect and I've seen light at the end of the tunnel. Am I going to lose all that and get the old lifestyle back? I don't want it.' I had got sick of being sick.

So I handed all that over and I changed – I started to change. I went out and had a drink and I got drunk, but the next day, I cleaned up and I put my heart and soul into getting better.

My first meeting at AA something clicked. It was an emotional experience. I got hope. There were people there who weren't drinking or taking drugs. At that time they were recovering. I found that other people had faith in me. Other recovering alcoholics – they told me I could make it. To give me faith in myself, you know, they told me where they had been: most drunks or addicts, you know, they tend to exaggerate and lie a bit, but I watch and I listen and that's how I have learned.

But I found that I did not really fit into AA. I had two fist fights in my first year at meetings because they tried to throw me out of meetings for talking about drugs. Throughout the years I've settled down and – you know what I'm like with my temper – it's ridiculous – and I thought well I've found something here and it's the only thing I knew that worked and they're not going to throw me out of these rooms – I'm fully entitled to be in here. The fact is that I was a heroin addict so really I wasn't fully an AA member even though I did have problems in the end with alcohol as well – you know, big problems. So myself and a few other addicts who were keeping quiet within AA in the early 1980s, we formed Narcotics Anonymous in this country. At the time there were five of us who were also recovering alcoholics. I always tell people that we started Narcotics Anonymous with a resentment, a bloody good resentment. It was out of a negative situation that something positive emerged. And you know, a good thing did come out of it, because there's 315 meetings now in this country. Narcotics Anonymous works on the therapeutic value of one addict helping another.

My earlier treatment for addiction didn't work because I wasn't ready then. When I had treatment at the hospital all that time ago, I was so mixed up, confused and drugs and alcohol don't help that situation. Drugs literally took me to the gutter and I was living in the gutter and I hated that lifestyle and I was ashamed.

As you know yourself, in the past professionals couldn't help me. You tried to point me in the right direction but nobody could help me – I had to find out myself. I believe that I went through many, many rock bottoms in life, you know, feelings of desperation, despair. When I came to that point of ringing the Samaritans, for the first time I became responsible and I asked for help.

I didn't have any faith in myself. I had fear. I had a lot of fear when I came off. I had to go through that procedure and I admitted my powerlessness over my addiction, and I do that on a daily basis. I have not had that desire to use, which is incredible, you know, and an old-timer said to me, an old-timer of AA, he said: 'Son, if you have faith within this programme of Alcoholics Anonymous, it's pretty similar to NA, you will never fear anything again.' And ninety-nine per cent of that has been true. The recovering people certainly gave me a sense of hope that if I follow this path it is possible that there is light at the end of the tunnel.

For the first time in my life I was really putting away my crutches and I had nothing else. That's the way I felt. Reality hit me smack bang in the face and I was just told, thank God, to simplify it, keep it simple. It's 'a day at a time.' These slogans that we use may sound *whatever* to other people but they are so important, to me anyway.

It was a learning process and the fear went. I've had a lot to learn in the past few years about relationships, the work process, about life in general. Fear of drugs did not enter into it. It was the fear of my own insecurities which are, are a hell of a lot of things, you know. I have always been insecure about relationships, myself, which I am not today.

I've been out the game now for fourteen years. I don't mix within a negative fraternity. Most of my friends are not drug users. I don't consider myself an ex-user – I'm still a recovering addict. My particular way of coping with abstinence was attending AA meetings and helping others who want my help. And three months later I became a founding member of Narcotics Anonymous in the UK. It gives me a sense of pride and satisfaction. I find that *giving* in life is the thing. Yes, you know, I'm a very selfish person, but, again, people gave to me and if they hadn't been there when I asked for help, where would I be? But I still find recovering addicts difficult because I think I've got to another stage. I'm not better that others but I've gone through so much in the last few years that in a certain way I think I've grown up, faced up to facts, and now I know a lot more about myself and so I don't get involved in a lot of negativity. You know, I believe that if you want to stay clean, you'll make it.

Faith to me is, I suppose, really a personal thing and I think my faith is in a power greater than myself. I do believe in myself more today than I have ever done. At that time that didn't come into the equation at all. I was totally unwrapped.

I've been through a lot of stuff which most people go through in life, you know, like illness, relationships, work, insecurities – not financially because I've been in work so far – and I've learned a lot about myself. Sometimes I've gone down into real depressions and I never used to believe in depressions but now I understand them. I'd go into a shell and I had to work on myself and talk about it in the best way I can or else just, just ignore it. I'd, you know, try to talk to myself. I'd try to find out what was going wrong with me and try not to over analyse it and take myself too seriously. Or I'd talk with fellow NA members whom I trust, who have the experience and who keep it all confidential, you know.

I've had sleepless nights, but it wasn't a deep black depression. I was just feeling down and just not feeling happy and content with myself. I did break up a relationship and I feel due to the kidney illness that I've had, I've really had to draw on some inner strength to cope with it and I am quite proud of that fact, but I have met other people with that same illness at the unit and it gives me that kind of strength as well because they are doing the same thing. A lot of times I've thought about dying and I don't want to die. I'm a fighter inside. I've even had fits of feeling down, suicidal, but I've talked about that and it's, it's only thought. It's shit, but where I live, in a high-rise block, I've seen fourteen people fall to the ground dead from jumping and I've thought, 'No, no.' So, you know, I had to work on it. I can't explain, but I didn't want to die.

I don't know if people grow out of addiction, but I don't think they do. I'm quite loose in life, you know, I take things as they come. As for me personally, I might pick up[1] tomorrow. I've said that for fourteen years and I haven't, because I know that if I did all that insanity would be back. I would be scared of that and I don't need to focus in on that. I need just to kick my own arse and get on with life.

I feel in my situation I am basically powerless over people, places and things. You know, people are going to call me names or do this, or do that, and they're going to make me react and it is no good going around trying to hit the world. It's just frustrating. You've just got to let go of all that stuff.

Growing up for me is maturity, making mature decisions. It's quite simple, you know, that I pay my bills, I become responsible for my actions and don't blame the drugs or society for everything. I don't complain to other people. I don't go on with, 'Poor me, this, poor me, that' because if I do, someone'll just pour me a drink next, you know. If you could live in my head for five minutes, you'd see how mad I was really, you know, but I don't act on those thoughts.

When I was using and living that kind of lifestyle, I wasn't growing up, I wasn't facing life on its own terms. I wasn't being responsible for myself. I wasn't being a responsible person. I'll tell you what, you wouldn't want to see me the way I was when I was worst. I had to grow out of that!

Even people who have been living in the gutter for a long time – the stereotypical picture of a junkie – can leave their addictions behind and move on into a productive life. Johnnie was in a much worse state physically and socially than some of the other narrators when he stopped using drugs. He had very little left to build on. He had a criminal record, no training, an erratic employment record, and lodgings on only a temporary basis with his birth mother who was threatening to throw him out.

Johnnie speaks most cogently not so much about the practicalities of living after he stopped using drugs and drinking, but about his struggle with despair at that time. He had had very little experience of getting on well with anyone up to that point, and true to form, he was angry and bitter about AA when he first attended meetings. He met with difficulties straight away, because not all members at the meetings wanted to deal with the problems of someone who used drugs as well as drinking. In other words, he came up against a barrier. He was not unconditionally accepted there any more than he had ever been in his life up to then, yet something got through to him. He sensed that here were people with integrity who had put alcohol-fuelled lives behind them. It meant something to him that the AA member he spoke to first on the telephone could say that she had not had a drink *that day*. For anyone who is addicted this is a powerful and intriguing statement to hear. How has that person managed it?

So what Johnnie speaks about is his struggle with himself. He discovered by listening to others at the meetings that he was terrified of his own insecurities. How many of us face this at a time of such vulnerability? He realised that his task was to come to terms with what he called the very angry child within him. But, as he says, he put his heart and soul into getting better. AA gave him hope and helped him to help himself. As for the precepts he was given, they were the things all members of AA are offered: to learn to take things as they come; that there's no point in complaining; to face the facts and to deal with depression, however difficult that may be. There can be little doubt that being sent by AA to the USA to learn about Narcotics Anonymous must have been a great boost to his self esteem. Someone believed in him.

Johnnie's disrupted childhood was an unhappy one with little continuity. Born of an Asian father and a very young British mother, herself one of seven children of a neglectful, alcoholic mother, he was put into care at the age of two. His father was reputed to have ill-treated his mother. Initially Johnnie was described as a bright, good little boy, and was fostered by a family with no children of their own. His disturbed, jealous behaviour on the birth of a girl in that family led to his rejection by them. In all, he was fostered by five different families, and by the age of nine he was in a children's home. At that point he discovered that his parents had never married, and he became aware of his mixed ethnic origins. He felt deeply upset and ashamed on both counts. Although he showed intelligence and athletic ability, his school days were marred by his emotional instability. Petty crime, mostly theft and uncontrolled rages, followed, and within three weeks of being initiated into injection by a friend, he became dependent on heroin and stimulants. After school, he had a poor work record and often quarreled with landladies in his attempts to settle in lodgings. Sometimes he slept rough.

He had two spells of inpatient psychiatric treatment, and three prison sentences, the last being eighteen months for possession of heroin. His former psychiatrist described his behaviour as a teenager as 'unpatterned and deviant when churned up and frustrated.' He summarised Johnnie's situation like this:

> An institutional upbringing deprived him of a chance to learn how to conform and maintain relationships. Socially he is a boy with very limited outlets and a low frustration threshold, and his stealing seems to be irrational and symbolic of stealing love. He has feelings of inferiority and a longing to belong to somebody, but having no one to belong to.

At that time he had been a constant disappointment to those who tried to help him, always in trouble as a result of stealing or violent outbursts.

His eventual settling into a creative life may have been the outcome of the first two years he had with his mother. Babies who start life with a close relationship, even if that is broken, find it easier to make secure attachments later. What is certain is that in his adolescence, when he was battling with conflicted feelings about his roots and having great trouble relating to authority figures, he was able to make a relationship with his therapist, his first psychiatrist, who understood him and took trouble with him. His relationship with the hospital as an institution was ambivalent. He rejected all attempts to persuade him to conform, yet he responded to the words of Dr. Rathod, for the letters he wrote from prison show that he had formed a bond with a much-needed father figure. Johnnie wrote:

> I'm sorry for letting you down, but please don't give up faith in me, for I mean no harm. I'm just mixed up and I feel alone. This I will overcome in time, for I want to live in peace and most of all I want respect. This I can only do myself. I promise you that I shall prove to you in the future that you have not wasted your time on me. I hate living like an animal.

He had no medical treatment in his final withdrawal from drugs and alcohol, but had the consistent, ongoing support of AA. He was able to be frustrated and angry in AA, saying that its members understood nothing about drug addiction, but he did not run away for long. He was selected by AA as one of six young people to be sent to the USA to learn how to set up NA groups in this country. From that point on he devoted his life to helping other addicts, both in NA and later in a statutory agency where he was employed as a drugs worker. Once he found a purpose in life and had supportive people around him, he forged ahead.

Rather than forming a single, lasting intimate relationship, he turned his own degradation and suffering to good use in helping countless others in a similar plight. From being a helpless victim, the changes in his life led him to find solace and fulfillment in helping drug users. It is not surprising that he found difficulty establishing the trust implicit in building one-to-one relationships after the rejections of his childhood, but he warmed to the 'tough love' of his ex-therapist first, and later to that of AA. This security enabled him to thrive.

In conclusion

A rocky start in recovery

For some, the early days after stopping are messy. They return for another drink or fix. They accept help, then get furious or disillusioned with the people who are offering this help. It is far from neat and tidy, yet they succeed in leaving their addictions behind. The despair Johnnie speaks about was gradually replaced by a sense of hope. The implication of what Johnnie says is that as therapists we need to keep up our hopes. However unpromising the outcome of a particular 'case' may look, we cannot tell at the time just what impact our words or our personalities are having on our patients. Crucial to his recovery was the fact that other people had faith in him. Therapists or friends who are caring for a person in the period shortly after they stop using drugs or drinking should stay alive to the possibility that this person may have deep issues to face, the very things they have been blanking out. Without the protective barrier of the drugs, they are extremely vulnerable.

Erupting emotions

The challenge for a person who has been attempting to blank out with drugs every 'difficult' emotion for years is to face these emotions without the protective blanket of the drugs. This is one strong reason why addicted people want to maintain their addictions. In Johnnie's case, as is far from uncommon, the emotional impact of his fear and anger did not deter him from facing his demons.

The issue of trust

An archetypal theme in mythology and literature is the hero's search for trustworthy supporters – human, animal or divine – even in the most inauspicious circumstances. Johnnie had not completely lost the capacity to trust people, as his letters from prison to his therapist show, but he had lost trust in himself. Waking up to the realisation that he was in danger of driving his mother to reject him yet again opened his eyes to the part he played in his relationships. At that stage he asked for help and found AA, a trustworthy source of support, however he behaved. It provided him with a model for 'facing life on its own terms.' Eventually he learned to trust himself enough to take responsibility for his decisions, but in the early days, as he simply puts it, 'I watch and I listen and that's how I have learned.'

Note

1 By *pick up* he means *start using drugs*.

Chapter 13

What I learned after I stopped drinking

Minette came to the hospital for help after she stopped drinking. Her drinking had brought her to the verge of collapse. She had outpatient appointments and joined the relapse prevention group, as well as becoming a member of AA. Later she became a drugs counsellor in a statutory agency, so she has thought about the problems of recovering from many angles.

It is fourteen years, two months and four days since I had my last drink. I find life very different now from the way it was in early recovery. It's a process, isn't it, about developing skills that were probably there, but were not used? It's a process of working through chaos, and making some kind of order or semblance of order out of so many things that aren't right: accommodation, work, relationships, plus your own kind of anxieties and fears. Early recovery is about identifying those things, because there's so much chaos. Once those things are sorted, once you have a foundation for your life, then it becomes easier. Until you get that kind of base level right, you can't move on, because there is no focus point. When you first go into recovery you don't have anything other than the fact that you know that you don't want to use any more, but that's not enough. The fact that you don't want to use isn't going to sustain you. You need to have all the other things that make 'not using' viable: a good relationship, a home, something to do with your time, – that's the biggest single area of concern. What are you going to do with the twenty-four hours of the day? That is still my feeling sixteen years on after going to my first AA meeting and since I identified that I had a problem. What are you going to replace not using with? So, it really is a process of focusing on the basis, the foundation of your life.

I suppose the thing is that when you come into recovery, you have no idea what your expectations are. I can't remember what mine were, other than the fact that I couldn't live the way that I had been living. So, maybe you don't have expectations. There are a lot of things you have to sort out. All you know is that you have to have a different life to the one you had. And I think that takes a good five years. Recovery takes a good five years before you can find your feet, because the chaos takes so long to sort out. It's not done in six months.

You begin to think about things in a constructive way, thinking through the process of dealing with change, because I think that's where a lot of fear comes to the fore in recovery, when people are unable to change their view. But, then I think that a lot of people who don't have an addiction suffer from that. More so. Moving and changing at different times in your life is very difficult. But I've kind of done that and I've coped with the fear of it. There are still fears, but they're normal fears, such as not being able to pay your bills, not being able to send your child to university. Realistic fears. I think they keep you on your toes. They make you actively seek change, because you need to do something about it.

The most difficult thing to change might be the reason that someone drank in the first place. And, I think a lot of it is about self-awareness, self-esteem, confidence, belief in yourself. I think society has a way of kind of not encouraging self-belief, and I think that comes in the work environment. I think if you're a giver, and you generally give of yourself in any given job that you're doing, I think people sit on that, and they take advantage of it. I was someone who perhaps didn't have the confidence to say, 'Hey, come on, I'm better than this.' It took me a long time to think, 'I am better than this; I can change this; I need to change this. You're not going to do it to me any more.' I can do the things they felt that I was unable to do. And I think that happened to me in the job that I was in for twelve years. Because there were so many things that I was good at, that I just did as second nature. There was no great song and dance about it. You just do it, kind of organisation management. But if somebody comes in new, and they make a big song and dance about it, inevitably they are going to be recognised. It's a bit more than not tolerating being put down. It's recognising that you have the ability to do certain things. Recognising it to such an extent that it doesn't matter what somebody else thinks. It's actually losing that feeling that I can't get anything, that I'm a real wimp, that I'm unable to do that. It's being powerful within yourself.

I think that the very core of a good recovery is having each segment within a circle balanced. You take your recovery in different forms. Because, if you're somebody that goes to meetings, you can continue to go to meetings throughout the rest of your life. You do some voluntary work; you take an active part; or you are interested in things that could make a difference. You have a home life that you develop and grow within. I think we continue to grow within our own family.

We recognise that our children alter, and have the ability to bring out the very best and the very worst in ourselves – so you kind of have to look at that, and take it on board. Sometimes my children say, 'Mum, I don't want you saying that. We don't like it.' You kind of sit back and you think, 'Well, why don't they like it?' But, they've obviously got the courage to say that. I never had. As a child, I could never have said to my mother, 'Don't keep doing that,' or 'Don't keep asking me that.'

Then there's your employment, knowing that your employment is only part of that day. It's not the whole twenty-four hours. So you have to have enough to do and then finish with work. But, I think the most important thing is being able to come home, shut the door, and think, 'That's it. I don't have to do any more.'

So yes, of course, life today is very different, because one has, or I like to think that I have a home; OK, it's got a mortgage, and it's got to be paid for. I've had full-time employment for nearly thirteen years, both in the commercial sector and in the health industry. My family has grown and I now have another daughter, I've got married, and the friendships with people that I probably had are on a different level. I haven't the same fears about going into a room full of people and thinking I don't fit. I *make* myself fit. I think I am as good as somebody else is, and I have 'achieved' in a different way. I am capable of doing things that I just don't think I'd ever have been capable of doing when I first came into recovery, but maybe I was capable of it, but I just didn't know about it, because using had become the obsession that it does, you don't allow yourself to do some of those things. I mean, you know, to be able to organise the events that I've done, in the places that I've arranged them in, you know – that's no mean feat. It takes organisational skills. What I've actually done doesn't seem real, whereas the using is real, but the achievements since that time I stopped don't seem real somehow. They are just two different worlds. So whatever years you miss out on, whatever development is suppressed, I must have caught up in some way or other.

Now I don't have to do anything in order not to drink. I'm fifteen years on, I don't have to think about it. There's coffee, there's Diet Coke. I'm very, very secure within not having anything to do about it. I don't have to be out there jigging and jiving, and going to meetings, and making sure that I'm noticed. It doesn't matter. So maybe that's the important thing. In real terms I do think about the time when I did drink. With the role that I'm now in as a drugs counsellor, I think about it quite often, which is in a sense unusual, because in my last job I didn't have time to think about it. But, I do think about it now in relation to some of the people I see as patients. Again, the thing is to get the person something better than whatever they've already got. If I see a patient, and they are sixty plus and they are drinking on a daily basis, what am I going to give them in their life that is going to be better than what they've got at the moment? You know there's a part of me that says, 'Why should they stop doing what they're doing?' I'm not going to give them anything different. I'm not going to give them a new social structure. I'm not going to give them a new job, a new home. Because in a way, none of those options are available to them. They are sixty plus. So I think about that again, in the sense of what are you going to give someone to fill up the time. What, go away and do jigsaw puzzles? I mean, I do tell them those things. And, I give them the most mundane things that I used to do myself in order not to drink. I use the knowledge I gained.

When you wake up in the middle of the night, because you haven't been able to sleep because you haven't had a drink, what are you going to do? Well, I know what I did. I can remember. I'd strip the beds. My house at that stage must never ever have been so hygienic. It was so clean it must have squeaked. My children must have squeaked, for Heaven's sake, all the cleaning and the washing and what have you that went on. Those are the things that I did. Those are the only things that you can do in the middle of the night when you've got children asleep in bed. You can't prowl the streets, so you clean windows or you sew. I've a great thing for tapestry and embroidery, and I still do that now when I have that sort of restless night. Now and again, you get woken at night, when you don't know if you're missing something, and obviously it plays on your subconscious and wakes you up. So, I do those things, and that's what I tell my patients to do. And, I think about it also when someone says to me, 'You don't understand how I feel. You don't know what it's like to be an alcoholic. You don't know the embarrassment. You don't know what it's like not to be able to tell your family.' So, yes, I think about it often in the sense that, no, I don't tell them I drank, but I think of a way of coming back to it. And, I think about it with the spouses of the patients that I've got when they phone up stressed or they can't cope.

I don't dwell on the time when I was drinking, because there's not very much that's good from that era. I mean, it would be wrong to say that there weren't really stupid, fun times that we all have as young adults, you know. Going to Calais and getting so plastered that you can't remember how you got on the ferry, but then half the nation does that every weekend. You know, you have to get it in perspective sometimes. And, I think of it when I see drink adverts on the television, and I think about it when my partner says, 'Why aren't you going to meetings?' I don't really need them all the time any more. Very, very rarely these days. But I go if there's an issue and I can't deal with it. I use it for that. That might seem wrong. It gives you good grounding. You go to a meeting and you hear someone sitting over there in the chair[1], how dreadful her life is, and all the rest of it. I tell you, it really puts it in perspective. My life isn't dreadful. My life today is just so different.

I think all my relationships have to be different from when I was drinking. They have to be more honest, by the very nature of not using, because addiction makes you secretive. So, they have to be more honest in that sense. The only thing I would say I was dishonest about now is my obsession with buying clothes. But I think I'm like a lot of women. I can still go out and buy something and bring it home and put it in the wardrobe, and then when I put it on they say, 'Is that new? and I say, 'No, I've had it months.' A lot of women do that. That's the one thing I'd say I'm not entirely honest with my family about. Otherwise everything is very open. They know where I'm going, who I see, where I've been. They know roughly on a weekly basis what I will be doing, whereas when you're drinking there's no way that you could make any plans.

I've got an eight-year-old now. If sixteen years ago one of my daughters had invited a friend for tea after school, there was no guarantee, one, that I'd have remembered, or two, that I would have been sober. That doesn't happen today, you know. It's written on the calendar, we know it's happening. I'm sober, I can do things with them. The friend comes back, as happened yesterday. We'll go to the park, they play on the swings, we play with the dogs, we'll go for a run in the car, things like that. I couldn't have done things like that sixteen years ago.

I think I'm more confrontative in my relationships. If my mother pisses me off, I tell her that she pisses me off, and I'll suffer the consequences. If she chooses to sulk because I've told her that she mustn't interfere, that's her problem. It's not mine. I try hard not to say what I think to my colleagues in the way that I want to say it.

But, you see, even at work, I would say if I wasn't happy about something. I suppose I would give respect where respect was due, but if I really felt that someone was out of order, I would tackle the situation. And, in the same way, if I know that I'm wrong, and let's face it, we're not always right, I'd remove myself from the situation, and I still do this today. I would go downstairs, out in the garden, and have a cigarette. I'd think about whether it was me, whether it's them, or whether it's both of us. And then, once my cigarette was finished, I'd come back and I'd tackle it. Whereas I could not have done that. I couldn't have even looked at the fact that maybe I was wrong, or maybe they were wrong. It was just a mess. And in my marriage I have to do that. I think a marriage is like that, you're continuously in a process of confronting things you're not happy about. You just have to kind of say what it is.

I think some people, although they've moved on and they've done different things, maybe their using was *everything* and still is, if you like. They've not been able to find any satisfaction within their lives or in what they've done. Maybe, they haven't got any faith or something, I don't know, but I think there are a lot of *dry drunks*[2] out there. For whatever purpose certain individuals used, I think their using was so powerful, so all-consuming. I mean, it's more than just a love affair. It is everything in their lives, and I think for some people, they have not been able to leave that behind. So although they have gone on and they 'confront' and they 'do things' and they do well in all kinds of ways, they have never really found anything that has the effects like using. I could probably count four or five people at the moment that I actually feel are like that. They have not been able to replace alcohol. I don't know if that'll ever happen. That's why, whatever you do, we have to remember that individuals are so different.

Undoubtedly the Twelve Step Programme has helped me greatly in recovery, because, without going into treatment, there would not have been anywhere else for me to go. The Substance Misuse Service, my GP, going to the hospital group where I could see my psychiatrist and my psychologist, were all good, but it was only for an hour and a half every Monday, so in a sense there was no way that that was enough, or ever could be enough. I value AA and the people that I met in AA.

Now and again, I ask myself – am I sick? I must really be sick to think that I've left drinking behind. I question my motives on that sometimes, but I think that is taking on board the Twelve Steps, quite literally in everything you think and do and feel. I think it is right to ask myself, 'I think I've moved on, but, let's get real, you're only a drink away from your next relapse, who knows.' I think the most fascinating thing for me, and it's not going to happen, is to think, 'If I have a drink, would I be an alcoholic straight away again? Would that happen to me? Or, have I learned to deal with the problems?' I won't test it because I won't tempt fate. I am not going to cock up my clean[3] time. I don't want to go back to being just a day clean again, I couldn't bear it.

The vast majority of patients I see, I tend to feel they don't deal with their problems, they just exacerbate them by their drinking. I still even today don't know if they are alcoholics or if they've got mixed up in a situation that they can't get out of. They've got themselves into this all-consuming habit. They haven't actually dealt with their difficulties within their relationship, within their marriage, or the fact that they've been made redundant.

I think I have a spiritual life. I'm a Catholic and that's quite important in my life. It's His will, whatever I do, I say, 'Would this be the right thing?' 'Help me out here, I'm struggling,' kind of thing, and inevitably that does happen. Now, I don't know whether – that's the whole thing about God – you don't know whether you've resolved that yourself, or whether God has intervened. And, I think that's where your blind faith comes in. So, yeah, the spiritual aspect of my life is very, very important, in all that we kind of do. Although we're not always ready to recognise that. And there's times when you want a more spiritual feeling inside and you struggle to find it. I was brought up a Catholic. It's always been there. Whatever people call their Higher Power, it is a faith. It's very hard not to believe that there is something greater than us, for goodness sake. I think just taking that on board, that there is something far more powerful than we are, gives your faith a spirituality.

I think we probably all start off thinking we're the centre of the universe and that when things go wrong, 'It's everyone else's problem and not mine.' 'It's not the drinking that's the problem, it's all the other things that are happening around me,' and not actually being able to focus on the fact that if you didn't drink you could resolve some of them. Those issues don't go away because you stop drinking. They're still waiting for you to solve them, to resolve them, to do something about them, to change them, which is what you're not able to do in the midst of your drinking. If I can't pay that bill, and I choose to ignore it, then that's about me. It's not the bill. It's the fact that I have chosen to make no active change towards resolving that bill. All I've got to do is pick the phone up and say I can't pay it, and they'll tell me how to pay what I can each month. I mean, generally you can do something about things – if you *want* to.

And I have to say my family is one of the most significant things in my recovery. So, my family has been the centre of what was going on, but I have been the centre as well. In a way, I have to have believed that I was important; otherwise, I wouldn't have been able to do the things that I was able to do. I have a life to live and I'm going to live it to the best of my ability. So, I think I have to include myself.

Then, God was very important. Definitely there is, there has to be, something spiritual. What I do and how I can help someone else is also important. Just helping other people, I help myself really. That helps my recovery profoundly. You see, it was the very 'self' that you used for. It's a long haul from that. It took me thirty-two years from the start to where I am today. I obviously didn't see myself as important.

My life had always been that I was a professional athlete. I ran for the UK overseas, and when I contracted broncho-pneumonia, I was out of training for a period of six weeks. I could not run, and for someone that had run every day of her life for a given period of time, that was a tremendous change in my life. A loss, whatever you want to call it. Whether it was the broncho-pneumonia, whether it was the combination of the drugs that I had given me, I was actually picking up my first drink at that time, I have no idea. I have no way of knowing. Whether that was my destiny, I don't know. Maybe I had to go through what I went through, in order to be where I am today. Because maybe over the last sixteen years there's someone that has changed because they've met me, because I happened to be in the situation I was in. Who knows? There has to have been a purpose to it all.

To pick up your first drink, and to recognise that that actually changed the way you felt, actually felt different. That's what happens. It makes you feel differently. That's why you do it. And any professional that tells me it's for a different reason, as far as I'm concerned, has no idea what they're talking about. It hits the spot and alters your whole constitution. You know yourself, when you have a glass of wine. Next time you have a glass of wine, drink it, allow it to go through your body and settle in your stomach, and you will feel differently. OK. You recognise that you're not going to have the next one and the next one, looking for that first feeling, that first emotion that made you feel different, because it is only the *first* one. It never works after that. That's always what you go for, whatever it is at that time. Why? Why for some and not for others? Oh well, I think it is a chemical reaction that affects some people differently. But I liked it, and I went back for more. And tragically, I went back for more for sixteen years, until I realised I wasn't going to get that feeling any more.

Minette's life story presents a sharp contrast to that of many of the other narrators in that she was brought up in an affectionate family with strong, but not oppressive religious beliefs and a stimulating experience of life outside her home. In her case, rather than having a troubled adolescence, a sudden unexpected episode of ill health put paid to her cherished ambition to become a professional athlete. Her low self-esteem may have arisen from this setback, or from subtle influences within her family. She is not clear about that, but the outcome was that as a young adult she became over-compliant and too eager for approval to fulfill her true potential.

Looking back at the time immediately after she stopped drinking, Minette says nothing at all about withdrawal symptoms. What she remembers is the difficulty of finding things to fill the gap left when she no longer drank. She also remembers that time as the time when she began to throw away her lack of belief in herself and to discover who she really was. She uses her memory of this now in advising others how to face a life without their favourite drug, and she speaks out of her experience, rather than speaking about it. She uses her experience as a point of reference without burdening patients with knowledge of her own past or present struggles, a knowledge they might well be unable to cope with. The practical side of this care is also, she would say, a way of making up for things she regrets about the days when her own drinking got beyond her control.

Minette's strength is apparent in her acceptance of not having all the answers and also in her ability to make use of her clear understanding of her own recovery to help other people. Many of the other narrators are involved in this, but Minette describes in detail how she actually does it.

She has a broad perspective, seeing the desirability of achieving balance in one's life, yet she can also offer strategies in precise detail to anyone who is facing the empty hours after they stop using drugs or drinking. She knows that she drank as an evasion of her problems, but she knows too that searching for the sensation the first drink brings is what actually draws the drinker on. Her strength as a counsellor is that she has a grasp of the crucial but often forgotten fact that change is difficult to embrace.

She was able to enrich her relationships after stopping. Most important was the relationship with herself, for she had been struggling against a burden of low self-esteem for years. In her relationships with others, Minette feels that she became more open and honest. In arguments she discovered that she could state her own point of view and stand her ground. Equally, she discovered that she could admit when she was wrong. She became able to accept criticism when it was justified, and to give herself enough time to ask herself, 'Is it her? Or is it me?' when something awkward came up in relationships. Because her realistic appraisal of herself helped her to stop underplaying her strength, she stopped worrying so much about what other people thought about her, and obtained a prestigious job. In that work, she discovered that she could deal effectively with people who were tricky and difficult.

Minette is not someone who speaks as if she knows all the answers. She has many unanswered questions about the nature of addiction to alcohol – could she ever have a drink without relapsing? Which comes first, the problems or the drinking? The vital thing is that she is able to tolerate these uncertainties, which is a sign of maturity. As she says, she is uncertain what approach to take with older patients who may well have fewer options for replacing their drinking or drug-using patterns of life with other activities. Perhaps it is not so easy for them to socialise or even go out? Maybe it is hard for them to change their habits or to face solitude with equanimity – and without their favourite drug? When we talked together she was worried about these matters, and thinking about how to approach the problems. Although she herself has gained so much from AA, she knows it is not everyone's cup of tea. There are no easy answers. For her, her faith underpins all her actions.

In conclusion

What is the message for therapists?

The time after someone addicted stops drinking or using drugs is a time when psychological help is of immeasurable value not only in preventing a relapse but in engaging in the process of rebuilding. Practical ways to deal with the problems that arise are symbolic of care of oneself – the converse of the self-destruction of the addict's life. Changes after stopping can be seen as falling into two categories: the practical activities needed to replace those of the addiction; and the changes in relationships. Secrecy tends to be a way of life for addicted people and greater openness in relationships may be hard for someone with years of the clandestine customs of addiction behind them. Some people will go to enormous lengths in life to try to avoid embracing change. Minette sees five years as the early stage of recovering. This may come as a surprise to some readers.

Not knowing

Minette makes the important observation about the time immediately after a person stops that they probably have no idea what their expectations of themselves should be. In their addiction people lose track of who they are. The first, tentative steps without the drug have to be taken with this as a starting point. This highlights how unrealistic is it to expect detoxification on its own to work miracles. In the relapse prevention group, we observed that people who continued to accept support seemed to find it easier to avoid relapses because they became involved in a positive process of growth.

Symptoms point the way

Minette could not throw off the shackles of low self-esteem until she had undergone the experience of repairing the damage caused by the effects of a serious addiction. That experience enabled her to embrace change, driven by her fears. This is a very different slant from the commonly held attitude that the consequences of addiction are inevitably destructive. Jung believed that symptoms reveal the true situation in someone's life, and can point the way towards what is lacking.

Notes

1 This refers to the form AA meetings take. A member takes the *chair* for one particular meeting, and has the floor for that meeting. They can describe whatever they wish about their drinking and their time in recovery. Then other members present have the chance to respond to what the chair has said.
2 In AA people who seem to be clinging to behaviour which they displayed when they were drinking, even though they are drinking no longer, are known as *dry drunks*.
3 *Clean time* usually refers to time a drug user has not been using drugs, whereas with drinkers, the more frequently used term is *dry time*.

Chapter 14

A most astonishing thing happened

Lawrence's first experiences of detoxification were at hospitals in London, where he was on the editorial staff of a national newspaper. He subsequently moved to our area, becoming a commuter. Following a relapse he was referred to our service where he had one-to-one appointments and was encouraged to come to the hospital group and to attend AA. The decision to drink can suddenly come upon someone who has been addicted in the past with no apparent warning even years after stopping. Lawrence thought he had mastered his problems with alcohol and for several years had simply chosen to drink soft drinks with his colleagues or in social situations. Journalism is a profession in which heavy drinking is common, yet he felt comfortable simply drinking fruit juice or Coca Cola – until one day. . .

I'm fifty-nine. I'm a journalist, but I retired early, last year, on health grounds, which had in fact no connection with alcohol. They were quite separate – internal plumbing problems. I think best left at that. As a family, there's my wife and myself. But I've got three daughters. All three are married and have careers in the professions. So we have been through all the business of the latest exam results. All the stress that accompanies that.

I regard my problem as still being drink, although I'm not drinking at the moment. I still regard myself as having a drink problem, because I think this is the safe way of looking at things. If ever I took a drink again, I would have the same problems that I had before.

As to whether these problems were related to my childhood, mine was a completely normal family. There was no stress in the family, nothing like divorce or difficulty over schools. Drink was a normal part of life. It wasn't an excessive part of life. It didn't dominate my family as a child. There were two of us. I've got a sister very much younger than me. Both my parents come from large families. There's no direct drinking problem. There's never been a problem for or against it. It was a working class family. My father was a commercial traveller.

My childhood was very pleasant, except, the only unpleasant times were the days that my school report arrived. Well, it invariably said that I could do better, except on one disastrous occasion when it said that it seemed I couldn't possibly do better, and I had a very nice let out on that one, because it was discovered that I'd had measles and was short sighted and needed glasses. I hadn't been able to see the blackboard for a whole term. So I got out of that school report very nicely indeed. Apart from that, a very normal childhood.

I left school at sixteen. The war was on. To me, my destiny was set out already. There was no question that at some point I'd go into the army and I wanted to get started on a career. I think I'd always wanted to be a journalist. I'd always had this fixation that I wanted to chase fire engines, which I suppose is basic curiosity. And of course be the first person to tell people that I'd chased a fire engine – and what I'd found. And so I started work on a local paper and I stayed there till I went into the army. I found that I did have a capacity for work. I think it was prompted very much by the idea that the higher the rank I got, the more comfort I got. The first ambition was to have sheets on my bed. So I did some work so that I had sheets on my bed. I ended as a staff captain.

The only action I saw was helping the civil authorities in India during their riot problems, helping the Indian police, when we were called out not infrequently in the later days. I stayed on until 1948. I could have left earlier but I wanted to see Indian Independence and I stayed on simply to see what happened. I thought it would be useful to me later in life. It turned out that it was. And we had a fair amount to do with the communal rioting leading up to Independence in August 1947. I saw a fair amount of tragedy and massacre. I saw a number of things that I wouldn't like to see again.

Then I came back home. I became a journalist, and I was in a way very lucky because I was part of an age group that wasn't well represented on newspapers at that time. They were looking around for youngsters in Fleet Street and I fortunately managed to get into it. There were very few of us in the age group that I was in. I became part of the higher editorial staff on a national newspaper. So I was success-ful, I had a good home and a very happy marriage – and yet!

It's very difficult to say how the 'alcoholic' drinking started. It's not difficult to say how I started drinking. I had first been in a pub, I suppose, when I was about sixteen, pretending to be eighteen and I'd had a drink once a week perhaps, but very small time – there was a shortage of beer. I might have a half pint a week or one gin and orange, something of that sort, nothing very much. There was a little more booze available in the army, but it didn't worry me at all, and I would go for weeks or even months without a drink. And when I first came back and started work again, I obviously had to relearn all that I'd learned and had forgotten, and a lot more – to get on in the job. In the early days of being married and getting started in the job over here, we were pretty short of money. There wasn't the money to drink. Apart from there not being any incentive. Being fairly newly married, marriage took up most of my time.

It never really hit me. Nobody ever said to me that I should cut down. I'd been drinking – fairly heavily and steadily – not, not heavily in the beginning, but steadily, and then fairly heavily toward the end of a period of about fourteen years, and I had been on holiday feeling very, very ill. I had been drinking on holiday in this country, and I decided that I couldn't stay on holiday any longer. I had to get back to London to get home again where I could simply get into my own bed and feel at peace with the world, and I went to see my doctor who simply said to me quite directly, 'You're an alcoholic and you need treatment.'

Nobody likes to hear the word 'alcoholic' applied to themselves and it came as a shock, but he meant it kindly. I knew that he understood that I had got a fairly stressful job and he simply said, 'You need treatment', and arranged it. Very, very sudden indeed. I went to see him on a Friday morning, I saw a psychiatrist at two o'clock in the afternoon at a hospital in London, and by three o'clock that afternoon I was in the psychiatric unit – having had a very large drink on the way!

Well, it's a very strange story. I went into treatment. I had treatment for six weeks, and at the end of that I was recommended to go to AA. I went to two AA meetings and decided this was not for me; I would do this thing on my own. I thought it was purely a matter of willpower – that I wouldn't drink. I wouldn't go anywhere near the places where I had been drinking – and for something like eight years – you have to remember that I have an alcoholic's memory, which is always an optimistic one – I was completely dry. I met the people that I normally met, I chatted with them in pubs and then just went home, having had orange juice, coca cola, whatever happened to be going at the time. I didn't even have wine at lunch time, I just stayed off drink completely.

Then a most astonishing thing happened. I had been in the habit of getting a lift home with a colleague of mine. He had a car parking place and he drove up each day and passed my door and took me up to the office, which was very convenient, because I didn't have to worry about my car being in the car park and my wife could have the car. Hundreds of times we must have crossed the same street going towards the car park, and all that I basically remember is one very beautiful July evening when we'd finished fairly early, round about six, we were crossing the road to go to the car park. We got as far as the refuge in the middle of the road. There was a pub on the other side of the road and for some reason which I cannot fathom out to this day, I said, 'Let's go and have a drink!' And we did.

During my time drinking I had no blackouts. It crossed my mind several times that I ought to cut down. Actually, people tended not to mention my drinking. I would be greeted at home with, 'Oh, you've been in the pub again.' That was irritating, but it was nothing more than that. I didn't feel guilty because I was in an environment where everybody drank. I think that had something to do with the escalation, certainly. I tended to mix more and more with people who drank more. We had a feeling of contempt for the weekend drinkers or the highly light drinkers, because they were just 'amateurs'. We were the professionals. I was in fact very lucky because the only effect that it had on me was a financial one. There were always acute financial worries in the later periods of that drinking spell.

I was not a drinker who started early in the morning, not till a lot, lot later. After I'd had that drink after crossing the road, I went through a period of years in which I had periods of sobriety, an attempt to go back to social drinking. Sometimes it seemed to be successful – I might go for two or three months purely social drinking. One or two drinks a week, two or three drinks at a time then, and then I found that it escalated, first of all over a period of, say, two months and then latterly over periods as short as two weeks, my drinking would go back to mammoth proportions.

I came to this local service twelve years later, sent by my GP. I think you straightened out my thoughts by emphasising again the fact that I was an alcoholic. This is one of the most difficult things that I've found. You can be told that you're an alcoholic, and you can look around and you can read books and you can see people who are alcoholics and know that you are like them. You accept that on one plane. Yet you don't accept it so far as you, yourself are concerned. You cannot believe that you are in the same position, although every ounce of ordinary common sense you have tells you this is the case. You don't accept it, and it's the beginning of acceptance that I think is so vital. Logic has no impact at all. You must get an understanding of it somehow that you are an alcoholic, that you are like other alcoholics.

There was never any threat from my wife that anything would be done. There were certainly emotional appeals that I had to do something, that I had to stop, and there were, as usual with alcoholics, there were the broken promises, the firm resolve that I was going to stop. Then having left London where I lived and then moved down here, I think the most remarkable and beautifully surprising discovery I made moving to Sussex was that the pubs opened at ten o'clock in the morning. I'd never been up so early and so active in my life as during that period! That in a way was contributory.

I'd had several bouts of inpatient treatment. I'd been for drying out periods, and I hadn't then made up my mind that I was going to stop drinking. I hadn't accepted that I was an alcoholic. But eventually, I made up my mind. I think honestly that somebody has to dig it out of you. Somebody has to bring forward to you, whoever it is – a psychiatrist, a doctor, your own GP, a good friend, AA – somebody has to bring it out so that you accept, more than just on the intellectual level. You have to accept that you are an alcoholic. And I think any help, professional or otherwise, to get to that stage is important. You changed the way I saw myself.

It then becomes up to the individual to work out a, a new, virtually a new life for himself. I did something that I said I would never do. I went back to AA. That was one thing I was advised by your people to do, and introduced to AA by them. So I went to AA. That was one thing. The other thing was that in the very first days of stopping drinking I avoided doing all the things that I thought had contributed to my drinking. I did not go to the town in the morning when I knew that the pubs were open at ten o'clock. I stayed away. I avoided temptation and I found myself things to make me far more active. Having retired and having more or less settled into a house, I worked out a plan of things that I was going to do. I tried to ensure that I wasn't empty-handed and certainly wasn't empty-minded, and whether it rained or whether it was fine, I knew what I wanted to do during the day and I knew at what times I wanted to do it, and I established, which I think possibly all retired people do – is that you take a share in the actual physical running of the home. That is, I think, fairly important. It means doing the washing up, that's one of the things. So you do that. You're not washing up at the Savoy. You're washing up at home.

I go to the relapse prevention group at the hospital. I find that meeting a very helpful one. It's not AA. It's got people in it who are still drinking, it's got people who come back and forwards, sometimes having decided that they're not going to drink and then drop off for a while, and I find that looking round at people who are still indecisive about their drinking and their drinking plans does me good. It's a reminder in front of you of what can go wrong – one of the dangers, I noticed – I've had about six lapses over drinking, having been not drinking for a while – and there is a difference between not drinking and being sober. Having been sober for a while I have slipped and I have not know why I have slipped. So I tend to beware of feeling euphoric about not drinking, and I need a constant reminder that there are people like me who are still drinking.

In my case, I think the answer has been to treat the symptoms, and not immediately treat the causes. I've worked it out in this way, that if I talk to somebody like you, who knows a lot of alcoholics and a lot about alcoholism, if I talk to you and explain things that happen to me, when they happen to me, I might hit, or you might hit on a reason for me drinking, that in itself would be at the moment unimportant. The fact is that I've stopped drinking by refusing a drink a minute at a time, an hour at a time, a day at a time, and at the moment go to bed saying, 'I haven't had a drink today' – that's enough for today. If I were to find the reason that I drank, I would then have a much more satisfactory basis on which to build my non-drinking.

Anyway, it seems that everybody in the family is very happy with the situation at the moment, and so am I. I'm happy with the situation. I'm going back to some form of journalism. I've got a new life, and that's it.

Lawrence's narrative highlights what can happen, seemingly out of the blue, to someone who thinks they have left the risk of relapsing into addiction far behind. He raises many of the most intriguing and hotly argued puzzles that baffle people in regard to addiction: the inevitability or otherwise of 'just one drink' leading someone who has been addicted to relapse; the question as to whether such an act invalidates all the previous time spent in abstinence, and whether that drink has been secretly planned in advance; factors affecting the likelihood of relapse; the relative import- ance or otherwise for an individual of discovering what initially caused the addiction; and finally, the relevance of the rational and the emotional factors which determine the outcome of treatment.

Of all the misunderstandings of the nature of addiction, one of the most damaging both for the person themselves and for bystanders surrounds the question of how lapses and relapses are regarded. While most people have an awareness that it is not helpful to try to persuade someone who has had a struggle to stop drinking to have *just one drink*, the implications of the difference between a lapse and a relapse are far less widely appreciated. Of course it is appropriate to warn of the hazards of dabbling with *just one drink*. For someone who has been chronically addicted to any drug and has stopped, this is a risky idea and can all too easily lead into a full-scale relapse, as it did for Lawrence. Yet a lapse need not become a relapse. Much of our time at the hospital was spent in preventing just that. What is crucial is that the individual has become aware of the danger he or she is in and has sought help urgently at this point in order to prevent a full-blown relapse. An acute sense of shame can prevent this. The person feels such a failure. The danger then is that they will try to blot out the feeling by continuing to drink and feel that all their efforts to stay 'dry' have failed. They may feel too ashamed to let anyone discover what they've done, but this is the very moment when they could stop; when they really need the help. First of all they need to be accepted by the therapist without blame and praised for having the courage to come at this awful stage when their self-esteem has plummeted because they feel they have jettisoned all their previous achievement. Even a few weeks' abstinence for a person who wants to 'stay stopped', as the phrase goes, is worth a great deal. Nothing can take that achievement away from them. They need to value it for its own sake. They may need to describe what has happened when they lapsed into drinking or drug use at tedious length, far from rationally and coolly, beating themselves up or blaming the outside world, before they can calm down. The essential thing at this stage is for the therapist to give an absolutely clear message that a lapse need not become a relapse, if they stop *now*. The very fact that they have 'confessed' and come for help shows that they don't want to be dragged back into a life of addiction. All their strength needs to be mobilised to stop beating themselves up for what has happened and their part in it, to take responsibility for it, and to put themselves in a situation where they can cool down without alcohol or drugs around. Maybe they can learn something from what happened when they can reflect more calmly, but this comes later.

Lawrence's experience illustrates the phenomenon of how sudden and unexpected a lapse can be. He had no awareness that he was going to go to a pub and have a drink. Here he was in the middle of London, on a seemingly perfectly normal evening after work with his usual travelling companion, when his eyes lit upon a pub across the road. It was several years since he had drunk any alcohol. He suddenly got the idea. It is probably true to say that psychologically speaking there is no need for a particular mental state to arise for a person who has once been addicted to alcohol or drugs to drink or use drugs again. Alcohol, being socially acceptable, is available everywhere and carries with it the stamp of sociability. There sit a crowd of people enjoying themselves. Maybe Lawrence envied those drinkers their capacity to drink, most of them without risk of harm of any sort. Journalists, along with members of some other professions, such as chefs and doctors, are particularly at risk. At the point when Lawrence had this relapse, he had not joined the self-help group which he later used to good effect. This meant that he was no longer keeping alive thoughts about drinking and not drinking, as he later did by belonging to the hospital group and AA. Perhaps his awareness of his needs and vulnerabilities had not developed sufficiently at that point to prevent a relapse. In other words, he had stopped drinking, but he had not fully realised the change in orientation in every aspect of life that is part of the process of recovering.

The problem of relapse exists to a large extent because of the physical effects of long-term heavy drinking of alcohol on the mind and the body. Once a person has been addicted to it, it seems that it is no longer possible for them to have just one drink, even years after they initially stopped drinking.

Whether discovering the causes of an addiction actually helps in the long term is an open question. Lawrence takes the line that he doesn't know how it came about that he developed alcohol problems. He feels that he must simply accept that he is one of those people who cannot drink and therefore must get on with creating a life for himself without alcohol. Taking this stance implies accepting the reality of one's vulnerability.

Lawrence felt in the period immediately before he initially sought help, '*I just can't go on.*' He speaks about how the discrepancy between an intellectual and an emotional acceptance of the reality of his situation was important. Unless the awareness touches the heart, he feels, there is little prospect of an acceptance of the need to change. Reasoning on its own is of no use. In the therapeutic dialogue with people at this stage, empathic understanding on the part of the therapist forges a constructive rapport. With some people, an authoritative, knowledgeable stance in the therapist will be welcomed, as with Lawrence, while for others that would merely offer something to kick against and reject. Lawrence was highly intelligent, but it was his emotional awareness that gave him the needed impetus to carry his decision through. He accepted the authority of his psychiatrist as that of a wise figure. Therapists often underestimate the value of their presence and their manner.

Lawrence's whole life has now changed, and he sees this as the result of conscious thinking and planning. He is aware of the triggers that might lead him to drink again. He finds it helpful to hear other people in the group talking about their uncertainty about drinking or not drinking, using drugs or not using drugs. Keeping this at the front of his mind helps him. I have noticed how scornful people who have never plumbed the depths of addiction can be about ex-drinkers or ex-users in remaining focused on this. They scoff at people for developing a new dependence on groups. Actually there is a world of difference between being *dependent* on a chemical substance and being *attached* to people.

Before problems arising from his addiction interrupted his professional life, Lawrence was on a high rung of the career ladder. After his final detoxification he took early retirement, and although this may have blocked his achieving higher status within his profession, he has been most effective in other ways in his local community. He has put his talents to work in vital local projects and he has been a great asset to the hospital group. He has also supported very many people who are in trouble with alcohol. He has mended the rifts caused by his drinking behaviour in his marriage and family in such a way that when you meet him and his wife, it would never occur to you how precarious his survival once was.

In conclusion

Liability to relapse

Whether an individual became addicted through having a troubled life, past or present, seems to have little bearing on whether or not they will relapse once they have left their addiction behind. Liability to relapse is simply part of the picture of addiction.

Different outcomes of stopping

Up to the most recent occasion on which Lawrence stopped, he appears to have attempted simply to subtract alcohol from the equation of his current life and trusted his decision not to drink again. The last occasion was different. He accepted the medical opinion that he could not drink as other people could. As a consequence he made radical changes which represented a re-orientation of his entire life, not simply drinking or not drinking. Lawrence himself draws the extremely important distinction between simply not drinking and what AA calls sobriety.

Searching for the reason for the addiction

As therapists, we have seen that some people use the impossibility of finding a definitive answer to the question as to why they became addicted in the first place as a reason for postponing the decision to stop indefinitely. It is as if they believe that a magic answer will appear which will do the work for them. Meanwhile the addiction is busy taking its toll. Lawrence shows how the question lost its relevance once he became involved in creating a different life for himself.

Therapeutic input

The therapist Lawrence spoke to at the hospital did not talk only about symptoms and amounts of alcohol. Lawrence says that talking to his psychiatrist, changed the way he saw himself. He also says that the impact was emotional, not rational. These simple statements of his hold the key to the secret of how therapy works.

Chapter 15

The new task

Problems in the early days after stopping

There tends to be a common assumption that the main problems in the days immediately after stopping drug use or drinking are the physical symptoms of withdrawal (see Appendices 1 and 2). Many addicted people claim that fear of these symptoms prevents them from stopping and they may use this as a pretext for continuing to use drugs. Theodore Dalrymple, describing his work as a psychiatrist in a hospital and a prison in the UK, observed this frequently with people he treated (Dalrymple 2006: 9–32), as does John Booth Davies (Davies 1997: 52–54). Throughout the narratives in this book it is noticeable that withdrawal symptoms are mentioned only in passing, and only by a few people, except by Lee, a man who is still addicted – whose narrative opens Part 4.

Quite apart from withdrawal symptoms, anyone who has just stopped after years of addiction is prone to be in an exceptionally vulnerable state. The effects of years of ingesting any drugs in an addictive pattern weaken the body. Every system in the body is likely to be in poor shape. Sometimes patients who had very recently stopped would come to the hospital group from their wards accompanied by a nurse, and they frequently resembled those who have just undergone serious surgical intervention. Quite apart from physical problems, anyone whose life has deteriorated psychologically and socially to a significant degree ends up in a state of infantile dependence on the aid of others.

During the addiction, the answer to any discomfort has been for the addicted person to use more of the drug to hide the pain. That is no longer an option. Days and nights have to be faced without the drug at a stage where emotions are raw. Detoxification in a hospital or treatment setting can ease the anxieties by providing continuous physical and emotional care and monitoring. Many detoxifications, however, are carried out in the community, and many take place without the aid of any agency at that particular time, as in the case of three of the narrators, who were not in any treatment setting, but had the help of AA.

Challenges to be faced

The primary task facing an individual who has just stopped drinking or using drugs is to avoid a lapse or, if it happens, to deal with it. Without accomplishing this task, there can be no growth. Cravings for drugs and the temptation to start again are inevitable at some point. Not only is the drug itself the lure, but also the milieu of the drug using. Imagine having to change your friends and acquaintances, and the venues where you are in the habit of meeting them, overnight. Yet that is what people who stop using drugs usually require of themselves. Leaving behind a lifestyle and acquaintances all involved in the same patterns of drink or drug use is no easy matter. How many of us would be able to face abandoning what has become a daily routine? Habits and lifestyle become so entrenched. Without them we easily lose our bearings. Some people say they avoid going out altogether at the start of their abstinence. It is with the intention of avoiding temptation that many people would choose to go into a treatment centre away from their homes to detoxify if they had adequate means.

Another snare is the substitution of a different chemical substance. As nearly all of the narrators addicted to heroin drank alcohol as well, it could have been all too easy for them simply to increase the amount they drank. In a town on the south coast, when the disruption of a social centre associated with the use and supply of heroin had a major effect on the dissolution of the heroin network there that was equal in importance to the arrest of dealers or the expansion of treatment services, many drug users simply turned to other drugs, including alcohol (Fraser and George 1988). Many drift gently from one type of addiction to another, and that other may be equally or even more harmful. A particular difficulty is that alcohol is so much a part of the normal social fabric today.

A formidable task is that of facing up to whatever damage, physical or mental, the addiction has caused. There may be permanent scars that will never heal, but painful, too, is the awareness of the life and opportunities which slipped by while the individual was in the throes of addiction and had little energy left for anything else. Some chances will never come again. Equally hard is the task of facing up to the damage done to other people. Guilt and shame come flooding in for many people when they sober up and the drug is no longer there for them to hide behind. The question is bound to arise in some form or another as to what part the person themselves played in becoming so entangled in a need for the drug. Could disasters have been avoided? This is particularly painful when there has been something like a fatality, perhaps a road accident caused by drunk driving. Self-recriminations in themselves only increase the agony. This is perhaps one of the reasons why AA has succeeded in helping so many people, by understanding the need to face the consequences of their actions and the need to make amends if this is possible without causing further harm (see Appendix 4, Steps 8 and 9).

Addiction frequently evokes disapproval in others. The sorts of recriminations someone who has stopped using drugs may face are: Can you accept the blame for what you did? As well as reparation to people you have hurt, can you find a way of forgiving yourself and moving on without an insufferable burden of guilt and fear? There can be a great deal of prejudice to face, and this can easily provoke resentment. What about the ignorance people can display in relation to recovering from an addiction, for example when they offer 'just one drink'? It is especially hard for someone who seeks the approval of others to shore up flagging self-esteem. Self-help groups are particularly useful in that everyone in the group is in the same boat.

The significance of practical measures

At the very start, the advice of AA tends to take the form of the strictly practical, *Keep it simple* and *One day at a time* being two of the best known slogans. Filling the long hours which were formerly spent either in seeking drug supplies or in being intoxicated is the task. Two vital objectives are served by this, the first being to fill that gap in terms of the actual time and the second, keeping one's mind off the drug. David Lenson, referring to ways in which the sense of chronological time is disrupted in addiction, describes how the use of the drug fragments the notion of time into discrete particles. The daily cycle of obtaining the drug, using it, having the 'privileged moments' of experiencing the effects and then feeling those effects wear off has its own coherence (Lenson 1995: 37, 50). After stopping, time assumes a completely different aspect.

Lawrence repeats to himself the mantra, 'Don't be empty-handed and don't be empty-minded.' While the advice is seemingly simple, it has profound significance, for this is the start of thinking about what one is doing, instead of just doing it mindlessly, as in the addicted days. Ordering each day implies more than that, and another point of great significance is that although the tasks may be practical, they are symbolic of caring for oneself and one's life. In psychological terms people become able to use their inner resources to discover or rediscover for themselves a self-caring capacity. Khantzian gives a deficit in such a capacity as a prime reason for vulnerability to becoming addicted in the first place, alongside the desire to blot out mental anguish from awareness (Khantzian 2003). This is a key concept, but it is important to bear in mind that self-care may fluctuate in an individual, rather than being a fixed attribute. In the teens, for example, longing for excitement and adventure often overrules caution. Fulfilling a day's practical tasks as best one can after stopping is the seemingly simple start of building some sense of achievement. Equally useful is learning to accept less than perfection in oneself when plans go awry. Interestingly, some narrators had no contact with AA, yet they speak similarly about activities which gave them a new focus such as yoga or participating in a poetry group.

Developing self-awareness

Not only did the narrators find themselves learning practical steps to prevent them from taking that drink or drug, such as drinking plenty of non-alcoholic liquids or eating sweet things, but they also started thinking about their own responses: 'How do I respond to my own tiredness?' 'Can I become aware of my mental states, my emotions, my body, and my reactions to other people and situations?' Rather than their distress being experienced as a bodily sensation, they began to learn how to tolerate an awareness of their emotions. For some people, it was the first time in their lives that they had been consciously aware of doing this. In their use of the drug they had found a way of avoiding awareness. Instead of blanking out emotions by having bodily sensations, now they started to tolerate awareness of the different emotions as they ebbed and flowed.

The significance of accepting help

'Aftercare', formal or informal, is of great importance. People who have become addicted vary greatly in the quality of the relationships they have had with others prior to their addiction, but during the period of their addiction their principal relationship is with the drug. After stopping they need something or someone to support them until they become stronger. To acknowledge that one can only survive with the help, care and nurture of someone else is a powerful experience. Emotionally one is at the mercy of these helpers, but as well as inevitably posing tricky problems, this presents an opportunity for learning.

In the hospital group, it was striking to note over the years how success or failure in *staying stopped*, as the expression goes, rested in large measure upon whether or not people could accept help and could go on accepting that help. We aimed to encourage people to listen to what was going on, to engage in the group, and, most important, to continue to attend without panicking and running away when the going got rough and the desire to maintain abstinence began to founder. Johnnie describes how he angrily slammed out of an AA meeting, but he was able later to overcome his fury with the group. Those who have been isolated and defensive may gradually come to see that nothing is demanded of them other than their presence. Many people become less defensive or aggressive and start to trust the group a little. It is a powerful experience for an individual who has lived in isolation under the shadow of addiction to be accepted by others at a time when they are beginning to retrieve or even discover aspects of themselves which have been effectively obscured from their awareness during the addiction or of which they have perhaps never been aware. Addiction, by its very nature, can make people behave in selfish, destructive ways which are not predominantly a part of their nature at other times in their lives. When they stop, they may be overwhelmed by self-reproach. Low self-esteem, sometimes disguised as churlishness, is an all too familiar picture in those who are addicted, whether this preceded the addiction or is a result of it.

Relying on others for support

If people can identify sufficiently with their helpers to listen to their advice, then they can start the process of discovering how to help themselves in dealing with the various difficulties which inevitably arise. However much cognitive mastery is important in learning how to handle difficulties, continual support is crucial when emotions run high. It is so easy to feel empty and discouraged at the thought of a lifetime without the drug which has become the object of one's desire, and this is the time when being able to turn to someone for support is vital. This experience of relying on a person or people rather than on a drug can feel new and strange. As one narrator said, 'I didn't have friends in my drug using days. I had boon companions who needed me to be using drugs to justify their own continuing use.' It is this experience of relying on a person or on people rather than on a chemical substance that holds the key to radical change.

There is another side to relating to somebody who helps you. Sooner or later they are likely to disappoint you in some way. They don't quite live up to expectations, but you still want their support. This situation itself offers an opportunity to experience the coming together of opposite emotions. The question is: can you tolerate their imperfections? This is what Melanie Klein understood as the challenge for the infant – to accept that they could come to feel 'love' and 'hate' towards the same person, usually mother, without the world caving in (Klein 1980: 176–236). She called this human capacity by a name some people find misleading, the 'depressive position', but the name aside, it is a crucial factor in every single relationship we have in life. It implies being able to tolerate our mixed feelings rather than idealising or demonising the person or people to whom we are relating. In fact I would say that this is what really enables people to have and to keep and to build relationships. The experience of being offered and accepting support that is 'good enough' promotes healthy development. It is a matter of accepting that human beings, including oneself, are prone to fall short of expectations. After stopping drug use, many people showed that this painful learning actually transformed their lives.

Facing the challenges of the early days after stopping promotes growth

The challenge of the very first days after stopping can be summed up as the need to deal with the lack of the drug and the aftermath of addiction – as much as can be done in the immediate present. In the process of developing the necessary self-awareness, individuals, free of drugs, can start to get to know themselves afresh, particularly in terms of their own needs and vulnerability. In practical terms, the task involves finding ways of dealing both with cravings for the drug and with problems caused by the addiction, and with filling the gap left by the drug. From a psychological perspective, the challenge lies in the process of becoming more self-aware and in accepting the support that is offered.

Laying the foundations of recovery

The physical and behavioural changes caused by stopping drug use are accompanied by a shift in the inner world, and such a change, however much it may be for the eventual good, can be confusing. Dealing with change can provoke anxiety in itself. It would be surprising if there were not a sense of loss, as well as a sense of relief, because of the gaping hole left after stepping out of the drug-dominated life. However, in spite of this being a very challenging time, the act of facing up to the task is what opens the way to a promising future. In a recent book Stephen Joseph and Alex Linley (2008) draw together contributions from psychologists working in various different contexts to explore the paradox that the distressing struggles associated with the aftermath of trauma can be accompanied by growth (Morland *et al.* 2008: 57). Similar to this is the growth and resilience shown by people in facing painful challenges immediately after leaving addiction behind.

Whether the addiction arose in the first place as a defence against painful experience, or on account of some aspect of the social environment, or as a search for something elusive and just beyond one's grasp does not alter the fact that at this stage the challenge of staying clear of the addiction makes one clear demand – 'To thine own self be true.'

Part 4

In the long term

Four narrators in this part describe what has happened to them in the long term. The first is still addicted, and his bleak story is told by presenting an interview with his former psychiatrist, who had not seen him for many years. The dialogue between them shows how difficult it is to penetrate beneath the surface of a life preoccupied with drugs. The other three narrators, by contrast, speak eloquently about what they have done since they left their addictions behind and about what is important to them now.

Chapter 16

A bleak picture: Hoping against hope

Lee is one of the original group of teenagers treated locally for heroin injecting in the early 1970s who belonged to the cohort of the long-term follow-up study (Rathod *et al.* 2005). His narrative shows what life is like for someone who is still addicted. He is once again engaged in outpatient treatment at the hospital, where the treatment policy has changed and methadone is now prescribed. Here he is speaking to Dr. Rathod, his former psychiatrist, who had not seen him for many years. While the other narrators spoke freely, Lee tends to respond in a question and answer style, hence the different presentation of this narrative.

LEE: I continue methadone use because I've always been drug orientated since I've been sixteen years old. It's always an easy way out of any mental problem. It was an easy way out, that's all. I was opiates free for six years, but I had a girlfriend who was unfaithful to me and I happened to bump into an old face. Then I started again and I escalated it. At first it gave me a great buzz. And then the buzz went down, as it always does. As your resistance builds up you don't enjoy it so much, so you up your intake. It's just *me*. I want to cut down now, but I'm not *allowed* to consult with my GP about any other treatment. That makes you continue the habit. Because if I was allowed to get some treatment from my GP, such as diazepam for during the day and temazepam of an evening for, say, four weeks, that would stop my drinking problem as well, but I'm not *allowed* to. That's been blocked by the hospital. I'm not allowed to take any other medication at all, otherwise my methadone will be stopped. It will be stopped in December anyway, and that's the time when I can go to my GP and get my alcohol problem out the way.

DR. RATHOD: They are not treating you for your alcohol problem at the hospital really?

LEE: No, just my methadone.

DR. RATHOD: I see. So Alan[1] doesn't concentrate on your alcohol problem much?

LEE: He does. Yes, he's very concerned about that.

DR. RATHOD: Yeah. But nothing is being done about it?

LEE: Not at the moment. He won't, he, mm – the only thing I know that he's said was that if my GP wants to deal with my alcohol problem, i.e. with the diazepam and temazepam, then he can take on my methadone as well, which he wasn't prepared to do.

DR. RATHOD: In what ways do you think methadone helps you?

LEE: Well, it doesn't, really. It's a burden. I'm on 10mg, which is very minimal, but when you stop that, within three days it really hits you. The last time that he cut me off, he cut me down from 30ml very quickly to nothing over a period of seven days.

DR. RATHOD: Well, that's not the same thing. You have been on 10ml for how long now?

LEE: About six weeks, three weeks.

DR. RATHOD: I mean, you can go on taking it, but don't give me that stuff that you're going to have a desperate withdrawal after 10ml.

LEE: I know what I went through in Holland when I come off of a large script. The withdrawal is very severe for me recently.

DR. RATHOD: But how much were you taking then?

LEE: I was on diamorphine[2] and methadone. So quite a lot. Yeah. Quite a lot.

DR. RATHOD: I mean, I don't mind you playing games with yourself – I'm just seeing the flaws in your argument.

LEE: There's always flaws.

DR. RATHOD: But 10ml is a very little amount.

LEE: Yeah, but all that will do, for that to be stopped abruptly, which I don't mind if he wants to, will probably push my alcohol intake back up.

DR. RATHOD: Yes. So in fact, that's your blackmail.

LEE: No.

DR. RATHOD: 'I can stop it if I want to, but you know what will happen? – I'll drink more!'

LEE: Well, no. He tells me I'll do that, which is probably right. He's going to cut me down to 5ml in about three weeks' time, and that'll be for two months and that'll be it then.

DR. RATHOD: OK.

LEE: And then, with a little bit of help. . .

DR. RATHOD: What do you think would help your problems? *You* say. What other treatment do you get here?

LEE: Nothing.

DR. RATHOD: Did you have any treatment at all in the Seventies? Because you used to see a chap called Dr. Rathod. Feel any benefit at all, or was it more a punishment than anything?

LEE: It wasn't punishment, no. I needed help.

DR. RATHOD: Yes, but what did it do to you? It didn't do any good to you.

LEE: No.

DR. RATHOD: You still continued to. . .

LEE: I know, yeah. It just. . . I suppose it's the people that I was with, everybody was doing it, and, you know, I know it was, 'This has got to stop!' but it was always in front of you, because everybody I knew was doing this thing. And it was always just, 'I've got to cheat.'

DR. RATHOD: Yes. So you've never been abstinent after any treatment? But you hope to?

LEE: Well I was for five years.

DR. RATHOD: But did you have any treatment for that?

LEE: No.

DR. RATHOD: You see, that's very strange. How did you get off for five years?

LEE: I sat through it for five years in Holland. I didn't sleep for three weeks, virtually. I drank a lot of spirits, alcohol, but I was just determined. And then after six weeks I actually got back to feeling somewhere near normal. You go through a lot of stages, in your body, different things. Some things don't take four or five weeks to come out. You get some very strange reactions. And then it settled down and I went back to work and I was OK and it was just a problem of the relationship I had at the time. Because I knew of heroin, it was a corner to run to.

DR. RATHOD: You know, five years is not a short time. You went through a hell of a lot of withdrawal. So it amazes me when you talk about 10ml and 'terrible withdrawal'. A chap who stood all this. Now you can say, 'But I was younger, doctor.' You can use that.

LEE: Oh, perhaps. Perhaps I was more physically fit for it. I'm definitely not now.

DR. RATHOD: How much were you taking at that time, before you started the cut-down?

LEE: What, before I gave it up completely? I was on two 30mg of diamorphine a day, and I think 40ml of methadone linctus a day.

DR. RATHOD: And how long were you on it?

LEE: I think that was about four years.

DR. RATHOD: So what made you suddenly go to Holland — this pilgrimage?

LEE: I was seeing a Dutch girl at the time. And it was an escape route. I went to get away from it. And these people — they guided me away from any of that. One of them used to be an addict. So he knew the situation and he was quite a good help, you know. He tried to keep me more occupied in other things, you know.

DR. RATHOD: Mm. But you drank quite a lot?

LEE: A lot, yeah. An awful lot. I think that's where I started to, you know, where my drink problem really took off, there.

DR. RATHOD: So, you substituted the one for the other?

LEE: Yeah.

DR. RATHOD: Yes. I see. What do you think would help you to stop the habit?

LEE: I've got all I need to help me stop the habit, which is a good home life. I just need to – how can I say without being – I need to be treated with the respect and a delicacy which I require – at my age, and for the amount of time I've been taking drugs? I've been taking drugs for twenty-eight years. And some people just really don't take that in. They don't understand. Perhaps they think they're talking to somebody that's only been taking drugs for two or three years. And it's been obviously a lot, lot longer than that. And it takes time to get it out of your mind.

DR. RATHOD: But, I'll tell you about a chap called Lee who did it years ago.

LEE: I know, yes.

DR. RATHOD: He didn't use that argument then, that he wanted to be treated with delicacy and respect. What happened to that bloke then? Was he a different chap then?

LEE: I just feel that I shouldn't have to go through what I went through then, which is, there was no other treatment available. I feel that in this day and at this time and in this country I shouldn't have to go through that amount of grief. It can be done gently, I'm sure, but also it's got to be me that wants to do it. *I'm* the main problem. Always. So it'll be me that wants to do it. Which I do.

DR. RATHOD: I don't think you are the problem, I have a feeling you're making yourself a problem. If I didn't know about the way you did it years ago, I would have agreed with you.

LEE: Mm. Yes, I have done it and it can be done. I've proved that myself. But now, I'm not very well at all, and I don't think my body would be able to take that. . . strain.

DR. RATHOD: Do you think your body will take continual poisoning?

LEE: Of course not, no. It's got to be stopped. Sure. It'll kill me in the end – at an early age.

DR. RATHOD: So when you say your body cannot take it, perhaps you are poisoning your body more than you think.

LEE: I'm sure I am, really. Because I know how I feel most of the time.

DR. RATHOD: So this is a contradiction, isn't it? 'I don't want to die, but I'm not doing much to. . .'

LEE: To help me not do it. Yeah. I know.

DR. RATHOD: Does that make any sense?

LEE: It makes a lot of sense but it's very. . .

DR. RATHOD: Don't use the word 'very hard'. If I had not known about you in Holland, I would have said, 'Yes, it is very hard for you.'

LEE: I think really it's probably more of a drink problem than drugs, now.

DR. RATHOD: Well, I was just thinking that if you could at least say, 'This donkey has been burdened with so much, so many things. He's a tired donkey.' You could at least take some load off his back.

LEE: And give me a rest, yeah.

DR. RATHOD: Couldn't you?

LEE: Yeah. But I want to, in a month's time.

DR. RATHOD: Well, the proof of the pudding — as they say.

LEE: Is the eating, yeah.

DR. RATHOD: So you don't get any drugs from anybody else?

LEE: No. None at all.

DR. RATHOD: Do sometimes your old mates give you any?

LEE: No. I don't really see old mates like that, if you like, because I don't think they're mates anyway. They want to have more people involved with them, because they don't want to be on their own. For somebody to put any addictive drug, any opiate, in any shape or form, in front of me, he's not a friend. It's the only way they keep you — well; it's like being on a leash.

DR. RATHOD: What is interesting is that — what do you think the treatment consists of? Is there any treatment really?

LEE: Well, I did it last Christmas, although — disregarding the methadone, it was the alcohol. Bad timing — it was right on top of Christmas, but I was getting diazepam during the day, that's Valium, and temazepam at night, and it's all on paper. Because I was coming virtually every fortnight for a blood test and it showed how my platelet count went to a reasonable level, so my liver count came down, so it was working. I cut it right out, totally, for a couple of weeks or something, and then I went in to drink sociably. Perhaps a Friday, like, you go down the pub to have a pint? Something like that, you know? It was on top of Christmas. People — these are family — good people, they really did go a bit too far with it. You know, 'Would you like some lemon barley water?' when we were eating Christmas dinner. I said, 'No, I'll have a glass of wine like everybody else has.' So I blew that one. I just need another go at it, which my GP is prepared to do. I don't think there's an awful lot you can do.

DR. RATHOD: What about things like Narcotics Anonymous?

LEE: I didn't like NA at all, because I'm not religious in any way whatsoever. I never have been from a very early age. It's not a new thing. And they are very religious and it didn't suit me at all. I did know some people there. I didn't like the way they operated. I don't like — I'm not going to sit in a circle when there's two or three people that are *ignorants*, basically.

DR. RATHOD: The same you would apply to AA?

LEE: AA? Well, I went to one here and it was another 'opposite'. All they want to do is shout all the time. And it just gave me a headache. I don't need that. A nice peaceful time — I'm forty-four now, I'm happy indoors, very happy indoors. I like my bit of space. That is me. I've got a nice wife and I can do it there. I don't need anybody else.

My mother supports me an awful lot. I'm trying to deny having a severe alcohol problem. That's what it is. I'm embarrassed to admit I've got an alcohol problem.

DR. RATHOD: Right. Why are you embarrassed?

LEE: I don't know. It's making me very ill and I hate to admit it.

DR. RATHOD: What other problems have you got?

LEE: Um. Well, I can't work, if that's what you mean?

DR. RATHOD: Yes.

LEE: Because I'm not well enough to work. Apart from that I haven't any other problems.

DR. RATHOD: You haven't any other problem?

LEE: No. I'm happy indoors. No other problems really. Only *me* really.

DR. RATHOD: Do you look back and say how you could have done things differently?

LEE: I *wish*.

DR. RATHOD: Yes.

LEE: I don't look back to see if I could have done anything different because there's no point. There's no point in looking back because it's too late. I've already done it. I used to do things like pigeon shooting and target shooting too, but the police won't let me have a licence now.

DR. RATHOD: So what's going to be the future of Lee?

LEE: I don't know. I can't put a date or − I can't see much in the future at the moment. I'm just plodding on day to day, hoping everything'll stay in place.

DR. RATHOD: Yes. [A long pause] Do you, underneath, when you sit quietly, do you feel optimistic or pessimistic about life?

LEE: I get very depressed on how I feel at the moment, and I do try to be optimistic, yes, because it's the only way forward.

DR. RATHOD: What depresses you?

LEE: Just having to rely on things. To rely on drugs. To rely on alcohol. My mother supports me an awful lot − gives me money. To have to rely on other people, when people should be relying on me at my age. I should be supporting them.

DR. RATHOD: Do you sleep well?

LEE: No. Not very well at all.

DR. RATHOD: What is the difficulty?

LEE: Just restlessness. I get up and have a cup of tea at turned three o'clock in the morning, watch the TV for a couple of hours, and I might go back to bed again for a couple of hours. It's very erratic.

DR. RATHOD: What is your best time of the day? Or is there no 'best' time?

LEE: There's no best time.

DR. RATHOD: All hours are grey?

LEE: − ish.

DR. RATHOD: They are all greyish. So life is not a very contented time?

LEE: It's not very colourful, no. I'm not very content.

DR. RATHOD: I mean, except for Michelle, it seems to me there aren't many stars shining on you.

LEE: No. That's exactly how I feel. If it wasn't for Michelle, I'd have nothing at all.

DR. RATHOD: Yes. Which is quite sad, isn't it?

LEE: Very sad.

DR. RATHOD: Yes. Do you sometimes cry?

LEE: Yeah, I do. I do, yes. I do get quite emotional. I think that's depression.

DR. RATHOD: Don't give me the jargon. Do you cry?

LEE: Yeah. I do cry.

DR. RATHOD: What do you cry about?

LEE: Um. I just wish things could be better. And I don't feel very well – all the time. And I get fed up with that, and I just wish things could be different.

DR. RATHOD: Would it be right to say that you have great difficulty in taking any advice?

LEE: Yes. You're quite right. Yeah. Um. Simply because I know how I feel inside.

DR. RATHOD: Advice means you surrender. You don't ask questions. Because then that is not advice. That is saying, 'Tell me the truth, but really I want to hear what is good about me. I don't want you to throw bricks at me.'

LEE: Yes. I know what you're saying. I want to stop this thing.

DR. RATHOD: Do you think you have the ability to stop?

LEE: I've done it before. I'm sure I can do it again.

DR. RATHOD: Do you believe that you have got the ability now?

LEE: Yes, I do.

DR. RATHOD: Then tell me, what is stopping you?

LEE: I just need a bit of help, medical help. I can't see me getting through it otherwise. Too many temptations out there.

DR. RATHOD: Yes, but life is full of temptations.

LEE: But there again, if you seriously want to do it – in here.

DR. RATHOD: You will do it.

LEE: And I do. But I feel that I don't want to go through what I went through in Holland again. I want to go through it with at least a little bit of comfort, instead of that.

DR. RATHOD: Yeah. Do you sometimes feel that you are going to die soon?

LEE: Yeah. Yes, I do.

DR. RATHOD: Yeah. And so you are saying, 'If I am going to die, let me die at least peacefully.'

LEE: If you're right, yeah.

DR. RATHOD: No, because if that is the situation, then I can understand everything you are saying.

LEE: It is like that, yeah. But I, then also I don't want to leave – I don't want to. . . leave and cause so much heartache to the people around me that I really do love. See, it's easy for me to go, just like that, finished, me gone, but that's very selfish. My wife, my mother, you know, it's. . .

DR. RATHOD: If you have lost faith, as I see it, Lee, you say you would like to be optimistic, but life is shades of grey.

LEE: Mm.

DR. RATHOD: You feel that you might die sooner than a person of your age. . .

LEE: . . . would do normally, yeah.

DR. RATHOD: So all these pull you back and you say, 'So if that is the scenario, why should I suffer?'

LEE: Mm.

DR. RATHOD: Does that make any sense?

LEE: It does, yeah.

DR. RATHOD: Because then at least one can say, at least this is the Lee that I am facing. And you have to carry him through, as best as you can.

LEE: Mm. Well, then – I could do with a bit more positive.

DR. RATHOD: Yes, but the thing is, Lee, you have never listened to advice. And I don't think you have changed.

LEE: Mm. No.

DR. RATHOD: You know what is the right thing for Lee, and your argument always has been, 'I know.'

LEE: It is, yeah. It is.

DR. RATHOD: What you call positive is what *you* think is positive. Not what *I* think is positive.

LEE: I can only say that I've been there, many times, and I know what it's like. Ask me, and I'll tell you what it's like for me.

Lee is now forty-four years old and in poor health physically and mentally. He has not been able to work for the past four years. His drinking has damaged his liver and his cognitive functioning – he cannot remember his landline phone number. The first part of this dialogue shows how he expends his energy in resentment at the treatment plan that has been proposed for him. By this time, the policy and staff at the hospital had changed, and a reducing methadone regime was offered. Neither the hospital nor his GP would prescribe the tranquillisers which he was demanding in addition to his methadone, for reasons which become clear as he speaks.

Lee's narrative presents a stark contrast to the others in this section, for it gives a brief glimpse of the plight of someone who has not been able to break free of addiction. Here is another narrator whose childhood was overshadowed by a tragic death, for his elder brother, four years older, died of cancer at home at the age of eight. He can remember being all too aware that his brother was in great pain. What a terrible memory! Like

Bernadette, it seems that he was haunted by his own and his family's pain. Such an experience marks a child as very different from his peers. As a teenager, he liked his own company, and often truanted from school. His drug injecting started in his teens and continued during his first marriage, which ended in divorce – his wife also used drugs. He sees nothing of the now adult child of that marriage.

He comes to the interview complaining. He has achieved nothing that he is proud of. He has no good feelings about his earlier treatment. It is difficult for Dr. Rathod to lead him away from details about his present drug use and treatment. This type of communication resembles the conversations of many long-term drug users who can hardly be drawn away from descriptions and arguments about the amounts, strengths, effects and availability of various drugs. These details can preoccupy them to the exclusion of virtually everything else. The addiction is in command.

What is most noticeable is how unwilling Lee is to take any responsibility for the situation he is in, and blames everyone and everything but himself. Here his attitude illustrates what Melanie Klein termed the *paranoid-schizoid position*, where the other person is seen in extreme terms as completely good or completely bad, with no grey area and with no tolerance or understanding towards the *human* nature of that other person. In this manner, Lee believes he is a victim, a role which prevents growth. In the midst of all this, however, from time to time he betrays a different awareness when he admits that he always has to cheat, and that *he* is the main problem. He presents a sad picture of trying unsuccessfully to hide from his despair and disillusionment. Dr. Rathod puts it to him that he is unwilling to accept any advice. Lee has not a good word to say for his current therapist at the hospital, although he goes on attending appointments to receive methadone from him. He is sorry for himself, but cannot take in any advice which might be useful to him. His argumentative stance cuts him off from anyone who challenges him. He will not listen. This is an example of a specific form of the isolation in addiction of which Smaldino and his colleagues write (Smaldino 1991).

The self-righteous air at the start of the interview, where he seems to be using confused emotion to obliterate his despair, collapses into something very different at the end, when Lee admits that his life isn't worth living. Here he does show a sense of responsibility, when he says that he will not kill himself because of what this would do to his wife and mother. He admits that he should be supporting them.

He expresses no pleasure in anything. All his statements are justifications for not making changes. He paints himself as the victim of an unhelpful world, trapped by people who don't help him, whereas he is really the victim of his addiction. He projects this on to others. He blames the police, for example, for not allowing him to have a firearms licence, while it is his own criminal record which makes this out of the question. He did have five years free of heroin, though he was not free of chemical substances, as he increased his drinking, using alcohol as a drug. But he says nothing good about those five years, apart from the fact that he proved to himself that he could stop. He blames the friends who helped and encouraged him for his increased use of alcohol, and he blames his return to heroin on his faithless girlfriend. He refuses to accept Dr. Rathod's suggestion that he may be overestimating the effects of stopping the small amount of methadone he is currently being prescribed. The addiction has taken over Lee's life so that in place of growth, there is deterioration. It has led him into an enfeebled infantile position, dependent on others. It has a life of its own which is sucking his life-blood dry. What was once exciting and pleasurable has enthralled him to such an extent that he now has no pleasurable life left.

In conclusion

A close-up of long-term addiction

This dialogue illustrates several features common to those who have been addicted for many years. Lee is extremely unwell, demonstrating many of the physical effects listed in Appendices 1 and 2, as he is addicted to both alcohol and methadone. He is also in despair and suffers from agitation and disturbed patterns of sleep. A common feature of people at this stage is a preoccupation with themselves and with their drugs to the exclusion of virtually everything else. Life has contracted to these elements, and nothing else can interest them. The drugs have 'got him'.

Relationships with others

It is sometimes impossible to tell whether an addicted person has always tried to lean on others, refusing to take responsibility for him or herself, or whether this is an effect of the addiction, but the outcome is a state resembling an infantile dependence on what the world can offer. All sense of being able to be effective without the drugs has receded.

A perverse element in addiction

In spite of all the harm drugs have caused his mind and body, the addiction has taken hold to such an extent that he persists in claiming to know best what treatment will help him: more drugs.

The role of the therapist

Lee has been a sore trial to his GP and to his therapist at the hospital. They have both persisted in resisting his wheedling and stood firm in facing the real problem – his angry refusal to take responsibility for his part in his predicament or even to consider their advice. This gives a glimpse of the difficulties therapists have to face. Their primary task is to create a space where the addicted person can bring themselves and their thoughts and feelings to someone who knows the score and will have the courage and patience not to collapse or run away under the burden of the patient's troubled presence.

Sometimes an addicted person will refuse to engage in trying to change, but blaming him or her will do no good. That would simply be to retaliate or to act out the addicted patient's own desire to blame, rather than throwing some light on what is going on. Nor must the therapist be intimidated into engaging in sessions when the patient is intoxicated. Making clear ground rules is part of creating a safe therapeutic space. Therapists need to see beyond and beneath the surface of someone's words. In this dialogue, Dr. Rathod makes some penetrating remarks at which Lee does not take umbrage. Here is a doctor with years of experience who forms a rapport. It is painful to witness such despair as Lee comes to admit by the end of the dialogue. Yet if people are not brought to the point of acknowledging the worst, they may never be willing to change direction.

Notes

1 One of the facilitators of the relapse prevention group, was Lee's therapist at the hospital at the time this conversation took place.
2 Diamorphine (heroin hydrochloride), a powerful opiate analgesic, is the name for medically prescribed heroin.

Chapter 17

A very major change for me

Geoff is an engineer, now in his late forties. He drank increasingly heavily from his teens until he was forty, when he had his last drink. He received outpatient treatment at the hospital after he stopped, having several months of individual appointments, concurrently with attending both AA and the hospital relapse prevention group. He later trained to be one of the volunteer counsellors at the hospital. Geoff articulates graphically how he perceives his development in recovery.

I had been introduced to counselling previously under the NHS some years ago when I'd been in a psychiatric hospital for three weeks because I'd stopped drinking suddenly. I dried out and they kept me in hospital for another couple of weeks, but it took me four years before I finally got to the point where I could stop drinking. I'd not been in treatment for some time.

I can't actually remember what day it was. It was one of those things – my drinking was such that I haven't been able to piece together those final events – but I do know that by the first of February I'd had my last drink. I had been in phases of trying to stop drinking for a while. My drinking had got me into such a state that I thought about committing suicide. I went to see my GP and said I was still drinking and she tried to get me into hospital or a treatment centre at that time, but there was no place, so she got me into the psychiatric hospital here, where I was for one night. But I wouldn't stay there, so I discharged myself.

When I went to the GP that day I was in such a state that I was unsafe to be on my own. She wasn't happy to see me roaming around. I have to confess that I was so drunk that I wasn't surprised. I went home – she insisted that I didn't drive home, she got the community psychiatric nurse, I think it was, to drive me home – and I went in to get an overnight case and a toothbrush, and to finish off the bottle of whisky that I had in hand. Apparently, from what they told me, I presented quite a coherent argument, but I have no recollection of it whatsoever! I used to have blank patches. I hadn't realised what a blackout was until I'd been in AA for some time and people talked about having no memory. I just went to sleep and that was it, and I hadn't realised at all what I'd done. In the group, I learned a lot more about my alcoholism. Up to the early days when I first went to AA, I never understood about alcoholism and what it really was. Even after I'd stopped drinking and gone to the group, it was some while before I really comprehended what alcoholism was.

The first few days there was a heavy temptation to take another drink, because I had stopped suddenly with no further treatment. I had no medication and I had discharged myself from the hospital and gone against the doctor's advice to drink a half a bottle that day, a quarter the next, etc. to avoid withdrawal fits and DTs[1]. One way or another I learned to resist that temptation. AA taught me to take plenty of fluid and plenty of sweet things to help me over those first few days. After the physical craving went, fortunately I didn't have a great deal of emotional or mental craving for a drink. That actually went when I took the step because I realised what drink had done to me and I didn't want any more drink. AA has a sort of programme as you know, and I did the first three Steps[2] at that time. I realised I couldn't do my recovery by myself, and I accepted a Higher Power, which for me was actually AA itself. I took those three steps. Looking back, I can see I actually did that at that time.

I did stop because by that time my life was falling apart. My wife and children had left me. I suppose I finally realised what my drinking had cost me. Because my drinking hadn't only cost me a lot of money. It caused me health problems, it cost me my job, my career, and I suppose all those things. Finally the realisation hit me at that point. It finally registered with me that I was the one who was drinking, and at that point I stopped putting it *out there*[3]. And that was the last drink that I had. Then I did engage in treatment. I had counselling at the hospital once a week for several months, and I came to the relapse prevention group on a Monday night, and I also went to AA several evenings in the week, which I'd gone to intermittently in the past. So that's where I ended up, if you like. Those were the influences leading into my recovery.

I'd found the counselling I had before very useful to dispose of a number of things, a number of, I think 'resentments' is probably the right word, things that had happened in my childhood that I hadn't ever talked to anybody about. I suppose actually since I've been in recovery, and doing the counselling course as well, I've realised that talking it through, things sound quite different, expressing them in words, to holding them in your mind, you know? You actually speak them out loud, particularly to another person, and it moves their power. There were two or three things dating back to my childhood, things I'd never spoken to anybody about, and I spoke to my counsellor about it, and then got rid of it. So that was one of the influences on my recovery.

Also there were a couple of people in AA whom I became particularly friendly with, who were particularly helpful to me. This lady, much the same age as myself, was going through the reverse of what I was going through at that time. As a recovering alcoholic, she was divorcing her husband at the time when my wife was divorcing me. We had a great deal in common, and we used to see one another very regularly. She was, I suppose, what AA call a sponsor and it was mutual support. I was able to support her from sharing my experiences, and it was a great deal of support, an ability to understand what was happening, because we had the other side being aired, if you like. And that was very, very, valuable.

It was a painful time. And it was because of that, because of the supportive element, and also, another lady, again much the same age as me, who also was very helpful, and gave very sound advice – these were two people who I'd known by now for some time, because I'd been going to AA for three or four years previously. I shared exactly what was going on in my life from day to day, and shared exactly what I felt about it. There was nothing in the sense of what was happening at that time that I wasn't prepared to talk to them about.

I think that is one of the things recovery has taught me, that in actual fact, bottling up these emotions or these feelings doesn't do me any good. I can't handle them by bottling them up, but if I share what's going on then I don't build up the resentments or the misunderstandings. They can grow out of proportion. If you share them, they don't disappear but you manage to handle them and they don't have the same power. You don't have that pain and that resentment within your mind. They go.

The physical cravings went away very quickly – yeah, they used to come back, I'd think it'd be nice to have a drink, but I found one way or another to say, 'That's not the answer,' or distract myself by doing something else – clean my shoes, go and have a bath, have a cup of tea, whatever it was. As I say, AA gave me the tools to get past those times, and they gradually went away. Just occasionally, even now, there are times when I think, 'Wouldn't it be nice to have a drink' – in a social sense – but I know that's not an option for me. I know that for me, drinking is not something that I can do. I definitely couldn't, and I just accept that. I used to worry about all the old things, like how am I going to cope with a family birthday, because I always used to associate drink with those good times, but again, I learned a few tricks from AA about not going to an event without being prepared for what you were going to do when someone said, 'Do you want a drink?' I'd say, 'Yes, I'll have an orange juice.' And that's progressively got easier, as you build up a bit of experience, you realise that not everybody does drink, especially with the drink-driving laws. You're not the social outcast you thought you might have been. I suppose the most glaring example is that at the beginning of the year I went on holiday to Cyprus, and at the end of the meal they'd come round with a liqueur, and put it on the table in front of you. And it was easy enough to refuse those, you know. I thought, 'What a change, Geoff, from ten years ago.'

One of the other major things that recovery's done for me, is, as I've touched on before, about 'putting the blame out there'. When I get into a situation, I tend now to ask myself, 'What was your part, Geoff?' Not to say, 'What did somebody else do?' or 'What effect did that have on you?' I tend to try to ask myself, if I look at what my part was, instead of blaming everybody else for it, then I think I've really taken responsibility for myself, if you like. It's part of recovery that I do actually have to take responsibility for things – I pause, because my responsibility can change. I sometimes do try to think, you know, 'What is it that's related to my having stopped drinking? What is it that's related to my having changed?' You see, my divorce went through, so I no longer have a wife, and my children went away. My children have grown up now, they have their own lives, so I don't have any children to support. I have never gone back on the career ladder. I was out of work for a long time, for three or four years, and when I went back I didn't go back into the position I had been in, because nobody would have me. I then moved job and found I actually could have a very comfortable living without taking on the responsibility, and that's good enough.

I'm an engineer. I've not gone back into management, but into actually doing engineering, from which I'd been quite divorced. What I do now is like going back to my roots. I get my hands dirty. I don't have the staff responsibility that I used to have. I am responsible for *myself*. When I was a project manager, I had responsibility for a staff of thirty, so I had all the staff responsibilities as well, such as career development and all that. And I don't have any of those now. I work within a team but I have nobody reporting directly to me. So there's been quite a change in the responsibilities that I have, I must say, both at home and at work.

I'm comfortable with the work that I do, it puts me back rather closer to the nuts and bolts of engineering rather than the paperwork, and my needs are less, I'm able to live comfortably on a lower income than I had. So that's been another change in my life. And I sometimes look at my life, the way it is, and ask myself how much it's a result of my not drinking, and how much of it is the result of some of the consequential things, and some of the decisions, if you like, that I've made as a result of that. So I live a life where I'm responsible for myself, but I don't have to be responsible for other people. I care deeply for the people round me, for my family, for my two daughters, and in fact for my ex-wife. Those relationships were totally destroyed at the time, the relationships with my daughters. The two of them went away, and one of them didn't speak to me for several months. I tried to work it out. I think it was about three years till the other one spoke to me. My wife, when she came to see me in those first days, was so frightened that she had to come with a companion. The relationship was really bitter. But in recovery, my relationship with my wife has changed considerably and now we've become good friends.

I have now got on good terms with both my daughters, although one didn't come to see me for a long time, but then came on my birthday, but she didn't invite me to her marriage. That was a pretty painful experience. But I had the support of someone from AA over that period and especially for that day. Things have changed so radically that we now all meet up for Christmas and birthdays. I am supporting my wife emotionally – she has what I believe to be terminal cancer. These relationships have all been restored. I regard this as a major achievement and the biggest outcome of my having stopped drinking. I didn't stop drinking to get them back. It wasn't the motivation, because I don't think it would have worked. I've talked to a lot of people in AA who have had similar experiences, some of whom have had the same losses, some of whom have not been able to re-establish their relationships.

I suppose really the other thing that I value is that I'm at peace with myself. Let's try and think what I'd like to say about it. I suppose I'm more self-confident. I have a better understanding of who I am, where I am, what I am today. I'd have been better off if I'd known some of these things when I was thirty-five. I'm not struggling to be what I think somebody else thinks I should be. I'm not struggling to be what my mother thinks I should be, for example. I don't strive to take on her expectations of me. I take what my own expectations are, but I don't take on other people's expectations of me. I suppose that's the biggest thing in knowing who I am. I do what I do. At work I've got myself into a situation where I'm content and happy with what I do.

I guess that one thing that I've done, is that I can say no. The other thing I've learned, which I was very poor at, is to accept the responsibilities that I am meant to take on. It happened at work the other day. Something had gone wrong, and we happened to be talking, and I said, 'That was my mistake, you know' – which was what had happened. And I suppose that's something I have learned, and I'm much more comfortable with. If I look back, I was always a bit of a ducker and diver. I was always quite prepared to see an angle whereby none of the blame would have been attached to me. But now, I'm happier just to say, 'Yeah, I screwed up,' and the world doesn't stop. The world goes on. It's really quite amazing. The work relationships go on. We get on and do what we have to do. It's quite strange because I can look back to when I was managing a team and I had to see that as a boss, I accepted that people make mistakes and things go wrong. I didn't have a problem with it, but with me it was a different matter. It's odd, isn't it? But I suppose again, you see, it's something maybe you gain with maturity.

But the fact that I'm actually able to sit here and talk to you like this is also another change. I wouldn't even have contemplated it, talking about the past or my attitudes. They were private things, they were mine. But now I have talked to counsellors, one-to-one, I have shared in meetings – I've learned all of those things. They all make life so much easier.

There are things that I'd like to achieve, but they're not the same things that I wanted to achieve when I was younger. When I was younger I was very ambitious, but I also saw my ambition in terms of monetary rewards. I don't any longer see the rewards being in that sense. I see the rewards in well-being of myself and in relationships, relationships with people. A massive change of attitude. I can also look back and say that I did actually achieve those things – a detached house, etc. – and that's also helped me when I look back on the hard times – they were balanced out by some good things. There were extremes. Now I'm better able to take a balanced view about it.

I think I have lost some of my pride. My pride was one of the things that – I'd have been too proud to admit the rather negative aspects of my life. And I think that that was possibly a major contributor to my drinking, and I would hope that if all these things were bottled up, I could share them now, or get rid of them. So I have got rid of a lot of that. I can look back on my achievements and be proud of those achievements.

I've always been a bit of a loner, right from when I was very, very young. I do recognise that. So yes, I made very good friends when I was going to AA, and I have retained those friendships, even though I don't go so much to AA. In fact, when I got into recovery all of my friends were people I knew in AA. I never socialised heavily with work colleagues, so I've never had close friends from work. I've never retained close friendship with people I've been to college with or school friends, except one person who used to sit behind me in the same class at school. So no, when I got into recovery, all my friends were AA friends, and I have retained these friendships, because, I have to say, one does get quite a lot from them. So, yes. I can look at myself and I know I'm a bit of a loner. I'm actually happy with my own company. I can go home and be quite happy – do some work, get myself a meal, then sit down and watch television if I want. I tend to be happy with my own company.

I'm not sure whether this played a part in my drinking or not. I think it may have done, and I can recognise, in a way, the danger in what I do at the moment, but I've said sharing and speaking about things removes their power to dominate in your mind, and I do realise that being a loner I never had that facility as a youngster, or in my earlier years, of having a close friend with whom I could share or unload guilt or whatever, and I do realise that there's a risk that I could cut myself off again. I have to watch the balance of isolating myself and going out. I know it's solitude which is quite different from loneliness. I'm not discontented. Of course I do have the capability of always going back to AA. There's always an open door there and, as I say, I don't go regularly, but I could go. I do still maintain the link because I do actually see that it has a value to me, if there was an occasion when there was no one else to go to, to talk about it, then that avenue is open to me. That's also a difference, because I recognise that. See, whereas twenty years ago I would never even have thought of it, and if I'd thought of it, I probably wouldn't have been able to.

Nowadays, I actually enjoy life. Most of the time I enjoy my work. My life is not perfect, but I enjoy going home and cooking myself something to eat and doing whatever I do, watching television, reading, I enjoy doing that. Equally I enjoy the likes of Sunday, having the family round – a super day. That was great. There have been occasions when a small group of friends have got together and gone off to the theatre and I've enjoyed doing that.

I don't have to be looking to the outside world for things, but I can do. It's there if I want it. If I want to go to the theatre, I can go to the theatre. Last year, I went on holiday by myself. Now, you know, if you'd have said to me ten years ago, 'You'll go on holiday by yourself and enjoy yourself,' I'd have said, 'You must be mad.' You know, I went away and I had a fortnight away and I really enjoyed it. It was a change, it was a break, and it was a different experience. I learned to do some things that I wanted to do. I decided to do some cycling. I was able to cycle in France. I had a really good time. And, yeah, I went by myself, and I'm going again next month. For my birthday, Jackie, my ex-wife, and I went out together.

How few people one meets who have radically altered their approach to life – apart, perhaps, from those who have experienced a religious conversion. Geoff mentions no affiliations with any religious group, and his 'Higher Power' he sees as AA itself, yet the changes he has embraced since he stopped drinking are profound. He has come not only to understand his own nature, but also his relationships with others. These changes in his life are at a deep level. By reflecting on his past and events in the present with his counsellor, with the two people in AA he confided in and with the groups, both AA and the relapse prevention group, he has achieved a remarkable reorientation in his approach to life.

Listening to the advice of AA led him to cope with the first days of withdrawal from alcohol. That was the practical side. Geoff is an engineer, and it is as if by engineering a more grounded life in terms of day-to-day living, this life has acted as a benign structure to support his awareness and appreciation of his emotional life. This, in turn, has enabled him to live differently. What AA also provided was the opportunity gradually to trust one or two people enough to work out what had gone wrong in his life and to discover for himself who he really was and what his values were. Letting himself trust these people, at the same time he found himself able to attend the hospital group and to engage for months in an important counselling relationship there. The key factor in bringing about this change was trust. He needed help urgently when he stopped drinking and this need pushed him into starting to open up about his difficulties. His counsellor, one of the group facilitators, was an excellent listener, a man of similar age and intelligence, who came to respect as well as empathise with Geoff, and the respect was mutual. To begin to open up to someone else about experiences and difficulties in life at a deep level is immensely courageous for someone who has previously shied away from this, but it is this step which can start to alleviate feelings of isolation. This has been an intense struggle, as is apparent in the way he expresses himself every time he speaks about discussing his feelings: '*You actually speak them out loud.*' He talks about having bottled things up. Things were sealed inside him to be brooded over when the bottle was uncorked. These toxic resentments had to be forcibly evacuated or they clung on in malign attachment within him.

As far as learning about himself is concerned, he had previously been driven by the needs and demands of others, but he came to recognise and understand his own needs and take account of them. The search for material rewards he dropped in favour of doing the activity he was really good at – hands-on engineering. This gives him far more satisfaction than taking responsibility for leading a team. He has become, he says, quite easily able to admit when he is in the wrong. In other words, he has dropped his highly defensive stance. He no longer demands of himself that he appear 'perfect'. He can replace false pride in a false persona with justifiable pride.

Losing the chance to live with his wife and children was part of the price he paid for his drinking, but he found ways to recreate the relationships on a different footing. This clearly means a great deal to him. So many people nowadays find it an impossible task to mend broken relationships, perhaps because they feel ashamed, or continue to blame their partner, or are simply too proud. It was fortuitous that he was able to be on good terms with his wife again when she developed cancer, and he was able to care for her throughout her illness to the very end of her life. But it was to his own credit that he had partially mended the bridge between them before that. He realised that it would be best to wait for his children to accept him again in their own time and he was patient enough to do so, in spite of his distress.

He has found that living on his own suits him. This has been part of discovering his true nature. While he was isolated by the shame and secrecy which accompanied his drinking, and even more by eventual rejection by his family, he now finds pleasure in his own company. There is a world of difference between isolation and solitude.

His former life collapsed through alcohol. I get the impression that as he grew up and established himself as an adult with a career and family, he felt driven to compensate for a feeling that he was never quite good enough. Material success meant a great deal to him because it gave him the desired status. But it was accompanied by a sense of defensiveness, for the structure he erected psychologically was fragile. He could never allow himself to be seen as being in the wrong. He hints at having had a great need to please his mother. He tried to compensate in so many ways, particularly by keeping up a good persona, trying very hard to obey the dictates of his demanding conscience. He drank more and more because he was dissatisfied with the results of his attempts. He found little satisfaction in life, forever wanting higher status and more approval. He tried and failed to make his life feel better by drinking, as a young engineering project leader, husband and father. His energies went into being always acceptable to others, always seeking approval. The trouble was that however hard he tried, there perpetually lurked a sneaking suspicion that it was not enough. People who suffer from inferiority complexes are fighting a continuous battle to prove themselves. Geoff used alcohol to help him to keep such feelings at bay as best he could. But alcohol, being what it is, came gradually but inexorably to erode his competence. As he had to drink more and more to stop experiencing withdrawal symptoms, so his home life, job and career all suffered a vicious downward spiral. He did make moves towards changing the situation, although it turned out that he was only flirting with change at that stage. He was deeply unhappy.

Now here is a picture of someone who, once liberated from living a rigidly defensive life through experiencing a complete collapse, has emerged from it and has grown and matured in the process. Perhaps a disaster is the only thing that could have pricked the bubble. Geoff doesn't speak about having had a *rock bottom* experience, but his collapse motivated him to discover who he really was. His story shows what a 'conversion' means. Although Geoff doesn't quote AA language very much, one can see how he has followed the basic principles of making reparation for the harm he caused while drinking, in such a way as to cause no further damage. He leads a life where he is self-aware and is honest with himself about his vulnerabilities and his potential too. He greets the chance of new experiences with pleasure and anticipation.

In conclusion

A function of drug use

We have seen that people who find themselves in an embattled state in life often use drugs as a prop, simply to keep going. It can be that they have taken on responsibilities that are too heavy for them or boxed themselves into a corner financially. Like Geoff, they drink more and more to escape from the unpleasant awareness of their situation – which makes it far worse, and usually far lonelier. It is as if they hate the prison they are creating for themselves, but they can't see a way out.

A gradual approach

The act of stopping successfully is often preceded by several 'unsuccessful' attempts. Though these attempts may seem little more than faltering steps toward stopping, they may each show the individual something of value. In this case, for example, the counselling Geoff had several years previously started an important process for him in helping him to come to terms with memories from his childhood. This did not, however, stop him from drinking more and more. It was part of the process of preparing to leave his addiction behind.

Re-orientation

Just as an addiction reflects some deep process in the psyche, so leaving it behind can bring about a radical re-orientation. This liberates the individual to understand themselves and see their lives in perspective. For Geoff, the re-orientation has been from fear toward trust. It is not the experience of the addiction itself nor his stopping drinking that has facilitated the radical change in his life, but the way he has engaged with his own 'rehabilitation' and continues to engage in developing as a person. He is on a path of individuation.

Notes

1 Delirium tremens may occur during withdrawal from alcohol. It can be life threatening if accompanied by fits. Its symptoms are shaking and visual

hallucinations, often of a paranoid nature. It can be medically controlled with tranquillisers.

2 The spiritual programme of AA.

3 By *putting it out there* the narrator implies 'blaming other people'.

Chapter 18

Stepping out of co-dependence

Stuart was addicted to a variety of drugs for twenty-nine years, from his early teens onwards. In his mid thirties, under the threat of losing his job, he was referred to the hospital. He attended appointments for a few months, speaking mostly about his alcohol and cannabis use, and he gained some insight into how much he was annoying everyone at work, but he ended this spell of treatment without making radical changes. He returned a year or two later and decided to enter a rehabilitation centre. Like many addicted people, he was entwined in a partnership where the drug-using pattern of the one has a profound effect on the other.

I went into a treatment centre and one of the stipulations was that I was clean and sober three days before I started. My drinking actually stopped three days before, and I smoked my last dope the night before. I thought dope was OK, but I changed my mind about that very soon. Once you've been in the treatment centre for maybe a day or two, then you're allowed to go out for a walk along the sea front, and I asked one of the guys that had been in there for a few weeks what the situation was with cannabis, 'It's still all right to smoke dope, isn't it?' And his reaction took me by surprise. He said, 'No, no, no. Of course you can't do that.' He said, 'It's mood-altering, isn't it?' I hadn't realised, because at that time I thought nothing at all about it. I didn't know what was going on with me, changing the way I felt. No, I hadn't realised that cannabis and all the other mood-altering substances had to go, had to stop. It's a programme of complete abstinence. When I went into it, I couldn't envisage a life without some kind of drug, whatever it was.

I was in that primary treatment centre away from home for three months. It used the Twelve Steps[1], and the length of time people stayed was twelve or thirteen weeks. Most people would go on to secondary treatment in a different centre, but it was decided I would do an extra week there and then come home. It was felt I had a relatively stable home life here. It was difficult being told that Louise and I were involved in a co-dependent relationship. It was definitely suggested that it would have to stop. I suppose the people running the treatment centre had seen it all before, and so there was only one way, and that was for me to know the truth of what was going on and to see that I was involved in a crazy relationship, all revolving around me, and my need to have mood altering substances.

One of the things to illustrate the point is that my personal counsellor asked me what I thought was important in the relationship, and I went through everything from love, being a good team, getting on well together most of the time, having common interests, and she kept asking me for more and more, and she then said, 'Can you think of something else that's important?' And, I really couldn't. Then she said, 'What about trust?' And that was it. That was the hub of it. I couldn't be trusted. I didn't trust Louise. I never trusted anybody else, I never had done. I only trusted *my* judgment. And if something went wrong, it was always somebody else's fault, not me. Incredible! I was in control. But the trust side of it – it never, ever occurred to me that that was fundamental in a long-term relationship. And no, I couldn't trust Louise. And that's a 'for instance' of how ignorant I was of normal life. I started to realise the dynamic between the two of us and how that worked. I saw how sick it was, not only in my partnership but in my relationships with everybody I knew.

A lot of people at the treatment centre were actually restarting their lives in a different place rather than going back to where they lived before. That was a very hard prospect, but I got to the point where I was prepared to do it, and it helped turn things round for me. Now, Louise actually did something herself about going to the Fellowship. About three weeks after I went into treatment, she attended a Fellowship[2], and that was something she made her own decision to do.

The way the group at the centre was done, there was a preamble to every session, to put us in touch that the group meeting was for our common good, and that there's no judgment, but that it was a safe place to share. After a while I got to trusting people as well, which I would never have dreamt of doing, and trusting what they told me. They were probably right when they said that when I got home that I had to consciously work at it with my wife. After so many years of thinking wrongly about things, about life, about people, you actually have to change the way you respond. You have to put yourself away from the centre of the world. You have to stand to one side and let somebody else be there. I know it's difficult for addicts, I expect its difficult for anybody, but you have to change. I went in to treatment, you know, because I knew I was dying. I knew I wouldn't last long.

Right back to my early teens when I was at school, I remember thinking, 'I'm not going to respond in the way people would expect me to respond. I'm going to change the way I react to things.' I decided that I would have no regrets. In actual fact, what happened was that I did exactly what I wanted to, and didn't feel guilty – I used to do *anything* rather than feel.

When I came home from the treatment centre free of drugs, there was a great blast of feeling. It's, it's like being exposed to something, I'd almost put it in terms of being exposed to something outside. That's how it feels, but it's inside, in your gut. I felt it was bashing me up. That spontaneity of feeling goes to a certain degree the more time you're dry, but at first it just hits you. So that left me very prone to breaking down and crying, because I just couldn't handle the emotion. Something would upset me or something would upset someone else and it would make me upset. I'd have an empathy.

I came back home, and I didn't make a conscious decision not to associate with the same people – it just happened. I was very vulnerable then but I was extremely happy. I'd a very big 'high', from the experience that I'd had. *I'd stuck at it.* I'd never stuck at anything before really. A lot of the time there, despite constantly being channelled into difficult positions, I've got some very happy memories that I'll have with me forever. But, I suppose what it was, was the *start line.*

I started going to meetings straight away. I went to NA. The trick is a day at a time. When you've only just cleaned up, the thought of ten years, a day at a time, is an impossible concept. But it does get easier. Seeing the truth of it. One of the things they don't say about it being a day at a time, is that it can be five minutes at a time – it doesn't matter, you can restart your day as many times as you like. That's one of the ways I got through the early days.

You know, if something upsets me, and I don't let it go and get it out or something, it'll just fester so I have to keep letting stuff go. The day you stop letting something go, you're right back to the beginning. That's what my life revolved around. I read a lot of literature, and talked about drugs to Louise. At the time, she was getting on very well. Things had been very bad in the past between us. Before we got into recovery, I used to try to control Louise's life and she tried to control mine. We'd keep watching over each other, winding each other up. I was invariably the guilty party, I was drunk, and Louise used to get off scot free. I understand nowadays how it works. Louise was the victim and what she never saw was that she was trying to control me, some of it innocently, some of it not. But when you're bound up in these things, it's difficult to see that anybody's responsible. And the responsibility, or the accountability, is one of the things also you've got to start letting go of, the guilt, because you're never accountable to anybody, you don't have to be. It's not necessary. Some people say, 'Oh well, it's an illness, you're not responsible for it,' and that's the simple answer. And you do gradually recover.

Life nowadays is different from what it was in early recovery. Then it was like having my eyes opened for the first time, all of a sudden. Now, there's still that excitement, but it's tempered with a feeling of some serenity, rather than going violently from one thing straight to the other. Balance. There's more balance in my life now than there's ever been. A lot more contentment. Better able to cope with crises. The real changes were all in the primary phases. Today, compared with my first weeks in treatment, it's like the difference between two people, the way I react. I can still get a very short fuse, but I can see sense in it, where I wouldn't have wanted to look at things. I wouldn't have wanted to go into any great depth – to avoid the pain. I'm braver now. I'd run away and hide and take lots of drugs so I wouldn't feel anything.

One thing that happened very early in treatment was that my father died. That was very difficult. One thing that always stands out about the couple of weeks when he was in hospital and we knew he wouldn't come out, was my reaction to that. Everybody around me was very sympathetic. I think I'd been told that morning or the night before, and my counsellor asked me what was happening and I said, 'Well, you know. . .' and she said, 'What's going on with you?' I said, 'What do you mean?' I was just very calm. Then she said, 'You're acting like nothing's happening.' And then I thought, 'That's it!' I just started crying, you know. I suddenly felt quite frightened. [Long pause. Stuart's eyes fill with tears] If that had happened before I was in treatment, I'd have just glossed over the whole thing and pushed it down and drunk, and felt sorry for myself. I was good at that. I didn't know what I felt, I didn't think about what I was feeling. All I knew was, I felt sorry for myself. I couldn't stand it. I hid my feelings and over the years, over twenty-nine years of using drugs, I got very good at it. That's what's changed. But I still kicked and struggled the rest of my time in treatment.

It's different now because I've got access to my feelings. One of the things I can do now, I can trust more people and I can trust my own feelings. It's really strange, because I think, 'That's happened. I can't do anything.' I recognise what has happened. I'm pushing something down. Normally, after a day or so, it comes out. Quite often it's to do with things where I don't want to admit my own responsibility for something. It's quite hard, that. Other times, it's usually to do with heavy emotional stuff. I'll still package it away. But these are the things that we know about in the Fellowship, these ways of learning to change. Sometimes I'll be really nice to somebody I don't like, or I'll do something for somebody and try my hardest not to tell them I've done it. I don't always succeed! Here I am talking about death, and that's a change as far as I'm concerned. And I try and remember that.

I do have fears about some things nowadays. A good friend, I think he's now out of intensive care, but last week he was in intensive care. He's already suffered the effects of drinking ethanol. He drank a load of that and ended up in intensive care in a coma, blind. He's got Parkinsonian Syndrome, terrible cramps. We know each other through the Fellowship. I couldn't put my finger on why it kept haunting me afterwards. And then a couple of days ago, it clicked: *fear*. Frightened the life out of me. It was the thought that it could happen to me. I know, it's a day at a time, that's all. So close to it. And the thought of relapsing. I know what I'd do as well. It hurts, I know. I've said I'm very comfortable, very secure, and yet I know full well what I'd do if I relapsed. I'd drink the bloody lot. I'd probably kill myself. I'd certainly land in hospital. Somebody said in a Fellowship meeting that if you put a glass of whisky in one hand and a revolver in the other, he'd go for the revolver. I knew exactly what he meant, because that's what it'll be. You might as well do it quickly, because I know there's no second chance for me.

The most difficult thing now is keeping myself away from the centre of things. The hardest thing is the spirituality of it all. I have a relationship with a Higher Power that I had to deny before. I always felt that there was something there, but the God of my religion was inaccessible because I was a sinner. What I've got now is what's known in the Fellowships as a 'Higher Power', which I happen to call God. It may not be everybody's interpretation, but it's where there's a different line between before I cleaned up and now. I wanted this exciting life, and the exciting life meant not being able to commit to something that would ever make me think about anybody else. I used to be my own 'Higher Power'. Everything I did or you did, or what everybody else did too, I looked at as how it reflected on me. There was no avenue for anybody else to have free will. I had free will till it was coming out of my ears! I was in charge! And one of the hardest things in early recovery at the treatment centre was to be shown quite clearly that I wasn't in charge. I had been in denial about that, amongst many other things. What was fundamental was that it was pointed out to me that possibly it wasn't a good idea for me to think of God being *in* me, because I would eventually start making the decisions again, and it's better that I look at God as being outside myself. It's really up to you what your Higher Power is, so long as it's not *you*.

Perhaps the hardest thing is to keep remembering to pray for someone that I don't like. The exercises like that I find very hard. While I might not do it on the day itself or the day after, if I've fallen out with somebody or had a disagreement with somebody, regardless of whose fault it was, mine or theirs, maybe a couple of days later, I'll pray for them. That's so different from the old me. I would have hated them to eternity. And I can still behave like that. The stuff that I concentrate on these days, more than staying clean, because that's now a way of life for me, not to use illegal substances, but I can still go shopping and spend money and stuff like that. At the moment, I've just sold a car and I'm going to buy another one and I'm going to spend more on it than Louise thinks, and it's a damn sight more powerful than she realises. So that's what I'm like. And so, no, I'm not always honest.

What's in the back of my mind a lot of the time is that I'm only ever that far away [indicating a tiny space with his finger tips] from blowing it and that frightens me. My temper frightens me, and sometimes my initial reactions to things. An old favourite of mine is to talk about people behind their backs, and I try so hard not to do it, but I can't resist it, I just can't resist it. Those are things that used to get me into trouble, and still do. I'm a bit better these days, but I still do it.

Thinking about the things that give me the most pleasure nowadays, well, immediately my response to that is, 'Well, what do I say here?' because I should say, 'My son.' But, I'm still pretty self-centred. I think it's a *wholeness*. I suppose that's still the addict, trying to control everything. It's not an easy one to answer. I'm very involved with my work. I get a lot of pleasure from it. I'm doing this course, which I'm not doing enough work for! I'm waiting to get this diploma. Once I've got that then maybe I'll be able to decide whether I want to stay put. It's a good business to be in but it's expensive to set up. It's a lot of hard work, I don't know how much of that I need. Long hours, middle of the night sometimes. I'm in a reasonably comfortable position at present, but not perhaps getting the responsibility that I want, but that of course may be a reflection on me. Occasionally, I feel restless about it, but a lot of the time the NA programme helps with concentrating on each day, not projecting too far. 'Let's get this sorted out first.' It's good that. 'Let's not be in such a hurry.' We moved here last year, but it's only recently, in the last couple of weeks really, that it's started to filter through that I might actually be planning to stay put here in this house, and not think about moving on. I was never happy where we were. Some of it was about the size of the house. It was too small. But of course, I was spending out on drugs and alcohol. So, I suppose I felt guilty. It was my fault. I was so out of it, except when I was working, that I couldn't really get anything together.

Until circumstances changed I couldn't relax. One of the things I got in treatment was that I suddenly realised that I wasn't constantly rushing around, trying to be in charge of everything. I can actually relax, which I never did. I could never settle. The only time I was relaxed was just before I fell asleep in a drug- or alcohol-induced stupor, then I would actually relax. In fact, I was stoned, comatose! And that was the only time I could really feel content. Nowadays, I like doing nothing. I like not having anything to do. I still have a problem when there are demands on me, and I don't want to do something. I suppose I enjoy to a certain degree the unpredictability of life. I can actually enjoy that, unless it all goes pear-shaped, but even then, I suppose, and these are all things that are so different.

Then again, I've got a terrible temper sometimes over work. I'll be honest, this has always been my thing. I always feel that I'm not as far up the slippery pole as I should be. It doesn't matter where I've worked, I've always felt I should be further up the pole, and that's the same here as it was the last place I worked, but this time I'm not using or drinking. I used to think I wasn't climbing up the tree because this person or that person didn't like me, or I'd rubbed somebody up the wrong way, and of course I now realise they knew what I was like. They may not necessarily have known that I was addicted, but they knew I was unreliable. When the same thing happens now that I've cleaned up, I do have to wonder what's going on. Is it because of me, or is it because of them? That is the point where I sometimes forget to say the Serenity Prayer[3], but that's when I *need* to say it.

Having children was something we hadn't even talked about. When we first met we might have talked about it. We didn't want children. It was only when we got into recovery that it became plain, very much, that there had been two reasons. One was that it would have got in the way of my drug using, and the other was that I would no longer have been the centre of the world. I'm quite sure of that. I also had a deep-seated realisation of how it would be for a child. You see, my father and mother both had alcoholic parents, and although they were neither of them alcoholic, they both were part of the dynamic. Maybe I picked up something at a far deeper level. There's a lot of talk about it at the moment – whether it's acquired, or inborn. Maybe I had a better feel as to what it might be like to be the child in that family, where parents or one parent was drinking. And also, I suppose I knew what I was like when I'd had a drink and it would have been dangerous.

I had to go through an incredible change before I could see it. I had it kicked into me almost. That's how it felt. Virtually kicked into me. And then I started to change. And that's one of the things that one realises, the family dynamic, and like I said, about breaking the chain. Before I cleaned up I just drank all the money. We were living in a very, very basic way. I suppose I seemed a little bit different, maybe, a bit exciting. Up to things perhaps I shouldn't be doing. Louise and I liked the same sort of progressive music, and we had quite a bit in common, but the thing that I think most of all was perhaps that we had a sort of sympathetic framework. We'd come together and help each other in what we needed. This was the other part of the picture. I never realised I could stand alone. I always needed somebody else to make me feel complete. And, that's another thing I learned early, very early on. I had to restart building up a personal history. That's what all this is about. And, I can, I can stand alone. The thing is, Louise and I are built the same way. And, when we've talked about things, that's what's come out from her too. That she couldn't say no. She too was shackled up. She has her own life. Yeah. She can make choices now.

Co-dependency is a term often used in the world of drug and alcohol treatment to refer to a situation where both people in a relationship are addicted or in danger of becoming addicted, and where the drug or alcohol use of the one affects that of the other. Often a therapist faced with this dilemma may feel that the only answer is for the relationship to end. Stuart's narrative illustrates how, if each individual decides to make changes independently, there can be growth within the relationship rather than a split.

Stuart speaks about the hazards in co-dependency: one partner trying to control the other, lack of trust, and destructive anger that goes nowhere. He was fortunate in having a wife who decided to take steps to help herself, and took that decision quite independently. It was as if it were only when each person in this couple had given the other the chance to breathe, that they could get on track once again – and that was only the beginning of the hard task of forging a more creative relationship. The marriage thrived after Stuart spent those three months at the rehabilitation centre. As he says, he and his wife had always had what he calls a 'sympathetic frame-work', which made a starting point for working out a new *modus vivendi*. Each had their own self help group to which they belonged and they read literature which gave them ideas on how to improve their relationship. Above all, they talked to one another about what they were experiencing at each stage of getting used to living without drugs.

Much of what they discovered to be of help to them could apply to any intimate relationship, but the trouble with addiction is that it precludes any intimacy and replaces it with what can only be called a negative destructive enmeshment. So for them it was like starting afresh. The new framework was based on a growing ability of each partner to stand on their own rather than needing someone else to feel complete. This entailed stepping back from attempts to control the actions of the other person, or wind them up by telling them what to do. It also meant being able to say no, and not having to feel accountable to the other. All of this involved trusting one another. In Stuart's case, he found it important not to let his negative feelings fester. In the past, each had had the habit of watching the other in order to cast blame, rather than each accepting responsibility for their own part in a situation. No longer need one partner become the critical accuser, while the other stands aside as an innocent victim.

Some life-changing encounters took place for Stuart when he went away from the town where he lived to the rehabilitation centre. He regards that as his *start line*. His counsellor raised a fundamental question which was an eye opener for him: Whom could he trust? Was he himself trustworthy? Stuart had come more and more to live inside a defensive stockade, and it was only gradually that he began to see that all the dealings he had with people were tainted by the same flaw. A second, most shattering encounter was again with his key worker. Stuart had hardly let the immanent prospect of his father's death touch his emotions. His defensive stance was in place, yet it took only a few thoughtful questions from the key worker to puncture his defences and free him to weep. He now regards this as a breakthrough of enormous significance: this was the point of his rebirth.

He knows that as a boy he used a deliberate decision to avoid having 'feelings' to enable him to break free of the protective family setting where he was the treasured son, the special one. He wanted to forge his own life, and heroin was most useful in promoting his cause. Unlike some of the other narrators, he had a good education, training and profession, so he actually had the scope to develop his potential. Yet psychologically his need for drugs led to his being less successful than he might otherwise have been in winning promotion because he was so unreliable. Every adolescent has to play the role of the hero to leave security behind and to seek dangers if they are to break free into adult life successfully, but not everyone has to go to such extremes.

Each of his parents had themselves been negatively affected by the drinking habits of one of their parents, and Stuart recalls that the conversation at home seemed to revolve around this background. This raises the familiar question: nature or nurture? Might there have been some genetic component which skipped a generation, meanwhile lying dormant in his mother and father? Or, alternatively, was the whole subject of alcoholism and its evils in some way the carrier of a miasma, a bad atmosphere, in the conversations Stuart overheard from his earliest days? When one's parents are very frightened of something, the fear seeps through and can become pervasive. Their attitude towards alcoholism was far from relaxed, and as is the case with any highly charged subject, it can develop a certain fascination for a child keen to explore everything, especially the forbidden.

Perhaps Stuart was seen by his parents, each with trauma in the past, as a vital symbol of hope. This is a heavy burden to carry. When he reached his teens, he felt torn between a desire to fulfill his parents' expectations and a wish to be free of the burden – or, more likely, he probably felt both things at once. He was not unaffected by his parents' ambitions for him, for he sees himself as having always been ambitious. Because he had had things pretty much his own way at home, I imagine it was especially hard for him to be bettered by rivals. Envy and rage are familiar friends to the ambitious narcissist, and bad friends at that.

His work in the new career he chose contains a strong element of helping people when they are at their most vulnerable. It is concerned with the formalities and rituals around death. It is intriguing to me that he has chosen this as a career, as he felt that he himself had several close brushes with death. Sometimes, he says, he is called upon to visit bereaved families in the night, soon after a death. It is apparent that he feels honoured. The formality and reverence of a funeral service is in striking contrast to the escapades of his wild days. Perhaps it is a much longed for antidote that reinforces a sense of wholeness in his life.

In conclusion

Co-dependency

When both partners in a couple use drugs, the situation is complicated, but the relationship need not end if both partners accept the need to change themselves, and don't try to 'make' the other change. It is a matter of each partner finding a way of standing on his or her own two feet.

The spiritual dimension

Quite apart from the changes in Stuart's marriage, the contrast between his life while he was addicted and since he left his addiction behind is stark. As he says, 'It's almost like two people.' Behind the changes he has made, there lies a spiritual element. Many people who become addicted have a fragile sense of self-worth, and for them, an awareness of God existing within themselves is precisely what can help them. In contrast, Stuart speaks about taking himself away from the centre of things. This works for him.

A problem at the root of addiction

In the previous chapter, the narrator was imprisoned by fear of failure. Stuart was imprisoned by his conviction that there was no point in having feelings. Often in listening to people who are or have been addicted to substances, it seems obvious that they have used the substances to bypass emotional upheavals or bad or bored moods, but it is rare to hear someone say that they took the deliberate decision to do so. Those who grow up with a strong sense of identification with the hero archetype and use drugs to enhance their experiences find it hard to accept the harsh reality that they are mere mortals. Stuart's bottled-up fury was volcanic in proportions. Stopping drug use involved facing both his fury and his gentler, loving emotions. This has enriched his life beyond measure.

Changes over time

It takes time for the personality to emerge from an addicted state. Stuart sees the difference between the person he was immediately after he stopped and the person he is now as the difference between two people. Because he is thoughtful and articulate, he describes changes often observed in people who have left an addiction far behind, but who are less articulate. Factors involved include having a sense of balance in facing the challenges of life, a continuing fascination with discovering how to relate well to others, and an ability to be one's own person.

Notes

1 Some treatment centres are closely linked to the philosophy of the Twelve Steps of AA and encourage their patients to continue to attend AA or NA after they leave the centre.
2 Al-Anon and Families Anonymous are the self-help groups parallel to AA and NA for the relatives and friends of people who are addicted to alcohol and heroin respectively.
3 The Serenity Prayer is read at AA meetings and often thought about in group discussions: *God grant me the serenity to accept the things I cannot change, courage to change the things I can, and wisdom to know the difference.*

Chapter 19

This intense relationship with life itself

Ben, like several of the other narrators, experienced a tragedy in his childhood. He was sent for treatment at the hospital as a young man on the order of the court, having been arrested for possession of heroin. He complied with this order, but heroin continued to play a part in his life in the following years, which he spent travelling the world, finally settling in Goa. There he eventually gave up using drugs without any treatment. In this narrative, Ben, now middle-aged and living in the UK, is speaking to the psychiatrist who originally treated him at the hospital. After their meeting, he wrote a letter saying more about his thoughts on their conversation. He has kindly agreed for me to include this letter.

The things that led to my stopping using heroin are very complex. It has to do with the things I really enjoyed apart from drugs that preceded my involvement with heroin. I don't know how credible this sounds, but being able to walk in the countryside and enjoy nature, the enjoyment of things like poetry, which I developed through my teens, as well as experimenting with drugs. I found that the more I got involved with heroin, the more it cotton-wools you. There's no joy in it. You don't feel pain; you don't feel pleasure either. It's the best sort of tranquilliser I know. But as time went on, what I used to do is I'd use it until I felt myself getting physically addicted and then I'd stop. I'd leave it alone for a while and then circumstances or whatever would happen and somebody would offer it to me and I'd decide to try it again, and as time went on so my tolerance built up, and my ability not to get physically addicted diminished. I found myself getting addicted quicker. The image that came to me at the time was of a web closing on me. That frightened me. Basically it was fear.

I can remember spending a day walking the length and breadth of town trying to score some heroin, going to everybody I knew, thoroughly depressed, with not even the money for my bus fare, just trying to get hold of something. I'd been smoking dope since the age of about eighteen, for several years anyway, and I had what I think looking back was a minor breakdown. I experienced intense anxiety, so I couldn't smoke. Up till then, I'd avoided LSD, that's another thing in the story. That hadn't been around, see, in the early days, it wasn't available. Then I was so depressed with this heroin thing and I'd read positive things about acid being used with alcoholics, you know, reorienting people to a more positive outlook. So I went round to a local person I knew and she gave me some LSD. That completely changed my perspective on life. Within five hours of this trip, effectively, I was looking back on the other thing. I can remember saying, 'What was that other stuff I used to do, god, you know, where was I with that?' And that gave me a different, much more open and optimistic outlook for a time. But the thing is, silly bloke that I was, I didn't leave it there. I started taking acid more often and of course, I ended up taking four microdots and having a bad trip. I was in a right mess anyway after that and went back to taking some more heroin eventually.

The last time I used heroin was in Goa. I had a lovely house there, with five bedrooms. What I regret is that my job now is working with children, teaching them natural history, and I wish that at the time I'd taken an interest in that. The time was wasted on the drugs. The last fix of heroin I had was morphine, and I just felt sickened with the whole thing. Afterwards, I felt awful physically and from then on I didn't use any more. I have to put it down partly to my love of poetry and things you could term *spiritual* and the acid experience. I didn't have to find any other drug. What I really found was other alternatives in life.

I started to get into meditation. I lived in a Buddhist commune for a while, for four years. This was with the Friends of Western Buddhism Order. I became a bit disillusioned with them for various reasons. Then I got married and recently I've been loosely involved with a group called the Creation Centre of Spirituality Movement. I subscribe to their literature. It's an ecumenical approach to religion. It's not saying, 'My way is the way,' which is the Friends of Western Buddhism stance, which is so sectarian – that was partly why I didn't want to know. When I got involved with the Creation Centre of Spirituality Movement, I found that creativity is a big part of it. I organised an ongoing group which used to meet weekly, and I used to read my poetry there.

There's another element in the picture: that's therapy. I've done a lot of therapy – humanistic and gestalt therapy. I had several private therapists. I did group work for a year, and I also did individual work for about two years, and that was very useful, looking at my life.

My brother was killed. . . my brother was killed in a fairground accident. I have a sister eight years younger than I am who was very seriously addicted to heroin for a number of years. I think she was in probably worse shape than I was. But I'm happy to say, she's fine. She's been off for about eight years now. Childbirth was the catalyst for her in giving up heroin. She never went back. I think she struggled for a while, but she coped with it.

My mother is now seventy-eight. I see her roughly about once every two months. I meet my sister maybe twice a year and otherwise keep in touch by phone. My Dad died when he was only fifty-eight. I was twenty-one. I wasn't really close to him, and I can remember a conversation about this at the hospital with you, actually. Saying how I regretted not having got to know him. But I have good memories of him. I knew that he was well liked by his workmates and so on, and highly thought of by people who did know him, and, as you said, those memories were precious. Better than not knowing at all.

My current job – I've only had this one for six months. I was redundant for a while, but now I'm a warden based at an ecology centre. It's to do with the environment. Basically my job is looking after a site, a park, and a stretch of disused railway line, and teaching children, bringing school groups, and teaching them about the environment. I do manual work as well and I bring school trips in. And the work that we do is to enhance it as a nature resource. Before that I had, well, I had a year as a gravedigger, and prior to that I had four years doing this job, the job I do now, but single-handedly managing a site – I'm in a team at present. Prior to that I had another nature park, but then the council withdrew the funding and that went down the tubes, so I was out of work. Occasionally I'll go out and do some gardening. When I was unemployed I did some old ladies' gardens to make a few bob and rather than leave them in the lurch, I still work for them.

The only time I was ever in trouble with the law was when I was arrested for heroin. I do have a drink. We'll share a bottle of wine once a week, Deirdre and I, but nothing else. I've been married for fourteen years. My wife is a housewife and a playgroup worker. I've got one daughter and one stepdaughter. We've lived where we are now for fifteen years and we're very happy there. As for heroin, I had a long affair with the mistress – then I just said goodbye. It was partly what I was saying, I mean, fear. . . But when I look back on what I did to my body, some of the things I got up to make my hair stand on end now. It's as if over time I became desensitised to what was appropriate. But somehow another part of myself was kind of looking, and mourning the things that I used to enjoy. So there was that voice too, plus my not wanting to cause my mother grief. I was in danger of dying really, overdosing or whatever, so there were a number of things that influenced me. Like my love of poetry – I couldn't write any more. I've only published in magazines. Just the odd one here and there. When I was seventeen I tried to get a book published. I got a very nice letter back!

Fear of dying was a big factor in my giving up. Well the thing, the affair, the love affair, went on – I mean drugs – went on for those ten years. I suppose it may just have been part of my maturation process. Maybe becoming responsible.

You know, one of the things I used to say to people was, 'Somebody up there must like me – the fact that I've got to where I am now.' Through no great willpower really. I mean, Christianity talks about 'grace'. It was like, you know, I was lucky enough to be the person I am, with the concerns and interests that I have, whereas other people perhaps didn't have those things.

When I got arrested, I'd stopped – part of my agreement with the court was that I'd come and see you at the hospital. I mean, to be honest, I just did it. It was a way of getting out of prison. I said I would do it. . . and also I stopped taking heroin, stopped taking drugs for a while, and I was suffering from all sorts of things, anxiety attacks and feeling a bit blown out. I asked you for tranquillisers and you gave me, I think, Stelazine – very heavy. Yuk – terrible, terrible stuff. That was the only treatment – and I came to see you once a week. I had to give urine samples to make sure I wasn't dabbling on the side, but that's all.

And also, with me, I grew up as a teenager with no sense of myself, with partly the involvement with heroin and with drugs. I was in that whole culture. I was finding myself a peer group with whom I could identify. Especially smoking cannabis, basically a bonding thing, socially. . . I felt quite good with myself in that group, that milieu, but, I mean, part of me. . . what I got from therapy, let's say, and from the Buddhist groups was a sense of myself as being OK. I'm OK, you know. I didn't get any qualifications. I left school at 15, but I'm still all right. I could, if I wanted to, I could have. . .

Stopping for me was gradual because I sort of went back, that time in Goa when I used once again. I had a feeling of remorse after I tried it and it wasn't all that good anyway. The retrial was disappointing. So why bother? For a while I did find it hard to cope without heroin, when I met people, especially people who were using heroin. Even today, occasionally, I meet people in the street who are obviously under the influence. If I empathise with them, I know in my gut, kind of, what they're feeling. I get a pang. You know when you see someone. . . but I don't get any urge to share. I feel sad for them. I didn't know NA existed at the time. I know it exists now. I've spoken to Phil. I was very, very pleased that Phil got in touch with me. Delighted, you know. Through Phil it was I heard about NA. I don't know whether it was around at the time I'm talking about.

Prescribing substitute drugs is not an adequate answer for drug users. It's not what people are looking for really. I believe what's at fault is something far deeper. It's a sense of themselves. I think they need some counselling or maybe some psychotherapy of some sort. They need somehow to acquire a good sense of themselves.

Ben grew up in a family deeply scarred by the trauma of the accidental death of a child. His father he remembers as an elusive figure who was not emotionally close to him and who died when Ben was twenty-one. As a young man, empathy with his mother's pain was partly what eventually led him away from dicing with the hazards of using heroin. He felt he could not risk hurting her further. It is noteworthy that his sister, now a mother herself, also had a spell of injecting heroin. Each person in a family where this sort of tragedy occurs is plunged into the need to find some way to survive. Communication within any family can become very limited in the face of tragedy. What happens is that each person is afraid of starting the others breaking down in floods of tears. Tears may be healing, but they are also heart-rending at a time when the family simply has to find a way of making the day work. No one is at fault if communication becomes limited, but this does further impoverish the family. A fairground is expected to be a place of thrills and pleasure. How terrible when it becomes a place of death.

Ben was drawn to a group of boys in their mid teens, nearing the end of their schooling, who were experimenting with drugs, partly as a way of exploring an activity which was illicit and therefore counter to their parents' strictures and those of authority figures in general. The youth culture of the time promoted this trend. School seems to have failed him. He is clear-thinking and articulate, yet he seems to have achieved nothing at school. Perhaps he was too preoccupied with grief to concentrate. Perhaps no one took the time to discover why he was underachieving. This can happen in large classes in secondary schools where teaching the subject matter can become the teacher's prime focus rather than concentrating equally on the learning processes of individuals in the class.

Ben says that he grew up with no sense of himself, and he believes that many drug users have problems of low self-esteem. He found his own way of exploring the world around him and within him while walking in the forest, in reading and writing poetry and in drug using. Expressing his ideas and emotions in poetry was an important part of his growing up. The memory of this later played a part in his growing disillusionment with drug use and his eventual stopping. It seems that, like so many drug users, at the time he became preoccupied with the drugs to the exclusion of other sides of life which he had treasured before the addiction flourished. When people write about the down side of addiction they often focus on the all too real risks to physical health. The loss of creative activities can be a wound too, once the addiction takes over.

Of heroin he says, 'I never felt so complete, before or since.' He writes of drug use as a distraction from the pain inside, illustrating the Freudian view of the function of addiction as basically a defence against psychic pain. Yet he also speaks of it being a part of his search for the creative side of himself, or perhaps even a search for who he was, for himself, reflecting Jung's view that addiction represents a spiritual search that has gone awry. The mundane materialistic world he found himself growing up in failed to provide him with the scope to discover what life meant for him. Later his travels in the East formed part of his search. Whereas Alfie and Stuart embodied the archetype of the hero as adolescents, Ben represents that of the explorer, seeking after truth.

Ben used one drug, LSD, to try to deal with the disadvantages of having become addicted to another, heroin. LSD was used in psychiatry in the 1970s in the UK under controlled conditions. The hope was that the patient would retrieve a memory of a traumatic event or events from their early lives which, it was hoped, they could then resolve with the help of therapy. It seems that this drug was effective for him at first, the only problem being that although hallucinogens do not create physical dependence, he wasn't able to stop after his first few successful trips. He found himself returning to heroin after a bad trip on LSD. He resented deeply his need for alcohol or drugs and described his panic when he had been sporadically stopping and starting in an attempt to control his injecting, saying, 'I found myself getting addicted quicker – the image that came to me at the time was of a web closing on me.'

Luckily Ben didn't come to grief, but came to a stage where he wanted to stop. Eventually he discovered that his retrial of heroin after a break was a disappointment. As well as the fear he felt of losing his life utterly to drugs, he says that it was his intense relationship with life itself that saved him. His ambivalence was what was hopeful, for he added, 'Somehow another part of myself was kind of looking and mourning the things I used to enjoy.' Many studies have explored the ways in which people stop drug using without treatment. These are critically reviewed in two chapters (Smart 2007, Carballo *et al.* 2007) in a book on self-change from addictive behaviours (Klingemann and Sobell 2007).

Ben came to realise that once-valued parts of himself were being overwhelmed by the 'addict' self – to his detriment. In this powerless state, the ego, in terms of the will, may collapse and surrender. Willpower no longer has the power to hold the personality together. It is at this point that people can become open to accepting help.

The vital factor in Ben's life after he stopped using drugs was that, as he says, he didn't have to find any other drug because he found more satisfying alternatives in life. He speaks about searching for the numinous. However we talk about another dimension in life other than the material and the mundane, Ben is not alone in feeling a yearning to experience it, and what is more, to live out of its richness. He wants children to see, to feel, to experience this. He has become an educator in the true sense of the word.

The parallels in Ben's recovery with that advocated by AA or NA are striking, although he was not influenced by either. Important at that stage for him was to live as a member of a community with a strong ethical sense of spirituality and commitment. He committed himself to Buddhism. To have lived as part of a religious community for the four years after he stopped using heroin I would guess would have been both supportive and taxing. It would have given him structure for his days and continuing reinforcement of spiritual values. He later moved to a less fundamentalist religious group in which he led a poetry group himself. He also married and became a family man at this stage. More recently his values have been reflected in his employment and in the work he does 'for free'. This is different from the narrators who speak about becoming drugs workers themselves, yet Ben speaks about feeling empathy in his gut for the heroin users he sees in the street, and I think his experiences with drugs have deepened his understanding of suffering and of the human condition. He has used this understanding in living a creative life at home and in his work as an environmentalist and teacher. He has put into practice his beliefs, which he lays out in his letter to his former psychiatrist, that we need a reason to live, that we need to learn to care for other people and that we need to honour our own vulnerability.

In conclusion

Drug use and deviance

Because it is against the law to possess, sell or use classified drugs without a medical prescription in the UK, the outcome is overall criminalisation of drug users. There are some people, however, like Ben, who have no history of deviance before they start to use drugs or at any time in their subsequent lives. His criminal record amounts to his one conviction – for the possession of heroin.

The search for a peer group

Finding and being accepted into a peer group is a crucial activity in the turbulence of adolescence. Some adolescents find a group which develops naturally from the friendship groups they have retained through their childhood, while for others it is more difficult. The fears and intense self-consciousness attendant upon growing up cast the young person into uncertainty about his or her identity. Nearly every drug injector treated at the hospital had been initiated into injecting within a group setting by an individual in that group. People in the groups tended to gather at weekend parties and share whatever drugs they had managed to obtain. A 'family tree' of those who initiated others was traced, and most of the injecting initiation could be traced back to three individuals (de Alarcon 1969).

Searching for the numinous

A further characteristic aspect of adolescence is the questioning of the meaning of life. Although this can and does take place in some 'institu-tional' settings such as schools or churches, it can also take the form of a more introverted search by the individual. The natural world and the artistic world can form the setting for such a search. Ben's adolescence illustrates this. Enhancing his perception of the world around him and extending the boundaries of his own consciousness by experimenting with drugs was also at that time a part of his search. Later, as he says, he no longer needed drugs.

Retrieving creativity

Looking back, Ben feels that his drug use was a waste of time. When he returned from his journeys of exploration, he found other ways to express his intense relationship with life. He returned to writing poetry, he committed himself to enhancing the natural environment and to helping children to appreciate it, so enhancing his spiritual life.

Ben represents those adolescents who experiment with drugs for different reasons from the many who have been in trouble with authority before they ever use drugs. He was lonely and alienated from the mainstream and was looking for some deeper meaning in life, as well as seeking for a peer group. Probably one of the reasons he seems to have been unable to benefit much from his contact with the service at that time was because he was simply evading prison. It is a hard task for a therapist to form a rapport with anyone who is forced into therapy.

The aim of therapy

Ben feels now that his addiction wasted his time and interrupted his development, but once he stopped using drugs, he retrieved valuable aspects of his life from the time before he became addicted. He discovered this capacity within himself, but his experience should encourage therapists who hope that they can work with their patients towards this end.

Ben wrote this letter to Dr. Rathod shortly after the conversation they had.

It was good to see you the other day. I would like to think that something of my experience may prove useful to other people. The reason I am writing is partly to clarify some of what I told you face to face, but also to reveal the truth that the task has not yet been completed. Is it ever? The struggle is to remain true to that in me which is essential.

As you know, addiction is in large part an avoidance of self. It has its roots in self-hatred. As a psychiatrist your experience, I think, will bear this out. Addiction takes many forms, but basically it's about avoidance. Whether your drug of choice is heroin or shopping or compulsive masturbation. The dynamic is the same – it's a distraction from the pain inside.

In many ways it's the culture that is addicted, we are bombarded on all sides by the pushers of various substances, all guaranteed to make us feel better. The flight into 'addiction' is always an option.

When you asked me 'how' I stayed free of drugs for so long, I avoided the use of the word 'spiritual'. By this I mean a 'sense of the numinous'. A way of relating to the world that perhaps has its roots in my childhood. As a young boy I served mass and took the idea of God seriously enough so that like many Catholic boys I thought of becoming a priest.

Later, as an adolescent (pre-heroin), I would walk for miles in the forest, with a copy of Walt Whitman's 'Song of Myself' or Ben Jeffries' 'The Story of my Heart'. You get the picture. I wrote poetry, composing Haiku about tree stumps! All of this adolescent verve was later submerged by opiates, but re-awakened with LSD, which in turn went on to take its toll on the foolish youth, now writing close to fifty years of age! The point I am making is, it was this intense relationship with life itself that saved me. I don't know if I made this clear when we spoke. Also my fear of losing my life utterly to drugs. The misery I would inflict upon my mother already bereaved of my brother John, dead in a fairground accident, if I should succumb to an overdose. Several of which came close to claiming me.

It is hard to give up our addictions. As a society we are heavily addicted to a range of things that we know are extremely harmful to ourselves and future generations. What we need are options to be made available. We are all so complex, what works for some may not work for others. We need a reason to live, a reason to be grateful to Providence for our existence. We have to learn to care for other people as well as ourselves.

Our giving up addictions has to be placed in a meaningful context. We have to rediscover our essential goodness, and to do this we have to honour our vulnerability, it is what makes us human. I am still in the process of learning to begin to do this.

I hope all of the overleaf doesn't sound too naive. If only it were a case of 'You know it's not good for you – give it up!' My Dad, having suffered two heart attacks, carried on smoking roll-ups till the day he died.

Drug addicts are people with emotional problems around self-esteem. I'm convinced of this. In many cases they are in search of an identity, a sense of self that is whole and entire. Heroin is, of course, just the ticket. I never felt so complete, before or since. This is its major appeal. So, where does this leave us? Not in criminalising people, nor, as we discussed, prescribing carte blanche to all and sundry. What is needed is prolonged counselling in a group context. I know this to some extent takes place already.

How do you get to the newly experimenting? The young people estranged from society by unemployment, abuse of one form or another, of which there are an enormous number? These are the ongoing generation of drug takers.

It has to be a matter of listening to our children. Of being there for them when they need us. With our own childhood's conditioning to struggle with, this is not always easy either. The school system, with its streaming of children, so that one feels good about him/herself while another develops low self-esteem. This I am convinced has to be addressed.

Care and empathy ought to be a requirement for all people working with children. Also venues for listening to and dealing with the deep concerns felt by many young people today, have to be made available. I'm getting on to something of a soapbox here, so I had better draw this to a close.

I don't pretend to know what needs to be done. It's an extremely difficult issue. However, I do acknowledge the integrity of your approach and wish you well.

Chapter 20

In the long term

In any type of recovery, the question arises as to whether or to what extent it is possible to return to life as it was before disaster struck. Addiction causes traumata which are so deep that the individual will have to tread a new and very different path if the addiction is to be left behind for ever. In a nutshell, this is a path of greater self-awareness.

The narrators in this section talk about their lives over the many years since they stopped using drugs, apart from Lee, whose interview illustrates what it is like to be still addicted after an equal number of years. His narrative displays not only his obsession with drugs and his fight against what he sees as an unfair and grudging world, but a terror of looking at where his life is heading. The others, by contrast, show how the new task which faced them immediately after they stopped evolved as time passed and became rewarding in itself. They illustrate how once freed from the shackles of their addictions, they went on to grow.

Triggers to change

In exploring precisely what has driven these changes, Geoff's questions reach the heart of the matter:

> What is it that's related to my having stopped drinking? What is it that's related to my having changed? I sometimes look at my life, the way it is, and ask myself how much it's a result of my not drinking, and how much of it is the result of some of the consequential things and some of the decisions that I've made as a result of that.

This shows how the process evolves from the point of stopping. It was not the fact that people had suffered the effects of long-term addiction, nor the fact that they had been able to stop and leave their addictions behind, that fostered this change in orientation, but the way they engaged in their personal struggles in the time after they stopped.

Development of insight

In order not to relapse once again into addiction, they had to do two things. They not only had to become vigilant against the triggers that could pull them back into drug using or drinking, but they also had to become sensitive to the characteristics in themselves that made them vulnerable to being pulled back. This was the spur to learn about themselves, a process which then tended to develop its own momentum. It existed on various levels. The day-to-day level related to behaviour. Think of the slogan in AA which warns against the particular hazards of being hungry, angry, lonely or tired (HALT). Once someone becomes conscious of their vulnerabilities they can take them into account and take responsibility for them. Some narrators realised after stopping that they had been shying away from any sort of responsibility for years.

Growing stronger

On a deeper level, narrators spoke about recognising and coming to terms with the traits in themselves to which they had long turned a blind eye with the help of drugs. Geoff had feared disapproval because he had always been insecure about his own worth. Stuart had tried to blot out awareness of his own flaws by envying and disparaging other people. Gerald and Johnnie had had no firm anchors in their young lives, and had frequently drifted into life-threatening dangers, lurching from one intoxicated crisis to another. These character traits don't disappear, but once they are brought into the daylight of consciousness, their poison is drawn. Linda admitted that she was still no good at finding a partner she could trust. Lawrence, being an exceptionally enterprising individual, knew that he needed to keep busy in order to keep out of the pub. The narrators speak about how they faced practical difficulties, but this went hand in hand with coming to a far more profound understanding of their shadow aspects. Each person faced the most self-destructive aspect of themselves and came to engage with it. This was often the very thing that had fuelled their addiction in the first place. It seems that while people were realistic about their flaws, they were not cowed by what they perceived, but could square up to them.

Taking responsibility

Minette and Johnnie spoke about taking responsibility in terms of paying their bills, but they also spoke about becoming more honest with themselves. It is not easy to accept the losses caused by addiction philosophically. In fact, like some of the other narrators, they took responsibility for an emotional need to be involved with people on a caring basis. They sensed that they needed to contribute their unique understanding of addiction to help others. In her book on the archetype of the scapegoat, Sylvia Brinton Perera describes how after people become able to disentangle themselves from the burden of being a scapegoat, as many addicts are in their families or in society, they will still have a special relationship with this archetypal theme. It becomes a focus and gives special meaning to their lives (Perera 1986: 98). It is this shift that lies behind the emotional significance of the dedication shown by wounded healers.

Many of the narrators chose different employment from whatever they had been doing before they were addicted. Because they understood their own needs better, they could not only see what didn't suit them, but they also became aware of their potential strengths. The narrators all knew of other people who had died through drug use. Survivors' guilt is an inevitable but haunting accompaniment to abstinence for people leaving addiction behind and is complicated by the awareness that their troubles were partly self-induced. In becoming helpers of others, this guilt may be partly assuaged. Many have become experts in helping others who have problems caused by drugs and alcohol, and this fits with the archetypal wounded healer model. It is interesting to ask whether their addictions can be called a phase in their lives, or indeed in their development. Are they equally addicted to helping other people or attending meetings of self-help groups and is this healthy for them? We all have people, objects and activities to which we are deeply attached if we lead healthy lives. The two founder members of AA asked an alcoholic whom they visited in hospital if they might speak to him, for their *own* sakes. One of them, William Wilson, writes, 'On talking to a man there, I would be amazingly lifted up and set on my feet' (Alcoholics Anonymous 1976: 15).

Relationship

In many instances the narrators' self-discovery took place in the context of relationship with the individuals who were supporting them. This, in itself, was a significant change from the isolation they were living in while they were addicted. Everything else follows on from two factors: a growing insight into themselves and a willingness to relate to others and to trust them. They discovered that the act of accepting help is not weak and despicable. Whether people became affiliated to AA or not, their development tended to follow a similar pathway. It could be described as allowing a support system for one's life to develop and then maintaining it. The practical and the spiritual go hand in hand.

Within this new orientation, development happens in spiral fashion. One thing leads to another, just as it did in the opposite direction, in a downward spiral into addiction. Getting to know themselves had many implications for the narrators. Apart from discovering where their strengths and weaknesses lay in the present stage of their lives, they were able to face problems as they arose and come to terms with the vicissitudes of life. New problems came along, but facing up to life, instead of hiding away in drugs, in itself brought a growing sense of self-worth. Challenges met successfully strengthen a person.

From the unproductive co-dependency that can exist in an addicted couple, partners can move towards recognising their own and each other's needs. Stuart learned that for his relationship with his partner to thrive, he needed to step back and allow some space. This was part of becoming honest with himself. He came to recognise that he could stand on his own. In time, partners can experience mutuality rather than dependence.

Inner dialogue

The more ordered cast of a life without drugs permits an inner dialogue with oneself which was largely missing in addiction. Narrators found themselves having new objectives in the long term, but they were realistic objectives. Having balance in life implies being in touch with the varying rhythms of stimuli and relaxation, company and solitude, work and leisure and with accepting the variations imposed by the demands of the outside world.

The ways people changed varied according to their personalities once they came to know themselves better. Whether this involved taking responsibility for their actions, becoming less bound up in materialism, dealing better with their slighted feelings, enjoying solitude or simply accepting the limitations of their lives without being crushed by them, depended upon the individual. But these are far-reaching changes, and each one of them is part of a creative spiral of growth – in Jung's terms, promoting the process of individuation. AA speaks about abstinence being able to develop into sobriety. This is true in that the chaos of the addicted life becomes something far more balanced. Any disastrous occurrence in life, such as an addiction and the havoc it causes, can remain simply a disaster. But it need not. Overcoming it can be the springboard for new growth and creativity. The task continues, but it becomes rewarding in itself and the process evolves into one of discovery.

Final thoughts

Addiction is not necessarily a death sentence nor a lifelong sentence. If someone who has been addicted to drugs stops drinking or using drugs and then succeeds in leaving the addiction behind, the process of doing so brings about change at a deep level. People become self aware after they stop because they know they need to do so in order not to relapse. Although that need may be the driving force at the beginning of their abstinence, there are many deeper benefits to the insight which grows as the individual comes to acknowledge the lasting effects of their addiction on themselves and on others and meets the need to forge a life without drugs. In creating a drug-free life from day to day, the practical and the emotional go hand in hand. Facing difficulties at this stage builds self-esteem.

After people stop, they need the continuing help and support of others. It is not a once and for all phenomenon. Relying on someone else brings with it a challenge: it is not necessarily straightforward. It can teach you something about yourself. It may show you things you never learned earlier, such as accepting the less than perfect in other people. This involvement is in complete contrast to the virtual isolation of being addicted.

What the narrators here have shown is how enriched their lives became afterwards. The defensiveness and chaos of their addicted days gave way eventually to new growth. Difficult and distressing as the time immediately after they stopped using drugs may have been, this distress was partnered by new growth and development.

The implication of this is that if an individual who becomes addicted can be sustained by whatever means are available, and the belief can be held by that person and by those concerned with him or her that it is possible to leave addiction behind, that individual, rather than being for ever impoverished, can go on to lead a creative life.

References

Addenbrooke, M. (2004) *An Enquiry into Psychological Aspects of Recovery from Dependence on Psychoactive Substances.* PhD thesis, University of Essex.

Alcoholics Anonymous (1957) *Alcoholics Anonymous Comes of Age: A Brief History of AA.* London: AA Sterling Area Services.

Alcoholics Anonymous World Services, Inc. (1976) *Alcoholics Anonymous.* Aylesbury BPCC: Hazell Books Ltd.

Bateson, G. (1971) The cybernetics of self: A theory of alcoholism. *Psychiatry, 34*(1), 1–18.

Biernacki, P. (1986) *Pathways from Heroin Addiction: Recovery without treatment.* Philadelphia, PA: Temple University Press.

Broom, K. M., Simpson, D. D. and Joe, G. W. (2002) The role of social support following short-term inpatient treatment. *The American Journal on Addictions, 11,* 57–65.

Burroughs, W. (1986) *The Naked Lunch.* London: Paladin.

Carballo, J. L., Fernandez-Hermida, J. R.,Secades-Villa, R., Sobell, L. C., Dum, M. and Garcia-Rodrigues, O. (2007) Natural recovery from alcohol and drug problems: A methodological review of the literature from 1999 through 2005. In H. Klingemann and L. C. Sobell (eds), *Promoting Self-Change From Addictive Behaviours.Practical Implications for Policy, Prevention and Treatment.* New York: Springer.

Dalrymple, T. (2006) *Romancing Opiates: Pharmacological Lies and the Addiction Bureaucracy.* New York: Encounter Books.

Davies, J. B. (1997) *The Myth of Addiction (Second Edition).* Amsterdam: Harwood Academic Publishers.

de Alarcon, R. (1969) The spread of heroin abuse in a community. UN Bulletin of Narcotics, *21,* 17–22.

De Quincey, T. (1907)*The Confessions of an English Opium-eater.* London: J. M. Dent and Sons Ltd.

Edwards, G. (2000) *Alcohol. The Ambiguous Molecule.* London: Penguin Books.

Fraser, A. and George, M. (1988) Changing trends in drug use: An initial follow-up of a local heroin-using community. *British Journal of Addiction, 83,* 655–663.

Goldstein, A. and Herrera, J. (1995) Heroin addiction and methadone treatment in Albuquerque: A 22-year follow-up. *Drug and Alcohol Dependence, 40,* 139–150.

Handelsman, L., Stein, J. A. and Grella, C. E. (2005) Contrasting predictors of readiness for substance abuse treatment in adults and adolescents. *Drug and Alcohol Dependence*, *80*, 63–81.

Hser, Y. I., Grella, C. E., Collins, C. and Teruya, C. (2003) Drug use initiation and conduct disorder among adolescents in drug treatment. *Journal of Adolescence*, *26*(3), 331–345.

Jackson, C. (1945) *The Lost Weekend*. London: John Lane The Bodley Head.

Joseph, S. and Linley, P. A. (eds) (2008) *Trauma, Recovery, and Growth: Positive Psychological Perspectives on Posttraumatic Stress*. Hoboken, NJ: Wiley.

Jung, C. G. (1963) *Memories, Dreams, Reflections* (A. Jaffé, ed.). London: Collins/ Routledge and Kegan Paul.

Jung, C. G. (1976) *Letters Volume 2: 1951–1961*. London: Routledge and Kegan Paul.

Khantzian, E. (2003) Understanding addictive vulnerability: An evolving psychodynamic perspective. *Neuro-Psychoanalysis*, *5*(1), 5–21.

Klein, M. (1980) *Envy and Gratitude and Other Works 1946-1963*. London: The Hogarth Press and the Institute of Psycho-Analysis.

Klingemann, H. K.-H. (1999) Addiction careers and careers in addiction. *Substance Use and Misuse*, *34*(11), 1505–1526.

Klingemann, H. and Sobell, L. C. (2007) (eds) *Promoting Self-Change From Addictive Behaviours. Practical Implications for Policy, Prevention and Treatment*. New York: Springer.

Lear, J. (2005) *Freud*. New York and London: Routledge.

Lehman, W. E. K., Barrett, M. E. and Simpson, D. D. (1990) Alcohol use by heroin addicts 12 years after drug abuse treatment. *Journal of Studies on Alcohol*, *51*(3), 233–244.

Lenson, D. (1995) *On Drugs*. Minneapolis, MN: University of Minnesota Press.

Liebeskind, A. S. (1991) Chemical dependency and the denial of the need for intimacy. In A. Smaldino (ed.), *Psychoanalytic Approaches to Addiction* (Chapter 5). New York: Brunner/Mazel.

McMurran, M. (1994) *The Psychology of Addiction*. London: Taylor and Francis.

Marlatt, G. A. and Gordon, J. R. (1985) *Relapse Prevention: Maintenance Strategies in the Treatment of Addictive Behaviours*. New York: Guilford Press.

May, M. (1991) Observations on countertransference, addiction, and treatability. In A. Smaldino (ed.), *Psychoanalytic Approaches to Addiction* (Chapter 1). New York: Brunner/Mazel.

Miller, W. R. and Rollnick, S. (2002) *Motivational Interviewing: Preparing People for Change in Addictive Behaviour* (Second edition). New York: Guilford Press.

Moos, R. H. and Moos, B. S. (2006) Rates and predictors of relapse after natural and treated remission from alcohol use disorders. *Addiction*, *101*, 212–222.

Morland, L. A., Butler, L. D. and Leskin, G. A. (2008) Resilience and thriving in a time of terrorism. In S. Joseph and P. A. Linley (eds), *Trauma, Recovery, and Growth: Positive Psychological Perspectives on Posttraumatic Stress* (Chapter 3). Hoboken, NJ: John Wiley and Sons, Inc.

Mott, J. and Rathod, N. H. (1976) Heroin misuse and delinquency in a new town. *British Journal of Psychiatry*, *128*, 428–435.

Office for National Statistics (2008a) *Alcohol-related deaths in the United Kingdom 1991–2008*. Statistical Bulletin. Retrieved from http://www.statistics.gov.uk

Office for National Statistics (2008b) *Deaths related to drug poisoning in England and Wales, 2008.* Statistical Bulletin. Retrieved from http://www.statistics.gov.uk

Orford, J. (2001) *Excessive Appetites: A Psychological View of Addictions* (Second edition).Chichester: John Wiley and Sons Ltd.

Perera, S. B. (1986) *The Scapegoat Complex: Towards a Mythology of Shadow and Guilt.* Toronto: Inner City Books.

Prochaska, J. O. and DiClemente, C. C. (1983) Transtheoretical therapy: Towards a more integrative model of change. *Psychotherapy: Theory, Research and Practice, 19*, 276–288.

Rathod, N. H. (1972) The use of heroin and methadone by injection in a new town. *British Journal of Addiction, 67*, 113–121.

Rathod, N. H. (1977) Follow-up study of injectors in a provincial town. *Drug and Alcohol Dependence, 2*, 1–21.

Rathod, N. H. (ed.) (1992) *Substance Abuse – A Layman's Guide.* West Sussex: Mid-Downs Health Authority.

Rathod, N. H., Addenbrooke, W. M. and Rosenbach, A. F. (2005) Heroin dependence in an English town: A thirty-three year follow-up. *British Journal of Psychiatry, 187*, 421–425.

Redfearn, J. W. T. (1985) *My Self, My Many Selves.* London: Academic Press.

Richman, J. (2000) Coming out of intensive care crazy: Dreams of affliction. *Qualitative Health Research, 10*(1), 84–102.

Robins, L. N., Helzer, J. E., Hesselbrock, M. and Wish, E. (1977) *Vietnam Veterans Three Years after Vietnam: How our Study Changed our View of Heroin.* Proceedings of the 39th Annual Scientific Meeting, Committee on Problems of Drug Dependence, Missouri (pp. 24–40).

Samuels, A., Shorter, B. and Plaut, A. (1986) *A Critical Dictionary of Jungian Analysis.* London and New York: Routledge.

Schoen, D. E. (2009) *The War of the Gods in Addiction: C. G. Jung, Alcoholics Anonymous and Archetypal Evil.* New Orleans, LA: Spring Journal Books.

Shaffer, H. and Burglass, M. E. (1981) *Classic Contributions in the Addictions.* New York: Brunner/Mazel Publishers.

Shontz, F. C. and Spotts, J. V. (1989) Interview: From theory to practice: The planned treatment of drug users. *International Journal of the Addictions, 24*(12), 1183–1228.

Smaldino, A. (ed.) (1991) *Psychoanalytic Approaches to Addiction.* New York: Brunner/Mazel.

Smart, R. G. (2007) Natural recovery or recovery without treatment from alcohol and drug problems as seen from survey data.In H. Klingemann and L. C. Sobell (eds), *Promoting Self-Change From Addictive Behaviours.Practical Implications for Policy, Prevention and Treatment.* New York: Springer.

Sobell, L. C. (2007) The phenomenon of self-change: Overview and key issues. In H. Klingemann and L. C. Sobell (eds), *Promoting Self-Change From Addictive Behaviors: Practical Implications for Policy, Prevention and Treatment* (Chapter 1). New York: Springer.

Tyler, A. (1988) *Street Drugs* (Second revised edition). London: Hodder and Stoughton.

Vaillant, G. E. (1995) *Natural History of Alcoholism Revisited.* Cambridge, MA: Harvard University Press.

West, R. (2006) *Theory of Addiction*. Oxford: Addiction Press. Blackwell Publishing.

Winick, C. (1962) Maturing out of narcotic addiction. *Bulletin on Narcotics*, *14*, 1–7.

Yalisove, D. L. (ed.) (1997) *Essential Papers on Addiction*. New York and London: New York University Press.

Zoja, L. (1989) *Drugs, Addiction and Initiation: The Modern Search for Ritual*. Boston, MA: Sigo Press.

Appendix 1
Alcohol

Metabolism of alcohol in the body

Blood alcohol content (BAC) is expressed as milligrams of alcohol per 100 millilitres of blood (mg/100ml). The liver of an adult can dispose of 8–10g or 10–12.5ml of alcohol in an hour, so that on average the BAC will drop by 15mg/100ml every hour. BAC determines whether the driver of a vehicle is legally allowed to drive.

Immediate effects of drinking alcohol

Ninety per cent of the alcohol drunk is metabolised in the body and ten per cent is excreted unchanged in the urine and breath. Initially it is changed to acetaldehyde, then to acetate and then to carbon dioxide and water. It is metabolised at the rate of 5–10ml per hour, and this rate cannot be hastened. However, food slows the rate of absorption and thus slows the rise in concentration in the blood. In addition, food protects the gut from the irritating effects of alcohol – hence the desirability of not drinking alcohol on an empty stomach.

Paradoxically, by depressing the parts of the brain that make us exercise restraint and judgment and keep us alert, as well as making us cautious and tense, alcohol produces a sense of relaxation and by loosening our guard, it helps us to socialise. However, it also depresses muscular co-ordination and our ability to react quickly to dangers. Alcohol is quickly absorbed from the gut, and more so on an empty stomach. In small amounts, alcohol acts as an appetiser, as it stimulates one's appetite by increasing the production of digestive juices.

The effects are in proportion to the concentration of alcohol in the blood, to the speed of drinking and also to the person's familiarity with the experience of drinking alcohol. Excess can result in making us uninhibited in behaviour – something most of us have experienced at one time or another. To illustrate the effects, a double whisky or large glass of wine (approximately two units of alcohol) produces a feeling of relaxation, obliterates the feeling of tiredness, but increases the chance of accidents as co-ordination is affected and reaction times delayed. Fifty per cent of people, however, will experience intoxication at this blood level, with slurred speech, obvious clumsiness and a delay in reaction time. After drinking four units, there will be increasing lack of co-ordination, a noticeable loss of emotional control, garrulousness and a tenfold increase in the likelihood of accidents. More severe accidents and deaths occur due to acute intoxication than due to chronic excessive drinking.

A dangerous condition called acute hypoglycaemia – lowering of the blood sugar – is likely to occur after ten or more units are drunk on an empty stomach, due to the brain's reaction to inadequate levels of glucose in the blood. The symptoms of hypoglycaemia are sweating, shaking, palpitations, feeling anxious, fainting and, on occasion, confusion. This hypoglycaemia is the result of alcohol interfering with the metabolism of glucose and glycogen in the liver. Alcohol also directly affects the brain cells adversely and this results in 'blackouts' in acute intoxication, when the drinker suffers from loss of memory (in varying degrees, depending on the level of intoxication) of events during drinking. Sometimes people arrive at their own homes without any clue as to how they got there.

Tolerance of alcohol

Tolerance is a natural effect of excessive drinking over a period of weeks or months. A person can consume larger and larger amounts without showing signs of intoxication. Surprisingly a person with increased tolerance can function adequately with much higher levels of blood alcohol than will a novice or a moderate drinker in similar situations. However, tolerance is never total in the sense that an excessive drinker is still liable to be intoxicated. At a certain point, tolerance is reversed, with the result that the drinker can no longer tolerate so much alcohol without feeling very ill.

The danger of cross-tolerance, the condition where drugs with similar effects are substituted one for the other, is common with excessive drinkers. They often experience anxiety (a withdrawal symptom) the morning after and are unaware of its connection with drinking. They may be unwittingly prescribed anti-anxiety drugs by their doctor without the true cause being established. The eventual danger of becoming dependent on the other drug is a real one.

Adverse effects of chronic alcohol abuse

The main organs affected are the central nervous system, the digestive tract, and the cardiovascular system. The foetus is especially vulnerable.

Central nervous system

The chronic nutritional and vitamin deficiencies associated with chronic consumption are said to be the main cause of common complications. These are peripheral neuropathy, chronic myopathy, cerebellar ataxia and Korsakoff's psychosis. The onset of neuropathy is insidious. The usual symptoms are aching and burning sensations in the periphery of limbs, especially the lower limbs. This is accompanied by cramps, loss of sensation, weakness and finally loss of power. Chronic myopathy, not so common, leads to weakness and wasting of limb muscles. Cerebellar ataxia is reflected in loss of balance and lack of co-ordination. Confusion and loss of memory, without any awareness of these symptoms, are indicative of Korsakoff's psychosis. This syndrome, also known as alcoholic dementia, is a condition where the memory, especially the short-term memory, is severely impaired. There is less disturbance of implicit memory, that is, memory for material of which one is not aware, than of learning and memory functions based on consciousness and awareness.

The digestive system

As excess of alcohol irritates the lining of the digestive tract and can lead to inflammation – many effects are not difficult to imagine. These result in chronic oesophagitis (oesphageal varices are a result of this and can cause haematemesis) and chronic gastritis. Pancreatitis is a rare but serious complication. The liver, being the organ where alcohol is metabolised, is especially susceptible. There is initially an excessive deposit of fat resulting in 'fatty liver', progressively leading to replacement of liver tissue with fibrous tissue (cirrhosis of the liver), and liver failure. The number of directly alcohol-related deaths in the UK has consistently risen from 4,023 (6.7 per 100,000) in 1992 to the highest of 9,031 (13.6 per 100,000) in 2008. In 2008, males accounted for approximately two-thirds of the total number of alcohol-related deaths (Office for National Statistics 2008a).

The cardiovascular system

While up to two units of red wine a day (especially in the over fifty age group) are said to protect against heart disease, chronic excess has the opposite effect. Coronary thrombosis and cerebrovascular accidents such as strokes are much more common in chronic alcohol abusers than in other comparable populations. Another complication is weakness of the heart muscle leading to congestive cardiac failure 'chronic cardio-myopathy'.

Psychiatric effects

Psychiatric complications are not uncommon in cases of addiction. These include chronic auditory hallucinations, which can be witnessed in the pitiful sight of 'full-blown' alcoholics living on the street loudly denouncing imaginary detractors. Delusions about the infidelity of one's partner are also found, but whether the frequency of male impotence is a contributory factor or not is difficult to say. Even more common is depression, especially in women. This can be severe.

Women and children

Dose for dose, women are more adversely affected by alcohol than men, maybe because alcohol is water soluble and a woman's body has less water content than a man's. A serious complication in pregnant women addicts is foetal alcohol syndrome. There is no agreement on safe limits of alcohol consumption for pregnant women. As for the effect on the foetus, stillbirths and spontaneous abortions are common, while in live births, evidence of foetal alcohol syndrome may be found. The babies are born with many malformations and damage to the central nervous system, which results in mental retardation, which is as common as one in three babies born to mothers addicted to alcohol.

Alcohol withdrawal syndrome

Besides hangovers, which are so common and transient, there are three other types of withdrawal effects. These are tremors, epileptic fits, and delirium tremens. Tremulousness starts within four to eight hours after the last drink. The person experiences nausea, weakness, vomiting, cramps and tremors of the hands. So far it may resemble acute intoxication, but some people also experience visual hallucinations of a frightening nature. The symptoms settle down within a few days or are relieved by another drink. Epileptic fits are much less common than in the case of barbiturate withdrawal. Delirium tremens, in its full-blown form, is a rare but serious neuropsychiatric complication of chronic excess or addiction, occurring in four to five per cent of cases. It starts within twenty-four to thirty-six hours of either sudden stopping of drinking or marked reduction in intake. It usually lasts four to five days, with complete recovery in the majority of cases. Its main symptoms are tremulousness, poor concentration, disorientation, loss of contact with reality, visual hallucinations of a frightening nature and persecutory delusions. Proof of all of these being withdrawal symptoms is that they are all reversible by drinking the appropriate amount of alcohol – a remedy not to be recommended. A classic description of delirium tremens can be read in Charles Jackson's *The Lost Weekend* (1945).

Treatment issues

Establishing treatment goals

Alcoholism presents itself in many disguises, such as problems of mood (anxiety or depression), or problems of relationships. The first goal is to help the patient to recognise that alcohol is a problem which needs attention, in other words to motivate the person to recognise the need to tackle the problem.

Controlled drinking – is it an option?

Most alcoholics would love to opt for bringing drinking under control and although this may succeed in the short term, controlled drinking is difficult to sustain over any length of time. If the person can abstain for six months at the start, then there is a chance that they will be able to control their drinking in the long term, but reverting to counting units is a thankless task which often spoils the enjoyment of drinking. Usually total abstinence proves to be the only sustainable goal. But the prospect of total abstinence forever is very daunting for the patient. The one strategy that we have found useful and which is advocated strongly by AA is the 'one day at a time' approach. Abstaining for a day does not sound very daunting and can be stretched from a day to a week and then further, with encouragement at every level.

Management of stopping

Depending on the severity of dependence, influenced by the amount drunk daily and for how long, one must be prepared for withdrawal symptoms of varying severity. These start usually within twenty-four to thirty-six hours after the last drink. Mild ones usually result in nausea, headaches, anxiety, and insomnia and weakness. These can be ameliorated with a short course of benzodiazepines or chlormethiazole (Heminevrin). However, there is a danger of getting habituated to these drugs if they are used for more than a week or so, adding another problem to be coped with.

Initially, for some patients who have difficulty in resisting temptation and coping with craving, short-term drug treatment can help. The drug acts as a deterrent. It is called disulfiram or Antabuse. It interferes with the metabolism of alcohol, resulting in accumulation of acetaldehyde. Acetaldehyde produces many unpleasant symptoms. Chief among these are hot flushes, intense throbbing headaches, vomiting, sweating, weakness and dizziness. These symptoms only occur if a person imbibes alcohol after taking disulfiram. It is marketed under the name of Antabuse in tablet form (200mg) in the UK. The patient knows that he cannot drink alcohol for about twenty-four hours after taking disulfiram. Usually one starts with three to four tablets first thing in the morning and gradually tapers the dose over a week to one or two tablets a day. A wise course is for the disulfiram to be administered by someone else to make sure. Disulfiram is not a cure, only a deterrent.

Initial abstinence is essential to the start of any treatment because you cannot reliably negotiate the objectives of 'treatment' with anyone under the influence of drink. Having got the patient to be abstinent, the next step is to negotiate the immediate (not the ultimate) goals. These are to learn to tolerate life without a drink for a short period and then to elicit the benefits of being sober. This should be followed by an explanation in clear and firm but sympathetic terms of the likely course of events if the patient were to resume drinking in the near future. This can only be achieved if the therapist can convey empathy and commitment to help the patient and establish a relationship involving mutual respect. The ultimate aim is to achieve not only sobriety but also the repair of the various areas of life which have been damaged – then alone will recovery have been achieved. Sustained abstinence is only part of the solution. Many patients find joining a fellowship like Alcoholics Anonymous to be very helpful. It is a fellowship offering committed mutual help. It demands commitment and honesty. AA also provides help for relatives through an affiliated group called Al-Anon.

There is a variety of treatments and venues available for helping patients. These are individual therapy, group therapy, self-help groups and behaviour therapy. Treatment is possible as an outpatient, a day patient, an inpatient or in residential homes. An alcoholic's chance of gaining sobriety increases with age (Vaillant 1995: 151). It is worth bearing in mind that over a third of alcoholics attain long-term abstinence.

Appendix 2
Heroin

There are various forms of heroin: crude morphine, which is sometimes called heroin; heroin 'base' prior to conversion to hydrochloride salt (brown powder); ninety-eight per cent pure heroin (injectable white powder, bitter in taste); crude or unpurified heroin (brown powder with a purity of between forty and sixty per cent); and smokeable heroin, adulterated with other substances such as caffeine, containing variable percentages of heroin. It can also be used as a liquid, but this is rare.

Heroin is the most common opiate drug of abuse. It is four times stronger than morphine, which is itself ten times stronger than raw opium. When introduced into the body, heroin is converted into morphine. It can be injected, either under the skin, into muscles, or into the veins (the commonest mode of injection); inhaled – a method of use known as *chasing the dragon*; sniffed or *snorted* – a method common in the USA; or smoked. When injected intravenously it reaches the brain within a few seconds.

Physical and psychological effects of heroin

Medicinal

Heroin is an exceedingly effective painkiller. It suppresses cough, depresses both respiration and bowel movement and causes nausea. It produces constriction of the pupils and this is often noted as a classic sign of use. Heroin is rapidly absorbed from most mucous membranes of the body – respiratory, nasal, and gastrointestinal. When injected intravenously it becomes effective within seconds. Ninety percent is excreted during the first day, but traces can be detected in the urine for up to forty-eight hours.

Psychological

As Thomas de Quincey (1785–1837) says in *The Confessions of an English Opium Eater*, 'Happiness might now be bought for a penny and carried in the waistcoat' (de Quincey 1907). After an intravenous injection, the effects are felt within ten to fifteen seconds and are very intense. In the words of former heroin addicts interviewed by us, 'the rush is fantastic,' and, 'there's a thrill like that of an orgasm.' The surge of euphoria, which is accompanied by warm flushing, itching, a dry mouth, and a heavy feeling in the arms and legs, lasts only a few minutes, but its psychological impact is much more enduring. The user prefers to relax and lie down in a state of reverie, and is prone to irritation if disturbed. In the case of sniffing and smoking heroin, the effects set in after ten to fifteen minutes.

Adverse effects of heroin use

Acute complications

Its most serious acute complication in the case of an overdose is a life-threatening suppression of the respiratory system, which can be fatal. In this case, the administration of oxygen and an antidote, naloxone, can be life saving.

Complications of chronic heroin use

Unlike alcohol or tobacco, heroin does not cause any permanent damage to health. Most of the medical complications arise not so much from heroin itself but from unhygienic injecting habits, such as sharing needles and syringes or not using sterile procedure for injecting. This results in local abscesses or cellulitis, in which infection spreads along the limb. Every organ is susceptible, but the lungs and heart are especially at risk. In addition, viral infection of the liver causing hepatitis A, B or C causes chronic disability and may cause permanent damage to the liver. Indiscriminate sexual habits often result in infection with the Human Immuno-deficiency Virus (HIV), followed by Acquired Immunodefiency Syndrome (AIDS), also known in Africa as 'the slimming disease'. HIV and AIDS are a global phenomenon of considerable gravity, not only for the addict, but also in the case of women, for their children as well, as HIV can be transmitted through the mother's placenta. These viral infections have very little in terms of curative remedies, and particularly remedies most sufferers can afford, although there are drugs to alleviate the symptoms and delay the full-blown syndrome. As most sufferers are young adults, the resulting effects on the economies, the health and the social services of the affected communities are enormous. To give an idea of the gravity of the problem, it is estimated that there are over five million people affected in Africa and a similar number in India. Heroin addicts become more prone to infections when they suffer from nutritional deficiencies and unhygienic living conditions. The major cause of sudden death, however, remains overdose of illicit heroin or prescribed substitute medication, mostly methadone.

Neonatal heroin dependency syndrome

Heroin easily crosses the placental barrier. This affects the foetus and can give rise to neonatal dependency syndrome in varying degrees, depending on the severity of the mother's addiction. The newborn baby looks under-nourished, is very irritable and restless, sweats a good deal and is prone to vomiting and diarrhoea. Its symptoms are reversible with the administration of small doses of opioids, such as Tincture of Opium, in order to enable withdrawal from the heroin. In terms of ongoing care, it is equally important to ensure that the baby will be well looked after when its mother is discharged from medical care. The mother's ability to look after the baby cannot always be assumed and continuing support and monitoring may be required.

The development of tolerance to heroin

Tolerance to heroin develops rapidly in comparison with tolerance to alcohol and anxiolytic drugs. It is characterised by decreasing sensitivity to the effects of the drug. This means that effects like euphoria or depression of the breathing or drowsiness become increasingly less intense and last for shorter periods. This would explain the need for larger and larger doses to produce the same desired effects. There is a varying limit to tolerance in each individual. There have been patients in our hospital who have injected four times the usual dose (5–10mg) daily and still remained up and about. Tolerance reduces equally rapidly after stopping. This can cause dangerous situations, as many users do not realise this fact and if they start using the amount they used before they left off, they are likely to suffer from an overdose, sometimes fatally.

Development of addiction to heroin

There is a popular misconception that 'just one fix' of heroin will cause addiction. Many of our patients were initiated into the use of heroin at weekend gatherings of friends, and then either used only at weekend parties for a certain period of time before use became more frequent or, in some cases, weeks or even months passed before they used again. For some, the first experience was unpleasant, especially the nausea or vomiting, but this did not deter them from trying again. Possibly seeing their friends' enjoyment when they injected it themselves encouraged them to persevere. Those of us who have been smokers will remember the first experience – unpleasant, but not enough to stop us, because of anticipated pleasures. None of our patients ever forgot who initiated them, when they performed the first injection, or their initiator, for the bond between the two had enormous emotional significance (de Alarcon 1969). Perhaps in this way it can be compared with the first experience of sexual initiation. The excitement, the anticipation and being part of a group of similar-minded people all helped in making the practice regular. People were invariably able to describe the experience in the most vivid detail.

For some, the onset of regular use was preceded by sporadic use and ambivalent motivation. On the other hand, if heroin use is regular and frequent, addiction sets in rapidly, as with all sedative/narcotic drugs that have a very short half-life and that are disposed of quickly by the body. Opiates and many sedatives and hypnotics belong to this group of drugs. The half-life of heroin is between two and three hours. With repeated use the user initially experiences increasing preoccupation with the pleasant effects of the drug and looks forward to the next occasion. As time goes by, the user starts craving for the drug and actively seeks it, is generally tense between the occasions of use and is markedly relaxed after the use. The contrast cannot go unnoticed. Addiction has now set in. Other changes in lifestyle follow. Previously valued pursuits like a career and relationships, as well as ethical values, may recede into the background and the pursuit of the drug takes centre stage. Now the addict struggles between two lifestyles: that of a 'normal' person and that of an addict, the one open and the other secret. The individual may have the illusion of being in control, but the reality is otherwise.

Heroin withdrawal syndrome

Withdrawal symptoms start within a few hours of the last use of heroin. A characteristic cluster of symptoms follows sudden cessation of using the drug in a heroin addict. This can come about by design (as many of our patients who are no longer addicted have experienced when they deliberately set about stopping use of the drug) or accidentally, if the addict has been arrested or admitted to hospital for an illness other than addiction. The symptoms are short-lived. They are severe in nature, but not serious or life-threatening, as in the case of alcohol, and complete recovery is usual within seven to ten days. The severity depends on the degree of addiction and how gradually the withdrawal or cessation is carried out.

In mild or in the early stages of addiction, withdrawal symptoms resemble mild flu, accompanied by a runny nose, sneezing, a 'hot and cold' feeling, and goose pimples, which give withdrawal its colloquial name of *cold turkey*. The person is also irritable and tremulous. In more severe cases there is also muscular twitching and quite painful cramps in the muscles, giving rise to the term *kicking the habit*. These symptoms are accompanied by nausea, vomiting, abdominal cramps and diarrhoea, which can lead to severe dehydration. Understandably the addict feels very frightened and restless, and the anxious look is made more telling by dilated pupils. Insomnia is common.

Some people go through a kind of protracted withdrawal syndrome during which they find it difficult to cope with stress, feel weak, develop hypochondriacal symptoms, feel apathetic and lethargic and have difficulty in sleeping. But these unpleasant after-effects subside with time. The most important elements in the management of withdrawal are constant reassurance that it will be over soon and ensuring sleep, if necessary with the help of medication. We have found that reducing doses of anti-anxiety sedative drugs, enough fluids, a comfortable bed and good nursing are enough for the addict to get through the withdrawal phase. Most hospitals, however, use substitute narcotics such as methadone in reducing doses for gradual withdrawal. One milligram of methadone will prove sufficient for every two milligrams of heroin. The other drug used is the opiate derivative codeine, given in 1200–1500mg doses. As patients' accounts of their intake of heroin and other drugs are usually unreliable it is desirable to manage gradual withdrawal in a hospital setting, if any prescribing of drugs, especially methadone or codeine, is involved. However, this is often not possible because of the financial strictures of the National Health Service in the UK, and so withdrawal with the support of medication is conducted on an outpatient basis, particularly in cases with no obvious anticipated complications.

The role of drugs in treatment

There are some drugs with specific effects and there are many of general use. Drugs with specific effects on the use of heroin are:

1 *Methadone.* This is a well-tried drug used to replace the use of heroin. It is usually advocated to alleviate the withdrawal effects of heroin but may be used to help a patient to stay off heroin, with the hope of gradually weaning him or her off any use of opiates. However, in practice this often does not bear fruit and a heroin-dependent person can become a methadone-dependent person. It is equally dependence-producing and many of our patients say that it is more difficult to give up than heroin. It is also rare for a drug user to use only one drug, and this is an added complication for patients who are being prescribed methadone. Its advantage, on the other hand, is more in the nature of social engineering. Because it is legal and reduces the hunger for heroin the addict does not have to be engaged in acquisitive crime to obtain money. It thereby also releases the person's energies towards becoming economically independent.

2 *Naloxone and naltrexone.* These both nullify the effects of heroin in such a way that if a person on either of these drugs does use heroin, there will be no 'high' and no euphoria. However, these drugs precipitate heroin withdrawal symptoms and should only be given to

patients who are free from the use of heroin and are determined to remain free.

3   *Leva acetyl methadone* (LAAM). This is another drug with similar effects. It has the advantage that it need be given only three times a week. The usual dose is 20mg.

4   *Buphrenorphine.* This also reduces the craving for heroin. The usual oral dose starts at 4mg daily, increasing to 40mg daily, but for recommended doses for a particular patient and for side effects, it is necessary to refer to the pharmaceutical texts.

Substitute prescribing is a favoured treatment for heroin addiction today, but it should not be valued at the expense of other treatments. If it can alleviate symptoms long enough for patients to reassess their goals, then that is fine. One danger is, however, that it may become an object of barter and dissension between patients and therapists. The findings of Goldstein and Herrera (1995), in a twenty-two-year follow-up study, that one third of their cohort in methadone maintenance programmes died prematurely are not reassuring. In England and Wales alone, 378 deaths were attributed to methadone in 2008, a rise of sixteen per cent from 2007, compared with 897 deaths involving heroin or morphine in 2008, a rise of eight per cent from 2007 (Office for National Statistics 2008b). As the cost of prescribing – whether it be of methadone or heroin – is high, it is vital that the benefits and disadvantages to the individual, as well as to society as a whole, in terms of crime reduction, should be adequately assessed on a long-term basis.

Drugs of general benefit in treating heroin users include those for the symptomatic relief of troublesome symptoms such as anxiety, restlessness and dysphoria, diarrhoea, and muscle cramps during withdrawal. Insomnia can be a troublesome problem. We have used minor tranquillisers to relieve insomnia as well as anxiety and irritability during the early stages of abstinence. However, as these have dependence potential, the duration of their use should be limited and the dose reduced quickly.

Appendix 3

Further reading

Readers who wish to pursue ideas in this book may find the following guidelines helpful. Details of the publications are given in the list of references.

The UK government-sponsored agencies Alcohol Concern and Drugscope have websites offering information at http://www.alcoholconcern.org.uk and http://www.drugscope.org.uk. The journal *Addiction* has its own website listing titles of papers at http://www.addictionjournal.org, as do similar journals on drugs and alcohol worldwide, which can readily be found on the internet.

Addiction: Mary McMurran (1994) is the author of a short introduction to the subject and Jim Orford's book *Excessive Appetites* (2001) has a history of the concept of addiction. Robert West (2006) has recently produced a book on the theory of addiction. Andrew Tyler's book *Street Drugs* (1988) and Professor Griffith Edwards' book *Alcohol: The Ambiguous Molecule* (2000) both offer essential information.

Psychoanalytic perspective on addiction: Howard Shaffer and Milton Burglass (1981) have edited a collection of classic contributions in the field of addiction. Daniel Yalisove's *Essential Papers on Addiction* (1997) offers a historical perspective on the contributions of Freudians.

Psychoanalysis and analytical psychology: Apart from going directly to the works of Freud and Jung, Jonathan Lear's *Freud* (2005) is a most accessible introduction to Freud's work; *A Critical Dictionary of Jungian Analysis* (Samuels, Shorter and Plaut 1986) gives clear and concise information on Jungian concepts; and *Memories, Dreams, Reflections* (Jung 1963) is the classic ghost-written autobiography of Jung. David Schoen's book *The War of the Gods in Addiction* (2009) opens with the complete correspondence between William Wilson and Jung in full along with a commentary. Information about psychoanalysis and related literature can be obtained from the website of the International Psychoanalytical Association (Freudian) and information about analytical psychology (Jungian) can be obtained from the website of the International Association of Analytical Psychology.

Longitudinal follow-up studies on addiction: Most recently these have been critically reviewed in Harald Klingemann and Linda Carter Sobell's book *Promoting Self-change from Addictive Behaviours* (2007).

Alcoholics Anonymous, Narcotics Anonymous, Al-Anon, Families Anonymous and other Fellowship groups produce their own literature and can be contacted by telephone or via their respective websites.

Appendix 4

The Twelve Steps of AA

1. We admitted we were powerless over alcohol – that our lives had become unmanageable.
2. Came to believe that a Power greater than ourselves could restore us to sanity.
3. Made a decision to turn our will and our lives over to the care of God *as we understood Him*.
4. Made a searching and fearless moral inventory of ourselves.
5. Admitted to God, to ourselves, and to another human being the exact nature of our wrongs.
6. Were entirely ready to have God remove all these defects of character.
7. Humbly asked Him to remove our shortcomings.
8. Made a list of all persons we had harmed, and became willing to make amends to them all.
9. Made direct amends to such people wherever possible, except when to do so would injure them or others.
10. Continued to take personal inventory and when we were wrong promptly admitted it.
11. Sought through prayer and meditation to improve our conscious contact with God *as we understood Him*, praying only for knowledge of His will for us and the power to carry that out.
12. Having had a spiritual awakening as the result of these Steps, we tried to carry this message to alcoholics, and to practise these principles in all our affairs.

Index

abandonment 6, 18, 21, 76, 80, 101, 105
see also lost child archetype

abstinence: initial 101, 122, 127, 189, 195; leading to sobriety 178, 189; total 103–4, 188, 189

acceptance *see also* surrender: and admission of being an addict 33, 63, 91, 96, 120, 123; coming to terms with reality 78; giving/receiving 29, 98, 114, 129–30; of imperfections 5, 128; of not having all the answers 114, 115

accountability *see* responsibility

acetaldehyde 65n2, 184, 188

addiction: and the aim of therapy 173–4; alcohol *see* alcohol addiction; ambivalence and 34, 35, 36, 38, 45, 87; avoidance of feelings as a root of 163, 164; being in love with the drug 44; blinding nature of 20; controlling power of 46, 79, 81, 82; as a defence against mental pain 19, 26, 45; destructive effects of 45–6; drug addiction in Western society 1; elusive searching for the reasons for 124; emotional reasons why people use drugs 37; as evil 46, 63, 64–5; growing up and leaving addiction behind 55; heroin *see* heroin addiction; interviews for research into long-term outcome of 8–10; isolation in 7, 11, 29, 43–4, 52, 143; Jung's understanding of 7–8, 11, 54; leaving addiction *see* leaving addiction; life after *see* life after addiction: early days; life after addiction: in the long term; lifestyle of 4, 31, 42, 43–4, 45, 127; and the

loss of creativity 170; and others' disapproval 128; and personal choice and responsibility 2, 158; perverse element in 144; psychological principles of addiction and treatment 5–8; range of drug use and 39–40; repairing damage caused by effects of 72, 98, 116, 127–8, 152–3, 154, 198; secrecy in 18, 20, 43–4; social environmental factors of 37, 41; swapping of addictions 36, 67; in thrall to 84–5; treatment perspectives 3–4 *see also* drug treatment; triangular model of 40–2; triggers *see* triggers of addictive behaviour; turning points from *see* turning points to leaving addiction; vulnerability to 2, 8, 42–3, 73, 81, 98, 123

adolescent rebellion 54–5

aftercare 129–30 *see also* support

AIDS 191

Al-Anon 37, 72, 165n2, 189, 197

alcohol abuse: effects on the body 185–6; cardiovascular system 186; central nervous system 186; digestive system 186; pregnancy and foetal effects 187; in withdrawal *see* alcohol withdrawal syndrome

alcohol abuse: psychiatric effects 186

alcohol abuse: treatment issues 28–9, 188–9; challenging an independent streak 27; controlled drinking 64, 188 *see also* controlled drinking; establishing treatment goals 188; management of stopping 188–9; sudden withdrawal *see* alcohol withdrawal syndrome